Norman Berdichevsky

The Left is Seldom Right

NEW ENGLISH REVIEW PRESS
newenglishreview.org

New English Review Press

Published by New English Review Press
a subsidiary of World Encounter Institute
PO Box 158397
Nashville, Tennessee 37215

Printed in the United States of America

Cover Design by Kendra Adams

ISBN 978-0-578-08076-5

First Edition

Contents

Latin America

Israel and the Middle East

Marxism and Its Political Theory

Three European Women of Courage Who Battled the Left and the Right

Acknowledgments

I have written this book and chosen its title primarily to reach all those, who, like myself grew up in an ultra liberal environment assuming that "The Left is Always Right."

I wish to express my appreciation to the World Encounter Institute and the editor of *New English Review*, Rebecca Bynum, and all its contributors over the past five years – they have informed, enlightened, entertained and amused me beyond measure. Once again, I also express my gratitude to my dear wife, Raquel, for her patience, counsel and guidance in helping to prepare this work.

--Norman Berdichevsky

Introduction

"Things fall apart; the center cannot hold; mere anarchy is loosed upon the world ... The best lack all conviction, while the worst are full of passionate intensity."—William Butler Yeats (1865-1939)

Although no older than the French Revolution, the political terms "Right" and "Left" have become banal and stale clichés which are often misleading guides that offer no clear indication about intentions, motivations, conflicting policy choices of political personalities and parties under changing circumstances. Both partisan political hacks and educated citizens who should know better, use them as synonyms for the good guys and bad guys. Jonah Goldberg's bestselling book *Liberal Fascism* shocked many readers who could not imagine how the two terms could be grouped together rather than stand as polar opposites.

It has already become a seminal work and the cause of apoplectic fits among those who have always conceived Left and Right as opposite ends of the spectrum, yet we know that "Politics makes strange bedfellows." Goldberg documents the most widespread violations of civil rights and centralization of power to occur in the United States since the Civil War, under the Wilson and FDR administrations, yet both these presidents continue to figure among the most outstanding heroes of many Americans today who identify with "The Left."

The purpose of this book is threefold:

1.   To further document cases in both the United States and abroad that verify Goldberg's thesis that a considerable segment of the American public is misled by the use of the terms "RIGHT vs. LEFT," which are cliché ridden, and often erroneous in their presentation of the most essential relevant facts and the conclusions drawn.

2.   To demonstrate that it is primarily the Political Left that has a vested interest in the continued use of this terminology due to the

considerable inroads made by the liberal media on public opinion. Many political pundits have drawn on the prestige of major writers and Hollywood celebrities whose work was shaped by a critical view of American culture as the epitome of alienation, hypocrisy and crass materialism in modern society. Their assumptions are that other cultures and societies are more authentic, "holistic," integral and devoted to a sense of solidarity and community. These views have been reinforced in popular culture, especially in film and popular song as part of the counter-culture that arose in the 1960s.

3.   To show that antisemitism was not inherently a part of many nationalist "right-wing" movements and that it is generated today overwhelmingly from the Far Left under the encouragement of the wealth and power of militant Islam.

Goldberg's book ought to have been written seventy years ago but let us simply conclude "Better Late than Never." It lays bare the century long manipulation of the terms LEFT and RIGHT in political science. There is an inherent bias in this terminology that favors the Left, a view enhanced continually by most of the mass media due to several generations of overwhelming bias in American literature and films. Those on the Left typically create a straw man, misleadingly confusing conservative and traditional values in favor of individual rights and limited government with the "extremist," "racist," ultra-nationalist, religious, antisemitic, traditionalist and "anti-popular" or "Fascist" forces that they call the RIGHT.

The mindless support of the American and European Political Left for radical and "revolutionary leaders" in non-Western developing countries has preferred to ignore or "explain" the enormous contradictions between those regimes and leaders they have supported as "progressive" and the accepted jargon of political science discourse that "LEFT" means enlightened, beneficial to the working class, liberal, secular and internationalist.

The dichotomy of LEFT vs. RIGHT obscures the basic similarities uniting them at their extremes. Both glorify and deify abstractions such as The Nation, The Working Class, The Race, The King, The Church and worst of all, "The People" promising ALL POWER TO

THE PEOPLE, albeit in the form of a demagogic leader who promises to wipe away all the humiliations of the past as well as the privileges of the "ruling class" once in power.

What is of no concern to both the Far LEFT and the Far RIGHT are real individuals and their inalienable rights to Life, Liberty and the Pursuit of Happiness as defined in our Constitution. These individual rights thrive best in a society under the rule of law and that means restraints on the power of the leader, party, race, church or class for whom they are impediments to "progress." For the political extremes, there are no restraints on power.

The book reflects my own thinking on diverse political issues as it evolved from my years of graduate study (1969-74) at the University of Wisconsin in Madison. My five years there brought me into close contact with the serene landscape of a beautiful nature as transformed by the generations of pioneers from Central and Northern Europe, many of them of German, Scandinavian, and Polish ancestry with family names of ten and twelve letters like mine who had played such a formative role in the development of the American Midwest and American character. It was here that I came to realize not only the beauty of America but the basic goodness and generosity of its people in the heartland - not the superficial and trite caricature of leftwing propaganda displayed so often by unthinking critics on both coasts who were as mindless then of the inhumanity of the Vietcong as they are today towards the Taliban and Al-Qaeda or the three generations of catastrophic Leninist-Stalinist misrule in Russia.

It consists of 25 case studies of major domestic and international crises, wars, alliances, conflicts, issues, personalities and elections that have been the subject of considerable media opinion and comment and most often by the use of the Left-Right terminology.

1. The Origins of the Right-Left Metaphor in the French Revolution.

Why do we continue to use it? Many students and observers of political affairs are aware that a single left-right axis is insufficient in describing variations in political beliefs. No simple diagram is sufficient to take into account social, cultural and economic issues, historical factors and the potential benefits and disadvantages of intended alliances and their consequences. This is all the more unpredictable in foreign affairs. Each chapter will analyze how contemporary observers were misled or surprised by actual events contrary to their acceptance of the simple Left-Right formula. It is probable that these terms will continue in wide use for years to come. They are often used synonymously with liberal and conservative but, as we shall see, this only increases the confusion. However lacking these terms are, discussion and comments such as, "He is a rightwing hack" or 'That is part of the rightwing conspiracy' or 'The Left is determined to win back its majority' are heard every day, at least in the frequent discourse of American politics. I will therefore also continue to use them and show where they need to be qualified.

THE AMERICAN SCENE

2. The Leftwing Tilt in Culture in Literature and Film

3. The Sixties Revisited: The Age of Aquarius

4. Can It Happen Here? The Incredible Prescient Political Novel of America's First Fascist President from the Democratic Party

5. The Gods That Failed But Still Enjoy a Favorable Press (*The New York Times* and the *BBC*)

6. Abraham Lincoln – Hero of the Left and/or the Right?

7. The Religious Left, Liberal Libels and the Censure of Senator McCarthy (How the Democratic Party and the Religious Left in the United States Helped Defame a Prominent 'Liberal' and Pave the Way for the Senate's Censure of Senator McCarthy).

8. Freedom of Religion - Not an Absolute Right Guaranteed by the Constitution (Ask the Mormons and the Serpent Churches).
    The debate over the ground zero mosque unleashed numerous erroneous comments asserting that the Constitution "guarantees" Freedom of Religion. It guarantees freedom of beliefs but NOT actions and the federal government has intervened numerous times to prevent

practices that threaten life, health and individual rights, especially of women and children.

9. The Stalinist and Daniel Webster

How the congressman most associated with the Leftward drift of the Democratic Party committed the most outrageous fraud and abusive vilification of his opponent in the recent Congressional elections and was scarcely criticized by the leadership and rank and file of the party apart from the remark that he went 'over the top'.

10. The Anachronistic American Jewish Affection for the Left Why American Jews Vote so Liberal and Why They Shouldn't. Will it ever change?

11. Collective vs. Individual Rights; How the Constitution Has Been Assaulted and Balkanized by Multiculturalism and Affirmative Action.

EUROPE

Right Wing Dictators Oppose the Axis

On the eve of World War II, various so called "Right Wing" authoritarian regimes of the conservative, traditional, national and religious type, namely Ethiopia's Emperor Haile Selassi, Austria's "Clerical-Fascist" regime of Engelbert Dollfuss and Kurt Schuschnigg, Poland's President and military leader General Jozef Pilsudski, Yugoslavia's General Simovic and his supporters in the armed forces and Greece's leader Ionnas Metaxas, all opposed the expansionist ambitions of Hitler and Mussolini. Even among Hitler's temporary allies, Finland's Marshall Mannerheim, and Bulgaria's King Boris III, as well as Spain's leader General Francisco Franco, there was no sympathy for antisemitism and each of them was instrumental in protecting their own Jewish citizens or allowing refugees to pass through their territories unharmed.

12. Fascist Italy and Austria Hand Hitler His First Defeat. Two Right Wing Fascist dictators (Dollfuss and Mussolini) openly confront and challenge Hitler. (Far Right vs. Far Right)

13. Franco, Fascism and the Falange: All the Far Right? Perhaps, But Not One and the Same.

The Spanish Civil War is consistently misrepresented as a simple struggle of Right vs. Left instead of the complex conflict it was involving regional issues, language, religion, land reform, anarchism, and the interventionist policies of the Great Powers. The Falange, portrayed as a "Fascist" party was in many ways an expression of workers and farmers opposed to big business interests, apathetic towards the Church, critical of the land owning classes and even schemed at one point to assassinate Franco. Moreover, the ultra-conservative and devout Catholic Spanish leader made Spain available for the refuge and survival of at least 30,000 Jewish refugees. (Far Right vs. Far Right)

14. The "Reactionary" King Boris III and His Crucial Role in the Salvation of Bulgaria's Jews in World War II

15. The Soviet-Nazi Honeymoon, September 1939 – June 1941; They Were Made for Each Other. (The classic case of how the Extreme Right and Left met, found common interests and became close temporary allies).

16. The Danish "Far Right" (Dansk Samling) Initiated the Resistance Against Nazi Occupation

17. The Two International Brigades; One Glorified (Spain) and the Other Forgotten (Finland)

Finnish-Americans and Canadians volunteer to help defend Finland against the Soviet Invasion and its Nazi Allies in the Winter War of 1939-40

18. Ionnas Metaxas, Autocrat, Monarchist, "Fascist" and Germanophile Who Led the Greek Struggle Against the Axis in World War II
Latin America

19. The Cuban Communist Party Support of Both Batista and Castro.

Masquerading the first sixty years of the party's history, the Cuban Communist Party and Castro regime pretend that ex-President

Batista was always a stooge of American and "right wing business interests" rather than their earlier line (1935-58) as the "popular" leader supported by the masses and Party. (Far Left Supports Far Right)

20. Peronism; Argentine Populism of the Right or Left?; Or Did it Matter?
    An example of Latin-American Populism that can be equally classified as Far-Right or Far Left. How such diverse personalities as Maradona and Che Guevara, iconic heroes of the Left and Evita and Carlos Gardel, icons of the Right all sprang from the same populist ethos that became identified with Peronism.

ISRAEL & THE MIDDLE EAST

21. How Israel Went from Darling of the Left to International Pariah. Fervent Left wing and "progressive" support for the Partition of Palestine and aid to the Israelis in 1948 has been totally forgotten by the willful amnesia of the Left.

Support for JIHAD on the RIGHT and the LEFT.

22. Connecting the Dots

23. Marx, Stalin and Opportunism on The National Question.
    The Left, taking its lead from Stalin and the foreign policy needs of the USSR proclaimed its 'scientific study' of dialectical materialism provided answers on all questions including the problem of "National Identity" and Self-Determination. The Left in much of the world followed the flip-flops from Moscow on which peoples and ethnic groups qualified as a "nation" with the right of self-determination.

24. Case Closed: The Utter Failure of Marxism-Leninism. The Negative Balance Sheet of Marxism-Leninism in Spite of All the Grandiose Promises Made to the "Left."

25. Three Courageous Women Who Battled the Left and the Right.
    Sigrid Unset, Oriana Fallaci, Pilar Rahola

Politics, it seems to me, for years, or all too long, has been concerned with right or left instead of right or wrong.

~Richard Armour (American poet and author, 1906-1989)

Cannon to right of them,
Cannon to left of them,
Cannon behind them
Volley'd and thunder'd

- Alfred, Lord Tennyson

1

Origins of the Right-Left Metaphor; The Trite Right-Left Dimension

How did the terms Right and Left originate and become part of the political lexicon? How did they become universally adopted? How accurately can this model delineate the real political character of a party, movement or leader? Are they outmoded? These are four essential questions that deserve more than a cursory answer in the introduction to the thread running through the 25 chapters that comprise this book. Can these terms easily be interchanged with other labels such as "conservative" and "liberal," "fascist," "socialist" and "communist"? Jonah Goldberg's epic bestseller *Liberal Fascism; The Secret History of the American Left from Mussolini to the Politics of Meaning* created a firestorm of opposition from those for whom the very title was an impermissible oxymoron.

The exhaustive documentation in *Liberal Fascism* of the presidential careers and administrations of Woodrow Wilson and Franklin Delano Roosevelt as well as the detailed analysis of Mussolini, Hitler and Stalin and those who were their original supporters and detractors left many of Goldberg's critics with egg on their faces. Many were simply totally ignorant of the facts and had to be reminded how their many misconceptions all stem from the same simplistic acceptance of the straight line or semicircular Right-Left Measuring Tool, based largely on economic and trade policy introduced in the last days of the French monarchy before the 1789 Revolution and its immediate aftermath of republican rule and the purely abstract and wholly arbitrary parliamentary seating arrangements that were introduced at the time.

Influenced by the exaggerated tilt towards the Liberal side of the political spectrum, too many Americans invariably accept the emotionally loaded doctrines of political commentary that Left = good and Right = bad in much the same vein as Orwell's Dictatorship of the Pig in Animal Farm: four legs = good and two legs = bad.

Today, not just economic policy but the entire range of major political issues is often debated under the rubric of Right and Left. "Free" Health Care, gun control, guaranteed abortion (euphemistically called Freedom of Choice), euthanasia, a more "equitable" distribution of income (sharing the wealth), generous subsidies to special interest groups, credits and welfare benefits for the needy, the growth of trade union power to enforce membership as a condition of employment, a limit on military expenditures, a hostile attitude towards established religion, and a general withdrawal from international commitments are automatically assumed today as falling within the liberal scheme of things (i.e. The Left) but were at times cornerstones of American isolationism and even Fascist regimes (i.e. The Right) as well as the rhetoric of 70 years of Communist misrule in Russia.

The book is also an attempt to more widely cover international affairs and demonstrate that in many cases of foreign policy, there has also been a simplistic portrayal of anti-American sentiment as stemming only from The Left when in reality much equally strident anti-American propaganda was an intermittent component of The Right in such diverse regimes as General Franco in Spain, the dictatorship of Juan Peron in Argentina, "Papa Doc" Duvalier in Haiti, and many ultra-conservative and reactionary religious Muslim states as well as a consistent element in Hitler's Germany and the 1930's Fascist regimes in Europe.

Lastly, it is my intention to present issues of policy and international affairs that cannot be pigeon-holed into a pre-ordained Right-Left continuum on a single horizontal axis (figure 1), but demand a more sensitive, multi-dimensional and complex model or paradigm. Slightly more sophisticated alternative models use a vertical axis with the most frequently used dimension, the degree of civil rights and liberties so that the upper right (high on both dimensions) are conservative libertarians and the upper left are anarchists. On the lower right are the authoritarian Fascists and the lower left belongs to the authoritarian hard-line Stalinist Communists, (see figure 2). This model too is quite inadequate in reflecting the reality of many issues and relations.

How the Right-Left Model Began

The most radical revolutionaries responsible for the overthrow of the old monarchical and aristocratic semi-feudal system prevalent before 1789 and their fundamental support for the slogans they chose to symbolize as "Liberty, Equality, Fraternity" left behind the indelible association of their seating position at the left side of the semi-circular shape of the Assembly Hall with other ideas identified as radical or progressive and democratic. It may well be that the terms were borrowed by the French from the British parliamentary tradition that supporters of the government sat to the right of the speaker while the opposition party sat to the left. Sitting among one's own party members became a practice in politics like the habit at a sports event where the home team and the visiting club fans prefer the comfort of solidarity beyond the range of physical and verbal abuse from opponents.

Eventually, after the Napoleonic period, the terms extreme right and extreme left, center-right and center left came into general use and by 1871 with the establishment of the Third Republic, the terms that began solely as seating arrangements were adopted by political parties who called themselves the Republican Left, the Center Right, and the Center Left (1871) and the Extreme Left (1876) and Radical Left (1881).

Undoubtedly the derivation of the terms has an even older origin and may well go back to the Bible where expressions like the "King's right hand," or "my right hand man" meant someone dependable. The right referred to the stronger, already established and morally just side or position. Forces that opposed the "natural order'"and the establishment could thus cast themselves as forces of change, opposition or novelty by using the term Left.

In general, politicians of the Left in Europe and their imitators in the newly established republics in North and South America generally endorsed and favored this designation whereas those not ardently in favor of radical changes generally disliked the use of these designations and preferred to be called conservatives, moderates or other names. They philosophically denied that the many different issues of public policy could be neatly arranged in a semi-circle or any single line continuum that would be valid across the entire political spectrum.

The Bible contains at least 25 unfavorable references to the left hand. In the best known example which also extols the right hand in the Gospel of Matthew, Jesus says: "*When the Son of man shall come in his glory, and all the holy angels with him, then shall he sit upon the throne of his glory: and before him shall be gathered all nations: And he shall separate them one from another, as a shepherd divideth his sheep from the goats: And he shall set the sheep on his right hand, but the goats on the left. Then shall the King say unto them on his right hand, 'Come, ye blessed of my Father, inherit the kingdom prepared for you from the foundation of the world.' ... Then shall he say also unto them on the left hand, 'Depart from me, ye cursed, into everlasting fire, prepared for the devil and his angels.*" (Matthew 25:31-34, 41)

The Biblical verses in The Book of Isaiah (Isaiah 41:8-12) make it abundantly clear that Israel stands on God's Right Hand. God declares to Israel in verse 10; "*I will uphold thee with the RIGHT hand of my RIGHTEOUSNESS.*" Israel was once indeed the darling of the Political Left on the international scene (see Chapter 18) but has been excoriated for more than two decades by almost all of the organized Left in Europe. Three notable exceptions are outstanding courageous female writers, and journalists, Sigrid Undset, Orianna Fallaci and Pilar Rahola (see Chapter 25) whose reputations for integrity had been formed by their opposition to the far Right. Nevertheless, by refusing to toe the conventional wisdom of the Left, they were ostracized and in response, threw down the gauntlet and refused to be cowed.

The custom of shaking hands originated in medieval times. It was customary when two men met, they would hold each other's right hand to demonstrate that they were not armed as weapons were usually carried in the right hand. Lefties could not be trusted because they could shake their enemy's right hand while concealing a weapon behind them with their left hand.

This tradition faulting the Left persists in many languages such as Latin, from which we derive "sinister" indicating suspicion and mistrust and evil although originally meaning simply "left." The French word for left is gauche, which in English means "awkward" or "tactless." The English word left comes from Old English meaning "weak." Why then, would the Political Left be so proud to bear this title? Apparently, it is related to the fact that the term indicates an unexpected, non-traditional and even elite status (all to be admired) since only about 10 to 12 percent of the population are left-handed yet they include notable personalities of great achievement such as Julius Caesar, Charlie Chaplin, H.G. Wells, Paul McCartney, Babe Ruth, Lewis Carroll, Nelson Rockefeller, and eight U.S. Presidents including Barack Obama.

Politicians on the Left over the past one hundred and fifty years have striven to inculcate the associations between their political views and the lexicon of politics that identifies the interests of the upper or dominant classes as "Right," and the "Left" as the sector expressive of the lower economic or social classes, and the "Center" with that of the middle classes. These associations are however often blatantly out of touch with the reality of voting behavior in many countries (notably the United States), regions and historical periods where countless other factors such as religion, ethnicity, historical memories, national interests, ethnic solidarity, and moral and philosophical values provide countervailing weights.

In the past, the associations of the Left with being part of a persecuted minority was doubtlessly encouraged by the real difficulties and disadvantages of being left-handed in society, especially in the use of many tools. Today, however the knowledge that Lefties are dominated by the right hemisphere of the brain dealing with music, art, perception, emotions, and other forms of abstract thinking aids in the belief that their views are culturally superior to the dominant right handed (and politically Right) majority. This view, however facetious and naïve, is held by many in the younger generation who identify with the political Left and believe that their supposed greater artistic sensitivity makes them "cool" as opposed to the "square" attitudes of their parents' generation.

Confusion Over Liberalism and Libertarianism

A major part of the problem is that liberalism, generally regarded today as being on The Left, originally was a viewpoint reflecting the beliefs in individual initiative, rights and liberties in both the economic and political spheres and opposed to the traditionalist, archprotectionist and aristocratic regimes of early 19th Century Europe. A liberal above all was in favor of a "hands off," or laissez-faire, policy. The United States was classically seen as an example of "liberal democracy." No less a statesman and spokesman for the new American republic, its first president, George Washington stated in 1790:

> "The Citizens of the United States of America have a right to applaud themselves for having given to mankind examples of an enlarged and liberal policy: a policy worthy of imitation. All possess alike liberty of conscience and immunities of citizenship. It is now no more that toleration is spoken of, as if it was by the indulgence of one class of people, that another enjoyed the exercise of their inherent natural rights."[1]

The central government was allotted a minimal role in the affairs of society and the economy as stated in the Constitution by the 10th Amendment, any exercise of authority not explicitly granted to the federal government was to be in the hands of the state governments. The function of government was not to provide direction for society or the economy, but the preservation of a "free environment" where individual citizens would conduct themselves as they saw fit as long as they didn't infringe on the rights of others. This has been thoroughly altered. By this definition, the strongest advocate of liberalism today would be The Tea Party in the United States but the common perception of the term "liberal" has, of course, been thoroughly revamped.

Some old European political parties, for example "Venstre" in Denmark (the word Venstre means Left in Danish), still represent the moderate right liberal view of free trade and strong protection of individual rights and liberties. At the time Venstre was established in 1870, the ruling party was called Højre (Right), the forerunner of the present Conservative Party. Venstre is currently the largest party in Denmark and was founded on the basis of free market liberalism and is regarded by observers as the traditional classic liberal right of center in favor of lower taxes, less government intervention in corporate and individual affairs and was originally strongest in rural districts. In the United

---

1 Washington's letter of August 17, 1790, to Moses Seixas and the Jewish congregation of Newport, Rhode Island in response to a congratulatory address to Washington when he visited their city. The account is on the Library of Congress website.

States, since the 1920s, "liberal" has generally meant the opposite. This of course confuses many Americans.

Today's popular understanding of the term Liberal is practically synonymous with The Moderate Left and closely associated with "big government," regulation of the economy, "progressive taxation" (soak the rich), and a so called "progressive social policy," that has come to mean gay rights, unlimited free speech, feminism, a special differential treatment of classes of citizens referred to as "Affirmative Action" and a foreign policy that provides assistance to help uplift the poor in many "third world" countries rather than any considerations of how national security interests are served.

How Many More Dimensions?

Several political scientists have argued for a more complex model with an additional vertical axis to arrange political parties (figure 2). Here, opinions diverge. It is no longer fashionable to use only individual civil rights and liberties. Some have argued for religious faith and traditional values. Today, most of the Left worldwide assigns religious faith to the Right as part of old fashioned traditional values yet, for a large part of American history, the Religious Left has been recognized as a powerful force thundering hellfire and brimstone against the Establishment. The so called "mainstream" denominations were primarily responsible for the campaign to end racial segregation in American schools and called for the censure of Senator McCarthy (see chapter 7) while the largest Evangelical sects today are strongly identified with the Political Right and are in the forefront of the struggle against abortion, pornography, divorce, and other issues that the Left has strongly defended. Most ironic and contradictory is the present attitude of many Leftwing political parties and regimes throughout the world that are reluctant to oppose a misogynist, intolerant, antisemitic and reactionary militant Islam or are apologetic about Western civilization (see chapter 22).

There is no more powerful image of the religious Left crying out in defense of the ordinary wage earner and against Wall Street than the sensationalist "Cross of Gold Speech" intoned by William Jennings

21

Bryan in the 1896 Democratic Party convention. Bryan, three times unsuccessful Presidential candidate and a former Secretary of State, likewise opposed any hint of imperialist involvement overseas and intervention in the affairs of other peoples or the slightest hint of colonialist adventures. This is the same William Jennings Bryan who was lampooned, ridiculed and defamed by Hollywood Producers in their wholly distorted and vengeful atrocity of a film "Inherit the Wind" (1960; nominated for 4 Academy Awards and praised by many "liberals" as an attack on McCarthyism as well as an historical account of the actual trial) dramatizing the "Scopes Monkey Trial." The film grotesquely portrays Bryan as a glutton and the epitome of religious reaction, fundamentalist Protestant Evangelical Bible thumping ignorance. The film is a total travesty of the actual court record.

Political scientist Hans J. Eysenck[2] sought another dimension on the vertical axis for a new model and believed that it was an essential element common to authoritarian personalities rather than economic theory that explained the frequent similarities of centralized political power. Both Nazis and Communists were tough-minded, aggressive, and strong believers in punishment for crimes against society. They resented any source of power beyond their control in the home, family, the church, the workplace and in the individual.

Eysenck was a veteran opponent of Nazism and was forced to flee to Britain where he carried on his research. He was equally hostile to communism and revealed the notorious antisemitic prejudices of the Stalinist regime and the hypocritical and luxurious life style of the USSR and East European ruling class of bureaucrats. Milton Rokeach developed his own two-axis model of political values in 1973, basing it on the concepts of Freedom and Equality as described in his book, *The Nature of Human Values*.[3] Although initially critical of Eysenck, Rokeach also agreed that there is a basic similarity between the polar opposites of the Far Right and the Far Left (Nazism and Communism) so that so called historical anomalies as the Hitler-Stalin Non-Aggression Pact of 1939 (see Chapter 15) were not really surprising. To reflect that the far

---

2 Eysenck, Hans *The Psychological Basis of Ideology* (editor) with G.D. Wilson. Springer. 1978

3 Rokeach, Milton *The Nature of Human Values, Individual and Societal.*, Free Press 2003. http://en.wikipedia.org/wiki/Political_spectrum - cite_note-Rokeach-12

Right and far Left bend towards each other, several new models such as a scroll or compass have been adopted (figure 3) to illustrate the curved space of the spectrum.

The lack of appreciation of the importance of geography and religious values is responsible for many miscalculations in the area of alliances and strategic interests that have often been more important than the economic and social policies of leaders who were cast as "authoritarian right" but were much more determined to soundly resist German and Italian aggression in World War II than the democratic and fragmented liberal-left coalition governments in traditional democracies such as France, Denmark, the Netherlands, and Belgium (see Chapters 12, 15 and 16).

As contemporary political scientist R.G. Price[4] maintains, the use of the terms "Conservative" and "Liberal" are problematic in themselves. He argues correctly that there are various types of "conservative Leftists" such as the Amish religious denomination which has rejected much of the technology of the modern world but achieved a prosperous economic order with a strongly conservative social base that requires mutual assistance in situations where individuals encounter unexpected hardship. The same may be said of the Israeli kibbutz movement until about 20 years ago.

The demand for secession in the American South that led to the temporary dissolution of the Union was a rejection of strong central government and would thus classify it as a "Leftist" ideology but on the economic scale, it was defending "freedom" by the demand of a small class of slave owners to continue their privileged way of life. Nevertheless, for many poor white southerners with no interest or sympathy for the institution of slavery, secession was the right to govern themselves without the interference of others with different social and cultural traditions and far removed from their homeland.

Art and Music

Nowhere is the similarity in the essential group-collective

---

4 Price, R. G. *Understanding the Political Spectrum,* self-published, 2007.

mentality of the Far Left and Far Right more apparent than in the attitude of their archetypical regimes to art in the fields of painting and music. Stalinist Russia and Hitler's Nazi Germany were of one mind on this issue – that art must have a "redeeming social value" for the benefit and the uplifting of the masses for the good of society. Stalin had this to say about art in 1946:

> "We should ask ourselves a question as to how dangerous are the 'avantgarde' tendencies in music and the abstract school of art and sculpture that is being imported from the West?

> Today, under the guise of innovation, formalism, we see it being induced into Soviet music and abstraction in painting. Once in a while a question can be heard "Is it necessary for such great people as Bolsheviks and Leninists to be engaged in such petty things and spend their time criticizing abstract painting and formalism? Let the psychiatrists deal with it!"

> In these types of questions you can sense the misunderstanding of the role of ideological sabotage against our country and especially against our youth, which is discernable. It is with their help that attempts are being made against socialist realism in art and literature. This is being done openly. In these so-called abstract paintings there is no real face of those people, whom people would like to imitate in the fight for their peoples happiness, for communism and for the path on which they want progress. …..To what can a bust of twisted iron sculpture, representing "innovation" as an art inspire us? To what can an abstract painting inspire?

> This is the reason why modern American financial magnates are propagating modernism, paying for this type of work huge royalties, which the great masters of realism may not ever see.

> There is an underlying idea of class struggle in the so-called Western popular music, in the so-called formalist tendencies. This music is created from the sect of "shakers" dance that

induces people to ecstasy, trance and makes them into some kind of wild animal ready for any action. This type of music is created with the help of psychiatrists so as to influence the brain and psychology of the people. This is one type of musical narcotics under whose influence a person cannot think of fresh ideas and is turned into a herd. It is useless to invite such people to the revolution. As you see, music can also fight."[5]

How right Stalin was! And Hitler! Hamburg in the late 1930s was the primary scene of young people who cultivated bee-bop and swing as an expression of anti-regime sentiment and is the subject of an excellent 1993 film *Swing Kids*. Benny Goodman records were the hottest item of this underground culture. The appeal of American Jazz music in the 1930s was a sure sign of opposition to both regimes that frequently lashed out at these "barbaric" forms of music as products of degenerate American society that "had been so corrupted under the influenced of Jews and Blacks." The Soviets would continue their attacks on American culture when rock and roll supplanted jazz.

The Bleeding Hearts of the Left

The brazen inhumanity of the Far Left in the 20th century posing as internationalists, humanists and pacifists is revealed in their actual stance on many issues in contradiction to their purported sympathy for the underdog and the oppressed. It is no wonder that many Liberals are called "Bleeding hearts." However, their sympathy is certainly not for "the meek who shall inherit the earth" as forecast by Jesus but for outcasts and brutal personality types. These won the support of the Bleeding Heart Left which insists that they are the "oppressed" who deserve a second chance. The Left traditionally opposes that convicted felons should be denied the right to vote.

For many crusading self-proclaimed leftwing writers, film producers, celebrities and artists, the more heinous the crime, the more

5 1946 meeting between Stalin and Soviet intellectuals to discuss and analyze the trends developing in Soviet art, music, literature and theatre - after the Second World War; reported in the Soviet press

the guilty perpetrators should be viewed as victims too (society is responsible) and their use of violence as a tool of redemption. The real victims of totalitarianism of the Left are counted in the tens of millions but the violence of Stalin, Mao, Pol Pot, Ho Chi Minh, was qualified by many as liberating or redemptive. It was a violence of the"masses" and gained its most enthusiastic supporters from the ranks of so called intellectuals in theory and the proletariat in practice. Mona Charen hit the nail on the head in identifying the hypocrisy and utter disregard for the similarities in the two evils of recent history, Nazism and Communism when she wrote:

> "The challenge posed by the two totalitarian systems of the twentieth century were comprehensive. They forced Americans to respond politically, culturally, economically, and above all morally. Liberals had no difficulty meeting the challenge of fascism. They found its barbarism despicable and said so. They feared its aggression. And they found its ideas disgusting. Even at the cost of 484,375 Americans (American fatalities in World War II), they were prepared to make whatever sacrifices were required to thwart and defeat that assault on world peace and simple decency.
>
> Antifascism came as naturally as breathing, which is as it should be. The Nazis, in the more than half century since their defeat, have become synonymous with evil in our intellectual and cultural life, again, just as it should be. And yet the Communists, whose crimes were nearly comparable (and the debate about which was worse is shabby and irrelevant), have never entered the evil category for liberals. Quick: try to think of a single movie about the horrors of Stalinism. This is not a failure of imagination. This is a moral meltdown."[6]

Even more complicated diagrams with two or more dimensions fail to show the nature of the political spectrum that frequently is curved at the edges (figure 3) as Far Left and Far Right diverge from

---

6 Charen, Mona, *Useful Idiots*, (Regnery Publishing, 2003) pp 260-261.

classical 19th Century liberalism and approach each other and may co-alesce and overlap in such phenomena as "populism" of various kinds such as the Peronist regime in Argentina (see chapter 20) or Huey Long's policies in Louisiana during the depression.

More complicated figures in the shape of diamonds and other odd shapes often lose any sense of a continuum. Some political scientists have devised extensive questionnaires with a point system to rank political parties and movements but these are usually unstable as they frequently cannot be used cross culturally. The diagram (figure 1) below is the American "classical one." Nevertheless it presents serious problems and disagreements because of the crucial role of personal liberty.

Figure 1- Traditional One Dimensional Political Spectrum:

LEFT   CENTER   RIGHT

Anarchy? Far Left -New Left-Blue Dog Democrats-Tea Party-Fascist -Nazi

Communism-Social Democrats-Liberals-Republicans-Libertarian-Anarchy?

There are still many disagreements on where to place anarchism, and libertarianism depending on the degree of state control vs. individual freedom. Even with a second dimension measured on a vertical axis (figure 2), there is not enough space to take personal liberty, nationalism, religious observance, moral and ethical issues (sexuality, abortion, homosexuality, euthenasia) into account.

Libertarians would claim that individuals have every right to do with their own lives as they see fit on the basis of individual liberty without any state control as long as they do not impinge on the rights of others so, nominally, they should be placed on the Right according to the concept of LIBERTY and that BOTH NAZIS and COMMUNISTS belong on the Far Left (most collectivist and authoritarian) of the spectrum because they restrict personal liberty and glorify the state and collective goals. In the United States however, those who support these liberties claim that the state (on the federal level) should ensure that they can freely exercise these rights without any consideration of public order, traditional moral and religious values and thus, are frequently portrayed as being on the Left side of the scale.

Where do the anarchists fit? This has also been problematic with the Right-Left scheme. Anarchy is defined as the absence of authority and law. Traditionally, being opposed to a firm authority put the anarchists on the Left. In several European countries, notably Spain, Switzerland, Russia, and Italy anarchists were active in various labor unions in which communists and socialists also participated. However, the anarchists and Trotskyite factions of the Spanish labor movement were brutally suppressed by the Communists who insisted on the order and authority of a strong central government and a regular army. For the 'true' anarchists, there was no place in the army for uniforms, ranks, military discipline or salutes. They believed in wholly voluntary cooperative communities not subject to codes, regulations, rules or subject to threats and coercion. Many of these groups also accepted sexual equality and tried to retain a large measure of autonomy by producing for themselves on a largely subsistence basis rather than function by specialized production within larger economic and consumer markets.

An anarchist with hatred of the Federal government and its policies to implement various progressive social programs led Timothy McVeigh to plan and execute the attack on the Federal Office Building in downtown Oklahoma City in April, 1995. McVeigh is always portrayed by the media as a Far Right fanatic because of his identification with "militia groups" yet, he had no philosophy or ideology of what type of society would replace the "tyranny" of the Federal government and should be considered an anarchist. Unlike John Wilkes Booth who was a Confederate sympathizer bemoaning the loss of the Southern cause or Lee Harvey Oswald's hatred of American capitalism, or various religious fanatics such as David Koresh of the Branch Dravidian Cult intent on ushering in a Last Days scenario, McVeigh stood for nothing except an anarchic individual hatred of the establishment, government and the vision of a world wide Leftist conspiracy that were all evil in his view.

As Goldberg demonstrated in *Liberal Fascism*, the exceesses with which Senator McCarthy was most often assailed and considered rightwing, an ugly nationalist strain, exaggerated exhortations to patriotism, jingoism, racism, nativism and a willingness to limit individual rights in the name of national security were precisely the excesses committed in most drastic form not by a senator and not by a Republican but by Democratic President Woodrow Wilson in his management of the economy, war and the Red Scares of 1919-1920. [7]

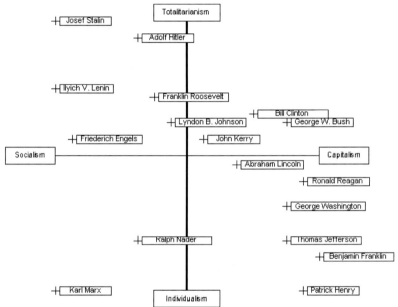

Figure 2, Source: The Liberty Papers Website[8]

One of many schemes to present a second axis of the political spectrum. This particular example illustrates the degree of control over the economy on the horizontal axis and the level of liberty as measured by individual vs. collective (state) authority. It is a bit more imaginative than many others by placing important historical personalities and locating them at their 'proper' position with respect to both axes. It is certainly accurate as the chart indicates, to claim that Hitler and Stalin are not so far apart.

7 Goldberg, Jonah *Liberal Fascism*, see Chapter 3 Woodrow Wilson and The Birth of Liberal Fascism, pp. 78-120.
8 http://www.thelibertypapers.org/2005/11/26/a-better-political-spectrum/

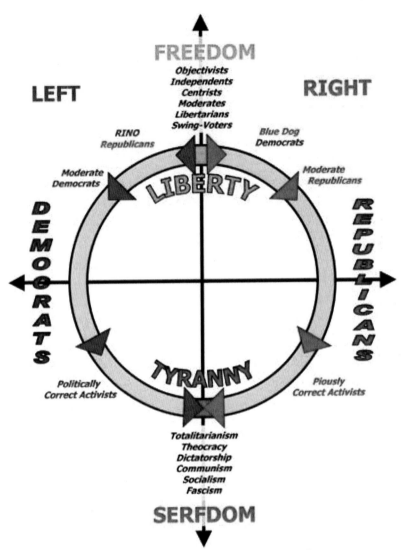

Figure 3 .Source: The Compass Thoughts Aloud; A Haven for Sovereign Rational Minds[9]

In figure 3 we see how the sides of the figure bend towards each other leading towards coercion, tyranny and serfdom at the bottom of the compass and towards freedom at the top.

9 http://www.thoughtsaloud.com/essays/the political spectrum/

2
The Leftwing Tilt of American Literature and Film

It is no wonder that long before the turbulent 60s, there was a strong attachment of many of America's leading writers and filmmakers with the Left. This has predisposed much political thought to follow the cultural trends perceived as enlightened, progressive, idealistic and cool.

The staple themes of American literature from Sinclair Lewis (*Babbit, Arrowsmith, Elmer Gantry*), through Arthur Miller (*All My Sons, Death of a Salesman*), Saul Bellow (*Seize the Day*), Norman Mailer (*The White Negro, The Armies of the Night, The Executioner's Song*), and Henry Miller (*The Air Conditioned Nightmare, Tropic of Cancer, Tropic of Capricorn, The Cosmological Eye*) are a corrupt, materialistic, puritanical, sexually frustrated and neurotic society that owes its fundamental values to American competitiveness. Europe, by contrast, may have poverty and aristocracy but holds out the promise of class, chic, style, refinement and the enchantment of a militant working class movement ready to rise to change the old world and usher in a new age while America has bewitched the poor working class slobs into believing they can share in the cake of affluence.

In *The Cosmological Eye* (1939), Henry Miller foresees an act of karma for America's sins that predates the attack of 9/11 by more than 70 years and expects some future act of cosmic vengeance:

> "Until this colossal, senseless machine which we have made of America is smashed and scrapped there can be no hope."

Never once did Miller or other successful critical authors who were outraged by what they found reprehensible in American society express any condemnation, surprise or shock at the excesses of totalitarian societies responsible for the deaths of tens of millions of ordinary people. However, they were often motivated to write in defense of convicted murderers in the United States to express their support of those outcasts whom they felt had acted out of desperation as "victims of society."

Their misplaced passion for the underdog continues today with automatic expressions of support on the Left for many murderers and rapists on death row, illegal immigrants, displaced Palestinian refugees, and even the 9/11 suicide attackers who murdered three thousand American civilians at work but who must be understood and their crimes also attributed to some legitimate grievance.

The War in Defense of Western Civilization against Islamist Fundamentalism and Jihad is rejected by many on the Left today who cannot accept that it is both a necessary and moral act of self-defense in their morally neutral, post-modernist view that no culture is better or worse than any other.

In a brilliant essay, Professor Sam Bluefarb has pointed out what must be the most revealing and atrocious example of intellectual sophistry that puts Miller alongside today's cultural idols who likewise follow an example of pacifism collapsing into idiocy. We have the advantage of more than seventy years of hindsight to evaluate Miller's preposterous proposal:

> "The surest way to defeat Hitler would, in my opinion, be for Europe to surrender willingly. I go farther—I say let him have the whole world. Can you see what would happen to his grandiose ideas [sic] if there were no resistance? Hitler, or anyone who seeks power, is only a force as long as he is opposed. Imagine laying out the problems of the world before him [and expecting him] to solve them. The man would die of brain fever overnight."[1]

Prof. Bluefarb reminds us that a similar proposal was made by another of the Left's great idols, the spiritual father of pacifism, Mohandas Gandhi during World War II, in which the Mahatma—"Great

---

1 Bluefarb, Sam "Henry Miller and the Pull of Gravity," *New English Review*, November, 2010.

Soul"—urged the Jews of Germany…..."*To go gladly to their deaths, and thus gain the moral sympathy of the world.*" Today, similar proposals coming from those who claim that we in the West are responsible for Muslim grievances are no less absurd. They think and act under the assumption that 1,400 years of aggressive Muslim expansion cannot be called provocation but only reactions to it by those under attack.

The "Pull" of the accumulated "Gravity" of the many authors, playwrights and other artists, intellectuals and academia is overwhelmingly towards the Left and has exerted its force for decades. Its compassion is reserved only for those on the fringes of society or Third World failed states and peoples. When it comes to any issue involving Jews who might be siphoned off from the ranks of the militant Left, there is no pity, humanity, sympathy or empathy. Those Jews who defend themselves and seek to live on the basis of their own integrity and individuality in Israel and elsewhere are now accused of betraying some higher nobler cause.

As long ago as 1958 this trend on the part of a significant segment of writers to dismiss Jewish suffering or reject the right of Jews to act in self-defense, was clearly seen in the interviews given by Leon Uris, the author of the best selling novel *Exodus* in explaining why he wrote the book. He had in mind successful Jewish authors such as Philip Roth, Saul Bellow and Bernard Melamud whom he called "professional apologists" for being Jews. Uris set out to tell the story of Israel's rebirth as the story of Jewish heroes rather than the psychological analyses of individuals who grew up damning their fathers and hating their mothers and wondering why they were born.

They are sarcastically referred to in Israel as "beautiful souls" by those who reject their elitism of supposed high moral values so out of place in the Arab Middle East and as remote from the real world as were the great majority of the victims of the Holocaust whose Jewish values prevented them, from attributing such evil to the Germans, made so poignantly real in the film, *Ship of Fools* (1965, based on the novel by Katherine Ann Porter).

Film

Two of the most honestly gruesome films of barbaric atrocities in modern times ever made are the Russian film *The Chekist* and the Polish film *Katyn*. *The Chekist* was directed by Aleksandr Rogozhkin (1992 Cannes Film Festival Award) but hardly rated mention anywhere in the United States. The unbelievable torture and mass executions seen in the film were all confirmed by *Pravda* in 1921-22. His acclaimed 2002 film *The Cuckoo* (*Kukushka*), won the Golden Eagle Award for Best Picture and is undoubtedly the most realistic and moving film made dealing with language barriers.

Katyn is the true story of the slaughter of 22,000 Polish officers in April, 1940 by Stalin's henchmen and based on the book *Post Mortem: The Story of Katyn* by Anderzj Mularczyk. It was nominated for Best Foreign Language Film. The Russian leadership has admitted Stalin's guilt for the Katyn massacre, finally turned into a dramatic film in the 2007 Polish production. It is an emotionally horrifying and draining experience. Both these films' producers and actors are brutally honest and graphically portray the unvarnished horror of the Communist regimes to their fellow citizens in Poland and Russia, something no Hollywood producer has dared to do and about which, most of the American public shows no interest.

Contrast this with the host of anti-Nazi films made during World War II that established Hollywood's patriotic reputation and the naked fact that no serious major Hollywood feature film has dealt with the epic battle against totalitarian communism. The films with a major international political theme made before American entry into the war hardly touched on the Soviet Union except for a light comedy like *Ninotchka* (MGM 1939).

During the war, Hollywood went overboard in its portrayal of the USSR and Stalin as a valuable ally with no serious attempt to condemn the atrocities of the regime that were already well known in the late 1930s and the 22 months of Soviet-Nazi cooperation from September 1939 to June 1941 (see chapter 15).

Hollywood's leftward drift extended in recent times to *JFK*, (Oliver Stone) a film that not just cast doubt, but spread malicious rumor and innuendo accusing the CIA and Vice President Johnson of complicity in the murder of President Kennedy and casting both the wretched and delusional assassin Lee Harvey Oswald and the unscrupulous New Orleans District Attorney Jim Garrison in a sympathetic light. The film changes reality by misrepresenting and inventing facts to fit the supposed conspiracy in which the CIA, the Mafia, Vice President Johnson are all cast in the shadow of suspicion and guilt.

Another travesty of the American cinema is *Gangs of New York,* (Martin Scorsese) a totally distorted account of the 1863 Draft Riots that outdoes Nazi and Soviet propaganda in its depiction of every aspect of American society and government as venal, corrupt and racist. The directors of these two films are considered among the 'most distinguished' in America. They are well known for their leftwing views and their films exceed in vituperative lies about American Society anything produced by Nazi and Soviet propaganda in their heydays.

The Romanticized Free French

It is hard for the average movie-goer under the age of 60 to conceive of a time when Hollywood responded to war and international crises with patriotic fervor and even took initiatives to explain complicated and difficult foreign policy dilemmas for the American government, yet this is indeed the background of many dramatic war films produced in the period of American involvement in World War II. The fall of France shook American public opinion so that even before Pearl Harbor, producers were researching for ways to represent the danger of Nazism.

Casablanca is the all time great hit, frequently voted "the most popular film of all time" in the United States (in some polls a close second to *Citizen Kane*). It, and four other "also-rans" deal with the role of the French in World War II, the Vichy regime and Franco-American relations.

These films come to mind immediately in the wake of the recent tensions between the United States and France. Three of them employed very similar plots revolving around heroic individuals, either American outsiders or expatriates in Europe and their confrontation with the Fascist Vichy regime or courageous French journalists battling the pervading atmosphere of appeasement. Three of these films even employed the same cast of characters, starring Humphrey Bogart supported by Claude Rains, Peter Lorre, Sydney Greenstreet and in two of them, his wife-to-be, Lauren Bacall.

Apart from the mega-success of *Casablanca* (1942), set in Morocco are the "also-rans," *To Have and To Have Not* (1944) starring Lauren Bacall in her famous debut and unforgettable line - "just whistle" and *Passage to Marseilles* (1944), both of which take place in the French Caribbean possession of Martinique and the French Penal Colony on Devil's Island (where Dreyfus was imprisoned). In *Sahara* (1943), Bogart plays an American captain and tank-commander rallying a motley collection of volunteers among Allied troops who include "Frenchy", a gallant Free French soldier.

Another film, *Cross of Lorraine* (1943), the symbol of General de Gaulle's Free French movement, deals with inter-French tensions and conflicts that played such an important role in 1940-42 when the American State Department recognized the Fascist Vichy regime and had to follow a policy of "correct relations" ignoring General de Gaulle, a policy that caused much confusion among the American public.

In all these films, the French are portrayed as a nation betrayed by its own leaders and opportunistic officials all too willing to collaborate with the Nazis. There is a small band of "Free French" who are presented as brave but also inept, disorganized and devoid of leadership. In the end, these Frenchmen are finally inspired to fight by the heroic Humphrey Bogart.

In *Passage to Marseilles*, Bogart, a French reporter, speaks out against appeasement and is framed by the authorities as a "troublemaker" likely to offend Nazi Germany. He is sent to Devil's Island for fifteen years after a street mob wrecks the printing presses of his newspaper that criticized French betrayal of the Czechs at Munich while the police simply stand by and let the mob do its work.

After escaping from Devil's Island, Bogart finds refuge on a ship bound for Marseilles. He tells Claude Rains that…. *"The France you and I loved is dead, Colonel. She's been dying for a long time. I saw her die in the Rhineland and at Munich. Now, her death is complete. I can stop lying and tell the truth."* In very similar dialogue in the other two films, Bogart tells other Frenchmen in exile who are full of doubt and indecision, that they must take a stand and fight the Nazis to redeem France's honor. After all, he had fought or sold weapons to the Ethiopians and Spanish Republicans – hardly the background one would expect from a nightclub owner in Vichy controlled Casablanca in 1942.

His words so shame the doubters that they kiss him on the cheek with the exclamation that *"We are so glad you are on our side"* (*To Have and Have Not*) and Claude Raines portraying the Police Commissioner decides to *"toss a bottle of Vichy water into the trash can"* (*Casablanca*). Since these events take place before Pearl Harbor, Bogart's action is his own free choice and not the formal obligation of an ally. He helps because *"it's the right thing to do,"* something which the Frenchmen seem to have difficulty understanding.

In all the films, one hears the repeated subliminal melody of "The Marseillaise." In Rick's Casablanca bar, it is sung openly in a brief act of defiance and Rick (Bogart) takes the blame. Casablanca has become a cult with its own following. Few films match its sublime mix of drama, romance, intrigue and adventure. Rick has a sentimental memory of the time he spent in Paris with his love Ilsa (Ingrid Bergman) before the war. The French surrender and ensuing confusion results in him losing Ilsa, only to regain her later and give her up so she can accompany a resistance leader into exile and carry on the fight.

Claude Rains plays the Vichy French police official "Captain Louis Renault" who provides protection for Rick's café in return for a share of the illegal gambling profits. This character at first typifies the cynical, corrupt and totally pragmatic Frenchmen who chose some form of collaboration with the Germans in order to survive. His devotion to "duty" is immortalized in the lines *"I am making out the report now. We haven't quite decided if he committed suicide or died trying to escape"*; his feigned sense of shock in having to close down the Café, *"I am shocked - shocked - to find gambling is going on here,"* only to be told by the croupier *"Your winnings, sir;"* his immortal reply to Rick who is holding a gun pointed at his heart, *"That is my least vulnerable spot;"* and his frank admission, *"I have no conviction, if that's what you mean. I blow with the wind, and the prevailing wind happens to be from Vichy."*

In the end, Louis has to make a choice and flees with Rick to Free French Territory, prompting the last line of the film from Rick; *"Louis, this could be the beginning of a beautiful friendship."*

A lesser known film, *The Cross of Lorraine* (1943), takes place in a prisoner of war camp where French soldiers are interned. Peter Lorre plays a sadistic and corrupt German prison guard. Hume Cronyn plays a French prisoner more than ready to work for the Germans in order to win extra rations of food and other favors. The other stars, Jean-Pierre Aumont and Gene Kelly, are two close friends who differ in their view of the necessity of fighting. They are depressed to hear the prisoners relate that their countrymen at home, especially the "wise ones," are collaborating. The muffled strains of the Marseillaise are continually repeated in this film until the very end. Sir Cedric Hardwicke, voicing dissent, plays a French priest who admonishes the prisoners that to resist and die fighting is better than to serve the Germans and thereby repudiate their "divine origin."

In this film, there are no American characters but the news alone that the Americans have landed in French North Africa and are fighting there with the Free French under "The Cross of Lorraine" (General de Gaulle's forces) is enough to bring elation to all the villagers where the two men have found refuge after escaping from prison. When spending the night at the home of an ordinary family, they realize how all the simple joys of life will be eliminated in the Nazi New Order and exult in the knowledge that they must fight to make that kind of world impossible.

Jean-Pierre Aumont's character is also plagued by the realization that before the war he had preferred the policies of appeasement and, therefore, he owes a debt to his friend Victor and those like him who saw the dangers of not fighting then. *"They wanted to fight and we didn't. We got all the Victors into this."* Even the character played by Gene Kelly - a traumatized man, broken by Nazi torture, who vows never to risk his life or even comfort for anything - is shamed by a teenage boy in the Resistance. The two friends and boy exult that *"It's war again! It's to bring happiness again to millions of homes that we fight."* (Just imagine a line of dialogue like this in a contemporary Hollywood film!).

At the end, the entire village population fights with rocks and bare fists against the Germans, burning their own homes in a Russian-like scorched-earth policy rather than submit. The film ends with the Cross of Lorraine fluttering across the screen to the exultant strains of "The Marseillaise." Rarely has the cinema portrayed such an out-of-character event for a nation.

All these films convey the incorrect notion that the opponents of Nazism were all to be found only on the Left – crusading journalists, radicals, liberals, bohemians and adventurers in the persona of Bogart rather than the reality in Europe of the politicians like Winston Churchill on the Conservative side of the political spectrum who were by far the strongest opponents of appeasement.

For all its faults, Hollywood, more often than its critics dare admit, hit the nail on the head in the past (i.e. pre-1960) in reducing complex issues and relationships to startling truths, sometimes even creating eternal myths. The motivation of the film studio in presenting the same theme in several films was the rescue of France's sullied, defeatist reputation in American eyes as part of wartime propaganda. Following Pearl Harbor, Hollywood clearly believed that the American war effort would be aided by the creation of a myth that France, the most powerful continental European power and democracy, our brothers-in-arms from 1917-1918 had not really been defeated but "betrayed" and that the Free French were worthy allies and still the bearers of liberté, egalité, fraternité.

This was an important goal because the Vichy regime had alienated American opinion both before and after American entry into the war. In July of 1940, the powerful French fleet based at Oran in Algeria refused the British offer to sail for British ports and had to be sunk. This was an enormous shock for American public opinion. The most powerful naval engagement of the war until that time proved to be the reluctant British decision to destroy a powerful and modern French fleet that, if fallen into the hands of the Axis, would have created a disaster for the British lifeline of supplies. The Vichy leaders, Marshall Petain and Admiral Darlan then called upon the French people to cooperate with Germany.

Finally the Vichy government severed relations with the United States on August 11, 1942 to protest the "invasion" of French territory in North Africa. For much of the American public, the "Evil France" has become identified with the enemy. The first American casualties in the "European theater" of the war against the Axis were caused not by German or Italian forces but by the Vichy French troops in Algeria! But, Americans knew too there was a "Good France" who remained their friend and looked forward to liberation.

Hollywood then was acting as the best conscience of the American people. It produced two other films that were both intensely patriotic and which glorified American valor as well as pointing out the lingering prejudices that should be eliminated in American society. In *Go for Broke!* the 1951 film starring Van Johnson, the outstanding combat record of the 442nd Regimental Combat Team was documented. It was the real life story of Nisei (second-generation Americans born of Japanese parents) soldiers fighting in the European theater. The unit became the most heavily decorated one for its size and length of service in the history of the United States Army as well as one of the units with the highest casualty rates. It also featured the conflict that Japanese Americans successfully resolved in putting aside feelings of hurt and humiliation due to the internment of many of their families on the U.S. mainland. Were this subject to be treated today as a film, it would undoubtedly have focused on the grievance these men legitimately had rather than their recognition that it was an issue that had to be set aside for the duration of the war.

One other film made during the war, *Sahara* (1943) starring Humphrey Bogart, had a clear message of promoting the brotherhood of the Allied cause and encouraging Italian-Americans not to despair. It recognized that a great majority of the Italian people were not willing allies of the Nazis and would, sooner or later, depose the Fascist regime.

What is perhaps most fascinating about many of these films is that they exploited a theme that the American public found easy to relate to then - whether it is better to stand up early and risk war, or try to appease a dictator who will never be satisfied with another compromise. It is an eerie reminder of events preceding the conflicts in Iraq and Afghanistan.

Hollywood Becomes and Remains Deaf, Dumb and Blind

Contrast these magnificent films with the hundreds of war, spy, Spanish Civil War (*For Whom the Bell Tolls*) and Holocaust films made since 1945 that continued to use the wartime anti-Nazi theme but never about any of the real life opponents of the Axis who were conservative even "rightwing" nationalist leaders (see Chapters 12-18).

The Fountainhead (1949) stands out as the ONLY film of a

political nature that intellectually argued against the Leftist themes of solidarity, the plight of the poor, the "just struggle" of the working class, the "new society" created in Soviet Russia and the greed of the wealthy and privileged. On the theme of the Cold War and the struggle of subject peoples under Soviet and Chinese Communist rule, there was essentially nothing but a few trivial Grade C films (for example –*I Married a Communist*) that had to be re-released under the less obvious titles of *The Woman on Pier 13* and *Beautiful but Dangerous*. Critics trashed the film for its "fatuous plot and cartoon characters," yet as a dramatic work it probably compares favorably with "the greatest film of all time' – *Casablanca*, differing only in the identity of the "bad guys."

What *The New York Times* labeled as "The Holy War of the Twentieth Century," i.e. The Struggle to Resist Communism and the Cold War, has not led any American producer to create a serious dramatic film involving the Hitler-Stalin, Pact, the Gulags, the now thoroughly vindicated charges of treason against the Rosenbergs, the evidence of Whittaker Chambers against Alger Hiss, the Korean War, the Hungarian Revolution, the Cultural Revolution in China, Pol Pot, Ceaucescu, the GDR or the collapse of the USSR. Can one imagine directors such as Martin Scorsese, Oliver Stone or Steven Spielberg dealing with any of these themes? Abroad, there have been a few serious British attempts such as *Dr. Zhivago* (1965) and *One Day in the Life of Ivan Denisovitch* (1971).

During the period of the Molotov-Ribbentrop Non-Aggression Pact (see Chapter 15) in which the Nazis and Soviets were close allies, the Soviet attack against Finland in December 1939 (see Chapter 17) provoked screenwriter Philip Dunne and actor Melvin Douglas to propose that the Motion Picture Democratic Committee, a group of activists identified with the Democratic Party, condemn the invasion. A hardcore insider group of Communist Party members using the organization as a congenial front insured the defeat of the resolution.

In his 1980 memoir, aptly named *Take Two: A Life in Movies and Politics*, Dunne wrote "*All over town, the industrious communist tail wagged the lazy liberal dog.*"[2] And so it has been ever since. This was

---

2 Although Philip Dunne participated in a noted demonstration with famous Hollywood actors against the House Un-American Activities Committee's investigation of Hollywood, he clashed with fellow members of the Screen Writers Guild whom he felt were "pro-Stalin"

noted in the 1930s by screenwriter Ayn Rand, the only one in Hollywood who had actually lived under communism. Communist party member Dalton Trumbo, known as the highest paid screenwriter in the business, viewed his profession as "literary guerilla warfare."

In 1941, before Pearl Harbor, religiously towing the Party Line, Trumbo wrote a novel, *The Remarkable Andrew*, in which the ghost of Andrew Jackson appears in order to warn the United States not to get involved in the war. This was so blatant that even Time Magazine sarcastically commented that *"General Jackson's opinions need surprise no one who has observed George Washington and Abraham Lincoln zealously following the Communist Party Line in recent years."*[3]

To gauge the influence of Trumbo and others in whitewashing Stalin and the Soviet regime, one has to view such films as *North Star* and *Song of Russia* (both 1943) that portray the USSR as a land of industrious workers and peasants living in simplicity but in dignity and abundance and dutifully following the guidelines of the Party. Even worse, *Mission to Moscow* (1943), starring no less a luminary than Walter Huston, accepted the charges of the 1930s purge trials against Stalin's former comrades and "explained" how the USSR had "generously offered Finland five times more land" (barren taiga) in exchange for the important security zone along the Karelian isthmus it had demanded just before launching its invasion in 1939.

Trumbo bragged in *The Daily Worker* that thanks to him and communist influence in Hollywood, the Party had quashed adaptations of Arthur Koestler's anti-communist works, *Darkness at Noon* and *The Yogi and the Commissar*. It is precisely this point that most of the House un-American Activities Committee missed in its investigations, the internal network within the screenwriters union in sympathy with the party line rather than the specific content of individual films that might be excused as part of the war-time patriotic effort to cast our Soviet ally in the best possible light.

Communists. He and the actors he appeared with came to realize that they had been naïve. Dunne's true anti-Communist sentiment was used by fellow travelers to denounce him as "secretly" cooperating with the Committee that rewarded him with uninterrupted employment as a screenwriter on major Hollywood productions during the blacklist period.
3 "Counsel from Hollywood", *TIME*. Feb. 6, 1941.

The Venona documents[4] and the memoirs of Hollywood personnel involved in the Communist dominated union activity and studio policies lends credibility to the justified investigations by the House Un-American Activities Committee. What is all the more notable is that the House Un-American Activities Committee was at first strongly supported by the Communist Party–USA (CPUSA) when originally introduced in 1933 on direct orders from Moscow because it was involved in uncovering Nazi and then later Trotskyite activities.

The actors and directors among the approximately 50 witnesses called to testify by the Committee who took the Fifth Amendment hundreds of times and were temporarily 'blacklisted' have entered the pantheon of Americana as the victims of the evil, racist, anti-Semitic, right-wing reaction as memorialized by those who idealize and idolize the witnesses who testified before the committee and in the best of all scenarios were naïve dupes. This was soon realized by a host of actors such as Ronald Reagan, Barbara Stanwyck, Lana Turner, Bette Davis, Humphrey Bogart, Danny Kaye, Gene Kelly and Lauren Bacall who originally went to the hearings with the intent of defending their studio bosses from what they thought might be slander and guilt by association but realized that the Communist Party was indeed strongly enmeshed in the studio's choice and rejection of scripts.

They were active in the IATSE (International Alliance of Theatrical Stage employees) while the Communist party-backed CSU (Conference of Studio Unions) attempted to force the studios to deal only with them. Even in the private field of talent scout agencies working with the major studios such as the William Morris agency, the Party had managed to obtain sufficient influence to steer the scripts of Communist writers and directors such as Ring Lardner Jr. and Bernard Gordon on to the desks of producers while soft-pedaling the work of their non-communist clients.

In 1999, the University of Southern California which is notable for its film school unveiled a sculpture garden dedicated to "The Hol-

---

4 The Venona Documents: Long-running secret collaboration of the US and UK intelligence agencies involving crypto-analysis of messages sent by Soviet intelligence to their operatives in the United States. These include evidence of Soviet espionage campaigns involving Julius Rosenberg, Alger Hiss, Harry Dexter White, the second-highest official in the Treasury Department; Lauchlin Currie, a personal aide to Franklin Roosevelt; and Maurice Halperin, a section head in the Office of Strategic Services.

lywood Ten" who were blacklisted as "victims" of the Cold War and heroes honored for their "Protection of the First Amendment" by refusing to testify. This is the result of the continued preference by many in Hollywood for wishing to "See, Hear and Smell No Evil" because they were committed to the prevailing ideal of those in the profession whose first allegiance is to anti-anti-Communism.

What has Hollywood produced lately? In *Reds* (1981), Oscar winning Warren Beatty plays American journalist and witness to the Russian Revolution, John Reed who makes the concession that the Soviet regime indeed "violates human rights" but nothing on the screen graphically portrays these violations. And today? We have *Syriana*, in which America's involvement in the Middle East and attempt to confront Islamist fanaticism is held to be solely based on oil and portrays the Arabs, the Arab states and Arab-Americans as the unfortunate victims of the global conspiracies and machinations of the CIA.

As long as they oppose the United States, even the most vicious adherents of the 8th century doctrine of fundamentalist Islam with its proclamation of Jihad and its denial of any civil rights or liberties, its record of violent anti-Jewish hatred, its contempt for the elementary rights of women and children, still qualify as "the good guys."

Hollywood producers made *Exodus* based on the novel by Leon Uris, the one unabashedly pro-Israel film only a decade after every Jewish movie producer had turned down making the film *Gentleman's Agreement* (1947; starring Gregory Peck) about polite anti-Semitism. It was made into a film by the great Greek-American director, Elia Kazan who was later turned on with vengeance for cooperating with the House un-American Activities Committee revealing communist influence in Hollywood. Uris himself had been in the front lines in Guadalcanal and Tarawa Island and felt an immense respect for the Israelis who had defeated the invading Arab armies and defied the legion of pro-Arab diplomats in the British Foreign Office and the leadership of the Labor Party (a sin the British Left has never forgiven).

In what must be one of the greatest ironies of film-making, it was none other than the notorious Dalton Trumbo, the arch-Stalinist, who had been 'blacklisted' for his refusal to answer any of HUAC's questions and spent seven months in prison who wrote the screenplay for *Exodus*. Apparently, this was one way of getting back into the good graces of Jewish film producers and movie goers.

One must stand and salute three Europeans with a long background of involvement in the Left and support for the Communist Party in their homelands. The three are worthy of redeeming the conscience of actors and directors everywhere. They refused to lend their names and art to suppression of the truth. They are the French actor and singer, Yves Montand, French actress, Simone Signoret, and Greek director, Constantin Costa-Gavras. The film is *The Confession* (French: L'Aveu), a 1970 French-Italian film. It is based on the true story of the Czech Communist Artur London, a defendant in the infamous anti-Semitic trial held in 1952 resulting in the hanging of eleven prominent former government officials, almost all Jews including Rudolf Slánský for spying (see Chapters 7 and 15).

The trial lasted eight days. It was notable for its strong anti-Jewish tone. Slánský and 10 of his 13 codefendants were Jewish. Just as in the purge trials of the late 1930s, the defendants were craven in court, admitted their guilt and requested to be justly punished with death. Slánský was found guilty of "Trotskiyite-Titoist-Zionist activities in the service of American imperialism." All the defendants were hanged in Pancrac Prison on December 3rd, 1952. The bodies were cremated and the ashes were scattered on an icy road outside of Prague.

The film dramatizes the life of Anton Ludvik, Vice-Minister of Foreign Affairs of Czechoslovakia who is arbitrarily arrested, imprisoned and put in solitary confinement for months without being told the reason why. It recounts the actual techniques of torture used in all the Stalinist show trials – sleep deprivation, brainwashing, walking aimlessly back and forth all the time, and drugs forcing the victim into confessing imaginary crimes and treason and repeating this confession in a public court. To play this role, Yves Montand lost 35 pounds. He had been shaken by the Soviet suppression of the Hungarian revolt in 1956 and for him, this role was settling a score with totalitarian communism and he said: "*There was in what I inflicted upon myself [for this role] something of an act of expiation.*"

We are still waiting vainly for such an act from Hollywood.

3

The Sixties Revisited:
The Counter-Culture Age of Aquarius

Those of us who were in our teens during the 1960s can appreciate the extent to which popular culture and politics have changed beyond recognition. We lived through that era as witnesses, spectators, demonstrators, civil rights activists, draft dodgers, drop-outs, beatniks, hippies, flower children, and participants of what some historians have termed the unraveling of society, the destructive generation, The Age of Aquarius, the great cultural revolution (before Mao expropriated the title for a totally different movement in China) and "the swinging sixties." Our children and grandchildren can consult and debate with their parents what the world was like before hard rock music, "the pill" and when the word "gay" meant merry. The consequences of what happened in the sixties were long-lasting: the sixties cultural revolution, in effect, established the enduring cultural values and social behavior since then.

The Sixties put a premium on physical beauty that created a new idolatry as well as a multi-billion dollar industry. Good looks were always an asset but apart from writers or painters whose work doesn't require them to appear before the public, talent, acquired skills and demonstrable achievements have now been assigned a back seat in a way incomprehensible to our grandparents. It is not only movie stars but singers, dancers, a host of television personality presenters and even politicians who owe their initial break to their looks. Would Barack Obama, Bill Clinton and Tony Blair have made it to the top in the pre-television era? Would a Harry Truman, Wendell Wilkie, Adlai Stevenson or a Clement Attlee do so today? Probably not!

Certainly a comparison of leading men contrasting Humphrey Bogart with Leonardo DeCaprio tells us much about the depreciation of strength and character as attractive male features. Only exceptional stars, such as Barbra Streisand and Bette Midler, bucked the trend and refused to have the nose job 'everyone' was convinced would improve their careers, whilst the late Michael Jackson, a plastic-man, turned himself into a freakish human wax figure in his narcissistic quest for the "perfect look." Our daily news is full of trivial and yet intensive coverage of the antics of various super-models and pop-stars. The late Anne Nicole Smith and Paris Hilton differ from celebrities of the past in that their "careers" have been totally devoid of any recognizable talent except sex appeal and outrageous notoriety.

The baby boom experienced an earlier onset of puberty than in previous generations (a biological fact), urbanization, rising living standards, the collapse of European colonialism following the exhaustion of the Second World War, mass communications (the transistor radio that allowed teenagers the independence of carrying their music around with them), and educational reform are identified as the structural imperatives that set the scene for a youth-oriented culture. It also drew upon the older 'angry young men' (in their 20s and 30s) of French existentialism, the Chelsea Set and the American Beat movement who had protested against the "rat race," British 'old school tie' snobbism, and shared a fixation with Cold War threats of nuclear annihilation and institutionalized racism.

My own favorite metaphor for the changes since my early teenage years was called to mind by the immense success of the epic musical "Hair" urging us "to let it all hang out" provoking the recollection that not one American professional major league baseball player before 1960 had long hair, a beard, moustache or sideburns (not to mention gold necklaces, tattoos, earrings and other paraphernalia that are so evident today). As the cigarette commercial opined, "You've come a long way baby." Nevertheless, today's stars, no matter how decked out, still chew bubble gum or tobacco and continually spit in all directions.

A major theme of the participatory uninhibited culture of the "swinging sixties" that has endured is the universal language of rock music, a merger of black rhythm and blues with white country and western music as the folk idioms of two down and out groups became elevated into a new international elite music for the young. The brass and reed sections of the old big bands, the sentimental crooners, the importance of melody and witty lyrics and traditional folk instruments fell by the wayside.

Anybody who doubts this can simply look at the sell-out stand-ing-room-only triumphal appearance in Moscow of Mick Jagger and the Rolling Stones. Brezhnev had dogmatically asserted that the Stones would never be allowed to perform their "corrupt degenerate" music in the Soviet Union. Now, rock music, Coca-Cola and McDonalds reign supreme in the former homeland of the New Socialist Man. The whole world as we knew it on both sides of the Iron Curtain has irrevocably changed.

The new music with its emphasis on the group and rock beat spread across the West replacing much of the older local/national pop-ular music as had chamber, symphonic and operatic music in the past for bourgeois society. Dance, beginning with the "twist," witnessed the separation of partners who no longer had to move in step with each other (or on each other's toes) and gave everyone freedom to move to the rhythm whilst fashion did away with men's hats and raised skirt lengths to new heights - launching an even more frenetic concern with hairstyles and youthful sexy figures. Carnaby Street in London set the pace and reversed the city's reputation as the epitome of conservative sophisticated chic and cool.

Many of the new trends, fads and fashions began first in the United States simply because its manufacturers were more keenly aware to provide a commercial and innovative response to a much larg-er youth market and then "image sell" its products to all those wanting to identify with youth and new exciting trends without accepting any necessary political message of rebellion, permissiveness, liberation, etc.

The truly revolutionary rise in living standards that brought affluence, massive migration from rural areas to the cities, a lifestyle of home and automobile ownership, access to higher education and a monumental change in the perception of women's role in society engulfed France and Italy, creating a new outlook of hope, optimism and forever eliminated the barriers that had once divided the more for-tunate, benign but stodgy Anglo-Saxon world from jaded continental Europe.

The more traditional patriarchal family-oriented societies of France and Italy could not withstand the dual pressure of affluence, youth empowerment and demographic strength (young people constituted an even larger percentage of the general population than in the United States). The enormous success of the first radio program and magazine specifically devoted to teenage interests, engendered envy among such traditional bastions of French society as the Catholic Church and Communist Party that launched their own competing copy-cat versions.

No memories of the sixties can ignore the political issues of the Vietnam War and struggle for an end to racial segregation in the United States (and the later prospects of 'multi-cultural societies' in Britain and France). These problems escalated the youth rebellion into a confrontation with the 'system' and the older generation in the United States and then almost in epidemic-like fashion in Britain, France and Italy. Much of the responsibility for the protest movements to engage in violent acts and demonstrations stemmed not so much as a spontaneous reaction to police mismanagement, but to the media penchant for confrontation. For a significant part of the demonstrators, the appeal of a romantic, revolutionary long-haired spirit of revolution made them frantically search for a new 'Revolutionary Class' to replace the proletariat, be it Third World terrorists, student radicals with their icon portraits of Che Guevara, the oppressive regimes of Cuba (see Chapter 19), China, Vietnam, North Korea or Albania, migrant workers or racial/ethnic separatists to bring down Capitalism.

The counter-culture served to unite not just those who were actually politically active but anyone and everyone with a disaffection for the older generation that had previously been expressed in elite universities, anti-racism, experimental theatre, the underground press, feminism, the homosexual cause, traditional anti-militarism, anti-colonialism, and solidarity with the plight of the Third World. All these groups embraced their various definitions of THE LEFT.

There was also a small but vocal anarchist lunatic fringe that either openly or secretly identified with the Weathermen, the Baader-Meinhoff gang, the Red Brigades, or the Black Panthers. The long hot summer of 1968 witnessed the unhappy coincidence of peak American casualties in the war, the televised rioting and brutal violence of Chicago Mayor Daley's police at the Democratic convention and the aftermath of the assassinations of Martin Luther King and Robert Kennedy.

An important part of the Sixties legacy is the romantic (but eroding) identification of youth, rebellion and THE LEFT as "cool." The triumphal election of Barack Obama is eloquent testimony to how far we have come since the Sixties – or is it? Has the election of Obama meant the end of racism? An Afro-American candidate (with 50% of his ancestry entirely "White") who wins 95% of the Black vote can only mean that, just as in the past, anyone with any Black ancestry is still regarded solely as Black by the great majority of the population in the United States. His racial ancestry (a category recognized on official government forms) and the fact of his official racial identity as Black (rather than "mixed" or "other") is testimony to the endurance of racial ancestry being determined by the Black component alone much like the Nazis regarded "mixed-race offspring" of Jews and Gentiles as essentially Jewish.

The infatuation with the counter culture of the renamed New Left rejuvenated former Leftwing hacks who had been embarrassed out of the public debate by the revelations of Stalinism. Some of this new youthful enthusiasm was of course not based on any reading of the orthodox texts of Marx or Lenin. Alan Bloom sharply analyzed the gulf between the two Lefts in his *The Closing of the American Mind*.

"The new revolutionary charm became evident in the U.S. in the sixties much to the distaste of old Marxists. There is also something of this in the current sympathy for terrorists, because "they care". I have seen young people, and older people too, who are good democratic liberals, lovers of peace and gentleness, struck dumb with admiration for individuals threatening or using the most terrible violence for the slightest and tawdriest reasons. They have a sneaking suspicion that they are face to face with men of real commitment, which they themselves lack. And commitment, not truth is believed to be what counts ... .The radicals of the sixties called themselves 'the movement' unaware that this was the language used by young Nazis in the thirties and was the name of the Nazi journal Die Bewegung. Movement takes the place of progress, which has a definite direction, a good direction, and is a force that controls men. Progress was what the old revolutions were evidence of. (pp 221-222)

"The imperative to promote equality, stamp out racism, sexism and elitism (the peculiar crimes of our democratic society, as well as war, is overriding for a man who can define no other interest worthy of defending. The fact that in Germany the politics were of the Right and in the United States of the Left should not mislead us. In both places the universities gave way under the pressure of mass movements and did so in large measure because they thought those movements possessed a moral truth superior to any the university could provide. Commitment was understood to be profounder than science, passion than reason, history than nature, the young than the old. In fact, as I have argued, the thought was really the same…the unthinking hatred of 'bourgeois society' was exactly the same in both places." (p. 314)

The recent case of District Attorney Eric Holder dropping charges against members of the so called "New Black Panther Party," observed on video in their uniforms and carrying police batons "discouraging" white voters and chasing away Republican monitors at the time of the 2008 election in Philadelphia, is the most blatant outrageous example of abandonment of the principles on which this nation was built. It is proof, if any more were needed, that Barak Obama's electoral campaign was a fraud and that instead of a color blind society we are in a new age where the administration relies on pandering to minorities to ensure its survival.

It didn't surprise me that apart from Fox News, this item was not reported at all by the *New York Times* and major network media except for interviews of the New Black Panther Party representatives accusing Fox News of "scare tactics." In these interviews, pains are taken to convince the audience that the New Black Panther Party has nothing to do with the "old Black Panthers" founded in 1966 in Oakland by Bobby Seale and Huey Newton with its explicit doctrine calling not just for protection of African Americans from "police brutality" but a passionate espousal of communist (Mao variety) ideology and Black Nationalism.

Watching the news on t.v. brought back my own confrontation with the Black Panthers then at the University of Wisconsin-Madison (circa 1970-71) where I was a graduate student and the similar total cowardice and neglect of their responsibility by University administration officials to protect their students on the campus. I attended a showing of the political cult film *Battle of Algiers* glorifying the terrorism of the FLN in their fight against French Colonialism (nevertheless, the largest number of victims were Muslims who refused to cooperate with the FLN). The event was also in support of Angela Davis, who was then trying to run for political office in California. After the showing of the film (the reason I had attended), several uniformed members of the Black Panther Party stood on the stage and posted several of their colleagues at the rear of the auditorium barring exit.

When I and several other students got up to leave; the uniformed "chairman" on stage (dressed in exactly the same get-up as the "new Black Panthers" but minus the clubs, who barred entrance to the polling booths in Philadelphia in the 2008 election), loudly proclaimed, "Nobody is to leave!"

I immediately shouted back that I had come to watch the film and had no interest in the rest of the event and intended to leave and that nobody was going to prevent me. This produced a cheer by another dozen or so students who followed me to the exits where the uniformed "monitors" looked doubtful about how to prevent us from leaving. I was prepared to use force but was very grateful that the leader on stage relented and gave orders to his henchmen to step aside and "Let the fascist pigs pass."

This was an event in which no one from the administration was present but my attempt to protest the lack of any supervision by the University the next day was met with the official response that I did not have "proof" of my allegations (unless I could contact others who were present and could verify my accusations). This was the line taken by a university that continues to call itself a great liberal institution of higher learning dedicated to education and the promotion of equality, harmony, tolerance and diversity. This was my realization that all I had come to believe about progress and being a "liberal" did not make me any less of a Fascist Pig.

4

Can it Happen Here? It Already Has!

It Can't Happen Here was a best-selling satirical political novel by Sinclair Lewis published in 1935. It aroused considerable controversy when published and in the years leading up to World War II. The plot featured the account of a crusading newspaperman Doremus Jessup, struggling against the newly elected fascist regime of President Berzelius "Buzz" Windrip, a populist leader whom some observers on the political Right assumed was a parody of FDR while others, particularly on the political Left rejected the possibility that a "popular" leader of the Democratic Party could possibly lead the country into a Fascist regime.

What makes the claim that Windrip is a Leftwing tyrant hard to refute is that he is painted in the image of Huey Long with the same demagogic appeal of a young, dynamic, charismatic "populist" from a humble background, full of charm, wit and promising "the poor and downtrodden" their place in the sun. He rails against the wealthy and his platform emphasizes that the "crisis" that gets him elected is due to the machinations of the Wall Street speculators. This resembled the new administration of President Roosevelt and his New Deal advisors as enemies of the "Wall Street crowd" that bore responsibility for the stock market crash and depression. Readers of the novel today who have been blinded by the political rhetoric of the misleading terms of Left and Right in common use, will nevertheless also find it "obvious" that a character such as Windrip, who was an outright racist and opposed "foreigners" and immigration, must be associated with the Political Right.

A closer and more realistic look at the characteristics of the National Democratic Party in the 1930s and today will reveal that indeed, the fear of a Fascist take-over in the United States was most likely then and is most likely to occur today as a direct result of a charismatic leader and collectivist policies that weaken the checks and balances of our representative form of government and the built-in safeguards of

53

constitutional liberties. They were threatened most aggressively in the 1930s by the attempt of FDR to create an enlarged Supreme Court as a puppet institution under presidential control and today, by the maneuvers of President Obama promising an enormous expansion of entitlements to a public conditioned by sixty years of expanded welfare benefits, to trade in their liberty for security.

In the novel, "Buzz" Windrip, a power-hungry politician, is elected President of the United States on a populist platform pledging to restore the country to prosperity and greatness, with the explicit campaign promise of giving each citizen five thousand dollars a year! It's simple; all he needed to do was print the money!

His opponent in the 1936 election is Walt Trowbridge, "*a Republican candidate for President, suffering from the deficiency of being honest and disinclined to promise that he could work miracles, was insisting that we live in the United States of America and not on a golden highway to Utopia.*"

The description of the fictional 1936 election campaign is prescient and has many parallels with the real one of 2008. Lewis, the first American to win the Noble Prize for Literature and generally regarded as an acidic, leftwing critic of American society, nevertheless predicted that if Fascism ever succeeded in America, it would be imposed by the Democratic Party winning the support of the masses, envious of those wealthier and more successful than themselves. The sophisticated but honest journalist Jessup, who is narrating the story, has a dilemma – whether to support the stodgy Republican Trowbridge (with all the old fashioned boring virtues of honesty and integrity) in his native Vermont during a time of crisis, or the dazzling Democrat Windrip with his fantastic promises. He eventually listens to the voice of reason and realizes that Windrip, for all his appeal to the masses, is bent on seizing the instruments of power to install himself as a dictator.

> "He wanted to follow Roosevelt and the Jeffersonian Party--partly for admiration of the man; partly for the pleasure of shocking the ingrown Republicanism of Vermont. But he could not believe that the Jeffersonians would have a chance; he did believe that, for all the mothball odor of many of his associates, Walt Trowbridge was a valiant and competent man; and

night and day Doremus bounced up and down Beulah Valley campaigning for Trowbridge. Out of his very confusion there came into his writing a desperate sureness which surprised accustomed readers of the Informer. For once he was not amused and tolerant. Though he never said anything worse of the Jeffersonian Party than that it was ahead of its times, in both editorials and news stories he went after Buzz Windrip and his gang with whips, turpentine, and scandal.

"In person, he was into and out of shops and houses all morning long, arguing with voters, getting miniature interviews. He had expected that traditionally Republican Vermont would give him too drearily easy a task in preaching Trowbridge. What he found was a dismaying preference for the theoretically Democratic Buzz Windrip. And that preference, Doremus perceived, wasn't even a pathetic trust in Windrip's promises of Utopian bliss for everyone in general. It was a trust in increased cash for the voter himself, and for his family, very much in particular."

Once in power, Windrip becomes a tyrant. He goes on to outlaw dissent after characterizing it as treason. He places his political enemies in detainment camps and creates a paramilitary force, the Minute Men who terrorize the citizens. One of his first moves as President is to make changes to the Constitution that give himself sole power over the country, rendering Congress obsolete.

When these measures are met by protest from the congressmen as well as outraged citizens, Windrip declares a state of Martial Law and with the help of his Minute Men, throws the protesters in jail. As he dismantles American democratic institutions, most Americans either support him and his "Corpo Regime," devoted to bringing relief to the "ordinary citizens" and enlarging the common welfare, his supporters wholeheartedly reassure themselves that fascism cannot happen in America. Eventually Windrip's hold on power begins to weaken. The economic prosperity he promises does not materialize, and more and more people flee to Canada to escape his government's brutality.

How fanciful, imaginative, ridiculous, far-fetched or accurate is it to compare charismatic populist President Obama to the character of Buzz Windrip? Take a look at some of the cardinal points in Windrup's electoral campaign platform in "It Can't Happen Here." During the very first week of his campaign, Senator Windrip clarifies his philosophy by issuing his distinguished proclamation: "The Fifteen Points of Victory for the Forgotten Men."

The VERY FIRST VICTORY POINT IS .....(1) **All finance in the country, including banking, insurance, stocks and bonds and mortgages, shall be under the absolute control of a Federal Central Bank, owned by the government** and conducted by a Board appointed by the President, which Board shall, without need of recourse to Congress for legislative authorization, be empowered to make all regulations governing finance. Thereafter, as soon as may be practicable, this said Board shall consider the nationalization and government-ownership, **for the Profit of the Whole People, of all mines, oilfields, water power, public utilities, transportation, and communication.**

Doesn't that sound familiar? The first year of the Obama administration and its "call for action" with the various relief proposals, the TARP, various "stimulus programs" and the President's proposals for cap and trade, energy, the banks sound like a rerun.

(2) The President shall appoint a commission, equally divided between manual workers, employers, and representatives of the Public, to determine **which Labor Unions are qualified to represent the Workers; and report to the Executive, for legal action,** all pretended labor organizations, whether "Company Unions," or "Red Unions," controlled by Communists and the so-called "Third International." **The duly recognized Unions shall be constituted Bureaus of the Government, with power of decision in all labor disputes. Later, the same investigation and official recognition shall be extended to farm organizations.** In this elevation of the position of the Worker, it shall be emphasized that the League of Forgotten Men is the chief bulwark against the menace of destructive and un-American Radicalism.

Does this sound familiar too? It should.

(5) Annual net income per person shall be limited to $500,000. No accumulated fortune may at any one time exceed $3,000,000 per person. **No one person shall, during his entire lifetime, be permitted to retain an inheritance or various inheritances in total exceeding $2,000,000. All incomes or estates in excess of the sums named**

shall be seized by the Federal Government for use in Relief and in Administrative expenses.

Isn't this what was/is called "Share the Wealth?"

(8) Congress shall have the sole right to issue money **and immediately upon our inauguration it shall at least double the present supply of money, in order to facilitate the fluidity of credit.**

(11) Far from opposing such high-minded and economically sound methods of the relief of poverty, unemployment, and old age as the EPIC plan of the Hon. Upton Sinclair, the "Share the Wealth" and "Every Man a King" proposals of the late Hon. Huey Long to assure every family $5,000 a year, the Townsend plan, the Utopian plan, Technocracy, and all competent schemes of unemployment insurance, **a Commission shall immediately be appointed by the New Administration to study, reconcile, and recommend for immediate adoption the best features in these several plans for Social Security.....**

(15) Congress shall, immediately upon our inauguration, initiate amendments to the Constitution providing (a), that **the President shall have the authority to institute and execute all necessary measures for the conduct of the government during this critical epoch; (b), that Congress shall serve only in an advisory capacity, calling to the attention of the President and his aides and Cabinet any needed legislation, but not acting upon same until authorized by the President so to act; and (c), that the Supreme Court shall immediately have removed from its jurisdiction the power to negate, by ruling them to be unconstitutional or by any other judicial action, any or all acts of the President, his duly appointed aides, or Congress.**

This too sounds like the "needed legislation" rammed through by the President's aides, Reid, Pelosi, Axelrod, and Rahm to protect and defend the "poor victims" (i.e. citizens) inevitably faced with ruin, economic destruction, and catastrophic ill health before the election of President Obama. Homeland Security Secretary Napolitano and Obama have already identified the dangers to their rule by labeling conservative Americans and even returning Vets "potential" domestic terrorists.

Added to their long list of "enemies" are pro-life Christian Evangelicals, anti-abortion Catholics, pro-Israel Jewish "neocons," conservative Blacks and Latinos, the Tea Party supporters, (whose behavior in public demonstrations has been almost impeccable compared to the mayhem and chaos generated by the many anti-war and anti-Bush rallies), gun owners, College Republicans, Sarah Palin, Anne Coulter, Michelle Malkin and Bill O'Reilly, talk radio hosts and conservative career women and housewives. Speaker Pelosi's comments that the nature of the grassroots Tea Party Movement is more like "astro-turf" and that she is "afraid" for the safety of ordinary Americans because she had noticed a swastika carried somewhere by someone are the two most desperate attempts ever made by a high ranking cabinet member of the government to demonize political opponents since the Civil War.

What about the points 3, 4, 6, 7, 9, 10, 12, 13, and 14 in Windrip's Platform that I omitted? They identify the enemies of the President, subversives, traitors and those who must be strictly kept under close supervision, namely radicals, Communists, Jews, Blacks, independent women and immigrants.

It must be remembered that until quite late in the Roosevelt and Truman administrations, the Democratic Party was the natural home of many Congressmen who opposed immigration, anti-lynching laws, and voting rights for African-Americans. Its 19th century heritage was as the Party of Slavery, Secession and Segregation. Today it has added another S – Socialism. The Democratic Vice President of the United States under FDR from 1933 to 1940, John Nance Garner, a former Texas Congressman, was considered one of the most reactionary members of the Congress with regard to his racist, isolationist, anti-Semitic, anti-Mexican, anti-Labor unions and anti-immigrant views and could well have matched "Buzz Windrip" more closely than any other Congressman in the 20th century.

The false and often irrelevant dichotomy of LEFT vs. RIGHT obscures the basic similarities uniting the two wings of political thought at their extremes that glorify and deify abstractions such as THE leader, party, race, church or class that embody THE NATION. Both ideologies at their extremes grant ALL POWER to a demagogic leader who, once in power, promises either to save the people from poverty, restore their heroic traditions and glorious past, redeem the nation and recover its historic borders, or wipe away the humiliation and the privileges of the "ruling class." Every demagogue whether labeled as a Rightwing or Leftwing dictator throughout Latin America, Europe, Asia and Africa has made the same appeal and it is always predictably anti-American, anti-Capitalist, anti-Jewish and anti-Israel.

Many imagined iconic heroes of the past consistently pushed their domestic agendas on behalf of the "common man" and the "poor" or for "civil rights" or "minorities" yet committed the worst abuses among our many Presidents in the direction of more and more centralized federal power – Abolition of Habeus Corpus (Lincoln), the "Red Scares" with their wholesale incarcerations and deportations of all those opposed to American entry into World War I (Wilson), and the internment of Japanese-Americans including those who were American citizens in "relocation camps" (FDR). The Left-Right continuum is a false paradigm. The extremes meet but it is more often the liberal agenda that leads the way to limiting individual liberties. The end result is the government's reach for unlimited power. Not only is it not true that "It Can't Happen Here," it already has begun to happen.

The Obama Health Care Bill passed by the Senate on March 23, 2010 is the most invasive imposition of the power of the Federal Government since Prohibition (ultimately repealed). It was fittingly referred to by Vice President Biden as "A Big F----- Deal!" Of course, that did not prevent the VP, the President, Cabinet members and Congress from exempting themselves from the provisions of the law.

Shifting explanations by the Democrats to justify the mandate of obligatory health care under the terms of regulating "Interstate Commerce" have shredded the Constitution and reduced its protection of individual and states rights to the First Ten Amendments (Bill of Rights) as the only ones not subject to constant Congressional and Presidential manipulation. Everything else is fair game. The fact that the new law has immediately been challenged as unconstitutional by no less than 15 State Attorneys-General is a rebuke to the Congress that so cheaply sold our birthright as American citizens.

5

The Gods That Failed
(*But still continue to enjoy a good press*)

A major reason for the continued popularity of the Right-Left model is the largely favorable attitude of the liberal media that traditionally dominate the news in the United States and in much of Western Europe. Deeply embedded in the model is the time worn value judgment that a noble, liberal tolerant and crusading press must be against any of the 'shibboleths' that are considered hallmarks of the Right, i.e. nationalism, religious values, and a narrow provincial outlook considered synonymous with prejudice.

The most influential book written about why intelligent, dedicated and noble men with the highest motives fell under the hypnotic spell of Communism remains *The God That Failed*, a collection of thirteen essays by Stephen Spender, R. H. S. Crossman, Arthur Koestler, Ignazio Silone, Richard Wright, Andre Gide and Louis Fischer. The essays chronicle the noble motives that drew these individuals to the Party largely through the cynical manipulation of their idealism and mistaken straw-man image of The Right leading to their choice of Communism and their ultimate disillusionment and sense of betrayal.

I underwent a similar experience with respect to lesser but still enormously powerful gods in the realm of ideas and a world-view that boasted, like the Kremlin, of being the 'vanguard' of progressive humanity and the ultimate reference guide for any political question or doubt. I refer to the two media organizations that for some remain idols in the pantheon of news gathering and interpretation. No evidence to the contrary, no matter how persuasive or corroborated by independent investigation, can match the unearned epithets of praise or the mantra of authority conferred on a statement by ..."I read it in *The New York Times*" or "I heard/saw it on the BBC."

I grew up with the same view inculcated by my upbringing and environment and, like the authors of *The God That Failed*, it took a long, arduous and painful journey to finally reject the two icons of "liberal" and "progressive" thought so identified with the LEFT that have masqueraded as the final court of opinion on any subject under the sun. How could it have been otherwise?

I grew up in the heart of the Bronx, in the Melrose-Morrisania-Grand Concourse section that in the mid-1940s was the most Jewish neighborhood in the most Jewish city in the world. That should be understood to mean "liberal," "secular" and "progressive" Jewish. My family and friends attended a local Orthodox synagogue (only the wealthy knew what "Conservative" or "Reform" was supposed to mean) as an outward form of respect - much the same as attending Jewish funeral services in a cemetery to honor a deceased relative. All those with a major interest in foreign affairs or literary ambitions read *The New York Times*. Everyone else subscribed to *The New York Post,* voted Democratic (or were closet socialists and communists), knew no one who openly voted for the Republican Party and as part of the conventional wisdom worshipped FDR, Edward R. Murrow and *The New York Times*, a triumvirate that symbolized enlightened opinion and the legacy of World War II heroism, internationalism, anti-isolationism and anti-racism.

Without a shred of evidence, anyone who opposed this enlightenment was consigned to the Dark Ages of the Inquisition, antisemitism, and the new looming specter of something called McCarthyism. It mattered not a whit that the senator from Wisconsin had no record or hint of any antisemitic connections or that some of his closest associates were Jews (and homosexuals). He was nevertheless cast in the role of Middle Western bigotry and reaction, just as two generations earlier the great silver tongued orator of the Plains, William Jennings Bryan, three time Democratic Party candidate for President, a symbol of popular sentiment against big business and Wall Street, was similarly ridiculed by *The New York Times* as a primitive fundamentalist evangelist "know-nothing." (see Chapter 7)

The dawn of a new decade already set the scenario of a heroic "Cuba Libre" under the benevolent rule of the new "Viva Zapata" image of Fidel Castro and teenagers like myself were posing in front of mirrors wearing a Cuban beret and struggling to grow a convincing beard and moustache. It was, however, shortly after Fidel's triumphant entry into Havana that my first confrontation began with the newspaper whose claim to publishing was the unchallenged "All the News that's Fit to Print."

Later on, in speaking to audiences about the nature of information gathering and the reliability of assertions posing as facts, I have labored to explain the crucial difference between primary sources that stemmed from eyewitnesses and ear-witnesses - the first hand evidence acceptable in court rather than hearsay, or the kind of second hand-information all too many readers assume are authentic because they appear as footnotes in a book or document. These may often be nothing more than the citation of information that has previously appeared in other books or documents, neither of which can be established as the testimony of a firsthand witness or contemporary with the event being investigated. What has repeatedly struck me and remained solidly implanted in my subconscious throughout my career in graduate school and in doing research on controversial issues is that…

a) *The New York Times* has frequently been fallible and

b) In recording and analyzing history, sources must be checked and doubled checked, (especially as I learned later; all the more so when the original is in another language).

These two lessons became more deeply ingrained with the choice of my profession in academia and in doing my own research and using sources that I knew were not original. It became all the more evident with the passage of time and my acquisition of foreign languages that were absolutely necessary in order to do the research I chose. In looking back over the past century, and in spite of the extensive international coverage provided by *The Times* and unmatched by any other American newspaper, I found that on several particularly "sensitive" issues, *The Times* also exceeded its rivals for its ideological bent contradicting its claim to publish "All the News That's Fit to Print," resulting in callous omissions and violations of essential journalistic ethics.

To start with the most recent first. On May 11, 2003, *The New York Times* devoted four pages of its Sunday paper in an unparallel expose and self-admission that Jayson Blair, a former and mediocre *Times* reporter had made up stories and non-existent "confidential sources" faked datelines, and plagiarized on a massive scale. That such fraud and deception could continue for so long would have hardly been excusable if the guilty party had been a third rate daily newspaper in a middle-size or small town with a long history of corruption, graft and a tradition of sensationalist journalism.

The admission by management that Blair had been given special favorable treatment because he was Black led to the forced resignation of the executive editor, Howell Raines who had helped the paper win a record six Pulitzer Prizes for its coverage of the September 11th attacks. How could a third rate reporter bamboozle the "most revered name" in American journalism with a transparent scam? The answer lies in the profound arrogance and blind narcissism that has seriously infected both *The New York Times* and the BBC. The biggest journalistic scam in American history should have been a cause for reflection and the need to introduce methods for cross-checking and verifying news stories before they see the light of day.

In another regard, the *Times* editors had never adequately assessed the extent to which their liberal political views and the shyness of the owners' Jewish identity had previously caused them to accept shallow and misleading coverage of important events. Foremost among these was the Great Famine in the Ukraine under Stalin in 1930-33, and the colossal dimensions of The Holocaust.

The deportation and starvation to death of millions of deported "kulaks" (the Soviet term for "wealthy farmers") and ordinary peasants in the Ukraine, Russia and Kazakhstan ranks as a genocidal crime of roughly the same dimensions as The Holocaust. It, however was committed in the Soviet Union during "peacetime." *The New York Times* botched both these stories in a manner that is despicable, the first due to their commitment to liberalism which meant a policy to excuse, forgive or "understand" the Soviet Union, and the second while "unintentional" was the reluctance of the Sulzburgers to give undue prominence to Jewish suffering lest they be thought of as too provincial and biased in favor of Jewish causes.

Certainly, the Ukrainian famine tragedy ranked as the greatest crime and news story of the 1930s yet it became a non-event, due in large measure to the cooperation/collaboration of the Soviet government and "the most distinguished newspaper" in the West. European reporters including members of the communist press in Western countries had no access to the affected regions but *New York Times* reporter Walter Duranty, stationed in Moscow since 1921, and acceptable to the Soviet authorities, was given special privileges to visit just those selected areas of the region where conditions were staged by actors on village-sets created for the occasion just as later the Nazis staged mock portrayals of "humane" concentration camps solely to impress visitors from the Swiss Red Cross.

What is even more disgusting is that Duranty actually knew the bitter truth of the famine but was blackmailed to continue to send false but glowing reports of overflowing granaries and plump, contented pigs and cows. Like the Blair fraud, none of the higher up editors attempted to query Duranty (A Pulitzer Prize winner!), check his sources or suspect that he might have been subject to pressure because the "news" of "progress" in the Soviet Union confirmed their self-delusions about Stalin and the USSR.

In his *New York Times* articles, Duranty repeatedly denied the existence of a Ukrainian famine in 1932–33.[1] He claimed *"any report of a famine is today an exaggeration or malignant propaganda"*, but admitted privately to William Strang (in the British Embassy in Moscow on September 26, 1933) that *"It is quite possible that as many as ten million people may have died directly or indirectly from lack of food in the Soviet Union during the past year."*

Appeals by Ukrainian organizations to *The New York Times* to posthumously cancel Duranty's Pulitzer Prize were rejected by *The Times*. The Ukrainian Congress Committee of America has been affronted and shocked by the decision of the Pulitzer Prize Board, and *The Times* not to withdraw Duranty's award which shames all those who have been honored by this prestigious award. The newspaper which was careful to amend an asterisk next to the name of Roger Maris when he broke Babe Ruth's homerun record doesn't have another one left for Duranty.

The New York Times hired Mark Von Hagen of Columbia University to investigate the charges against Duranty and concluded that Duranty was a frequent voice of Soviet propaganda and that *"For the*

---

1 August 24, 1933

64

sake of The New York Times' honor, they should take the prize away". The *New York Times* sent Von Hagen's report to the Pulitzer Board and washed its hands of the affair by leaving it to the Board to take whatever action they considered appropriate.

Just as disturbing, although, perhaps more understandable, was the reluctance of the Sulzburger family, committed Reform Jews with views favoring assimilation, long known opponents of Zionism, to relate the true dimensions of the Holocaust and give it greater prominence. In this respect, many other newspapers and government agencies in America and Britain must also bear responsibility.

Even some Jewish community leaders were reluctant to plead too hard for measures such as bombing the extermination camps or allowing a special displaced persons quota for Jewish refugees for fear of being accused of favoring Jewish interests. *The New York Times,* precisely because of its Jewish ownership, large readership and many reporters and employees, did not want to be seen to take the lead in pleading any special or parochial Jewish cause. This remains largely true to this day with a few notable exceptions. Of course, today, *The New York Times* champions the cause of multiculturalism for each and every distinct racial and ethnic group and frowns on assimilation.

What is also almost comical, however, is that this same newspaper today pleads for special consideration on behalf of Muslims among America's immigrant population who may be suspected of either being illegal immigrants or sympathetic to terrorism and Muslim extremism. So eager is the paper to avoid the taint of being accused of racism, that it bends over backwards to find extenuating circumstances to excuse extremist opinion among American Muslims or in any way holding them suspect of not being patriotic.

This is THE editorial line of *The New York Times* and it is stronger now than ever. For those who write most of the opinion pieces and those who eagerly seek confirmation of similar views, NOTHING IS SACRED. Nothing deserves to be regarded with devotion and/or patriotism. These are sentiments that are out of bounds and considered suspect. Is this part of the journalistic code of ethics? On September 2, 2007, N.R. Kleinfeld took issue with the continued call to Remember 9/11! His Front Page opinion piece entitled "As 9/11 Nears, a Debate Rises; How Much Tribute is Enough?"

Clearly it is already too much for *The New York Times*. The writer quotes Charlene Correia of Acushnet, Massachusetts who is identified only as a "nursing supervisor" without any explanation as to why her views deserve to be cited as representative for the entire country or if she is a relative of the victims or survivors. Mr. Kleinfeld assures us that "Few Americans give much thought anymore on Dec. 7 that Pearl Harbor was attacked in 1941" (A date to live in infamy but not for Mr. Kleinfeld or *The New York Times*).

Even generations ago, and when the issues involved had no significant bearing on American interests, *The New York Times* had a view that proclaimed its elitist viewpoint that "Father Knows Best." In 1905, when Norwegians demanded to separate from Sweden, the paper reacted to lobbying activities by Norwegian-Americans and severely criticized *"those among them who tried to influence our government in favor of Norway."* It took its favorite position then of "100% Americanism" (and of preaching from the grandstand):

"Norwegians naturalized in this country have ceased to be politically Norwegians. If they had legitimate complaints, these should be set forth in a bill of particulars." Several weeks later, however, *The Times* affected a judicious tone, advising its readers to *"defer to the knowledge possessed by the President"* (Teddy Roosevelt).

Of course, times and opinions have changed but what is common to *The Times* editorials for the past hundred years is an elitist tone that only those with Ivy League degrees and a residence in Georgetown or Manhattan are qualified to judge major foreign policy issues. It mattered little to the Sulzburgers then that 99.8% of the Norwegian people voted in a referendum to separate from Sweden (women did not have the vote but if they had, the result would not have been different or even a greater pro-independence result). Their opposition to Norwegian independence, or Zionism, or Senator Joseph McCarthy or William Jennings Bryan's candidacy, or Ronald Reagan's presidency with his romantic notions of "winning the Cold War" and his "dangerous Evil Empire delusion" were all part of its cosmopolitan world view that regarded any "narrow," nationalist, patriotic or religious loyalty and sentiment as reactionary and any radical departure from conventional academic wisdom as adventurist, reckless and irresponsible.

For *The New York Times*, their audience is global and they seek to portray events from what they consider a "global perspective." Their employees are recruited worldwide and are aware of the line their employers pursue. This means first and foremost NOT to appear as presenting an identifiable American identity. The same conclusion can be made "in spades" regarding the BBC! Anyone who still has a warm, glowing positive recollection of the BBC from World War II's memories of the blitz and the noble RAF should remain locked in their time machine with the dial permanently set at 1939-45.

I hardly expected a BBC retraction or correction of announcer Lyse Ducett's horrendous hundredfold magnification of Lebanese dead in the conflict between Hizbollah and Israel ("100,000; mostly civilians" as she astutely emphasized) in the BBC in America August 14, 2007, 8:00 EST transmission. No, no danger; No retraction, No correction, No apology (at least not to my knowledge) from the news gathering agency that continues to boast it is the "most accurate in the world." Their selectivity and slant in news reporting have been well documented for some time including self-evaluations.

In January, 2004, the BBC's 'Panorama' program broadcast an investigation into the events leading to the death of David Kelly, a government weapons expert who killed himself on July, 18, 2003, after he was revealed as the source of a BBC report critical of the government's justification for the Iraq war. The program was broadcast a week before Lord Hutton led the judicial public inquiry into Dr. Kelly's death.

Kelly, an employee of the Ministry of Defense, was found dead after he had been named as the source of quotes used by BBC journalist Andrew Gilligan. These quotes had formed the basis of media reports claiming that Tony Blair's Labor government had knowingly "sexed up" the "September Dossier," a report into Iraq and weapons of mass destruction. The inquiry opened in August 2003 and reported on January 28, 2004. The report cleared the government of wrongdoing, while the BBC was strongly criticized, leading to the resignation of the BBC's chairman and director-general. The report was met with widespread skepticism by the British press and general public. (From the Wikipedia on-line encyclopedia.)

A report commissioned by the BBC Trust, "Safeguarding Impartiality in the 21st Century," published in June 2007, stressed that the BBC needed to take more care in being impartial. *The Evening Standard* and *Daily Telegraph* claimed that a new report on media bias showed the BBC *out of touch with large swathes of the public and is guilty of self-censoring subjects that the corporation finds unpalatable.*[2] The United States, American society and popular culture are routinely treated by the BBC with scorn and derision. In October 2006, Chief Radio Correspondent for BBC News since 2001 and Washington correspondent Justin Webb said that the BBC is so biased against America that deputy Director General Mark Byford had secretly agreed to help him to "correct" it in his reports.[3]

A veteran reporter of the BBC, Peter Sissons swallowed 20 years of the BBC's arrogant know-it-all Leftist slant on the news and when he finally quit in January, 2011 had this to say:

> "Left-wing bias? It's written through the BBC's very DNA. For 20 years I was a front man at the BBC, anchoring news and current affairs programmes, so I reckon nobody is better placed than me to answer the question that nags at many of its viewers - is the BBC biased? In my view, 'bias' is too blunt a word to describe the subtleties of the pervading culture. The better word is 'mindset'. At the core of the BBC, in its very DNA, is a way of thinking that is firmly of the Left."

My own personal confrontation with the BBC began in London in 1993 when I was called upon to translate and voice-over in English a speech of then Prime Minister Rabin in the Israeli Parliament (Knesset) in which he delivered a stern warning to terrorists. I was chauffeured in a limousine to the studio at White City (The White City building houses most of the BBC's current affairs, factual and learning programs such as Panorama, Top Gear, Watchdog and many others) to listen to a recording of Rabin's speech that promised harsh retribution for further acts of terrorism. I had to be content with only a 19 second clip in which I practiced four separate times at imitating a "particularly harsh and cruel" voice, as requested by the BBC news manager overseeing the recording. He wasn't satisfied until the last rendition when I

---

2 June 18, 2007
3 Media Guardian article Monday 5 November 2007. Website accessed 18 November 2007

gave it as much cruelty as I could imagine was Hitler-like.

But the nail in the coffin of the BBC's claim at being a reliable source of information was my own personal letter of complaint over an error of fact, not an opinion or a charge of selectivity or bias. I have two letters of apology (in which the word "apology" is never mentioned) from Carol Deakin "Accountability Assistant, News and Current Affairs Department, dated November 30, 1995 and June 10, 1996. The error involved no area of current public policy or any 'agenda'. It was simply a matter of the casual ignorance and elementary wrong assumptions that stem from the fact that in its mighty empire, routine checking is left to a hired staff with no sense of what is required to substantiate information and search FIRST HAND SOURCES. The fact is that mistakes are repeated over and over again simply because they appear in print in books even by distinguished authors who do not have the requisite knowledge of the original language to verify the source.

Perhaps the most widely believed myth that emerged from The Holocaust and that is still widely believed thanks to Hollywood, Leon Uris (author of the best-selling novel *Exodus*) and the BBC as well as at least half a dozen Jewish historians who have written widely about the Holocaust and commented on the rescue of the Danish Jews and their safe passage to Sweden in October, 1943, is that the Danish King, Christian X (grandfather of the present Queen Margrethe II), in an act of solidarity with his Jewish subjects, volunteered to put on the yellow-star armband when the Jews were forced to do so by the German occupation authorities (see chapter 14). He never did so. The German occupation authorities never ordered the Jews in Denmark to wear the yellow armband. The myth stems from the book and Hollywood film *Exodus*. Very few readers bothered to read Uris's remarks in the Forward to the book: "*Most (i.e. not all) of the events in Exodus are a matter of history and fact. Many of the scenes were created around historical incidents for the purpose of fiction.*"

Queen Margrethe has been thanked so many times by guests for her grandfather's supposed action that she has written in her autobiography that this mistaken belief has caused her considerable embarrassment. The Danish Foreign Ministry has issued a special 24 page booklet[4] in English on the Occupation of Denmark 1940-45 and confirmed that this story was a popular rumor and nothing more. King Christian was a puppet king with no real power. He did not choose as did other monarchs such as Wilhelmina, the Queen of Holland, and Haakon VII, the King of Norway, to flee to England and help in the establishment of a government in exile. During the first three years of the occupation, Christian warned his fellow countrymen not to participate in acts of sabotage against the German occupation forces. This was the government line which he adhered to and which also guaranteed Denmark a special relatively mild status, including no discriminatory measures against the Danish Jews (until the planned deportation in October, 1943).

The King was certainly a decent man placed in a difficult situation. In 1942, he wrote a letter to Marcus Melchior, the Chief Rabbi, expressing "relief" that a fire at the synagogue in Copenhagen did not cause extensive damage. He and the Queen had attended special services at the one-hundredth anniversary celebration of the synagogue in 1933. A photo of their presence on that occasion was published in Life magazine in 1943, without an indication of the actual date, thus leading to the common perception among many Americans that the King was demonstrating public criticism of German antisemitism. Both the King and cabinet ministers expressed their views on several occasions during the early years of the occupation that there was no need to adopt any legislation affecting Jewish citizens because "There is no Jewish problem in Denmark." The armband myth in the Leon Uris book thus fell on fertile ground.

From May 5-9, 1995, the 50th anniversary of V-E Day was celebrated all over the world with a fabulous 4 day extravaganza of events culminating in London with a gala reception at the Guild Hall attended by over fifty heads of state. British and World television had considerable time to prepare for this event and do any required research. Yet, BBC presenter Vivian White, in his commentary accompanying the entry into the Guild Hall of the assembled heads of state remarked that...Danish Princess Benedikte, (the Queen's sister who attended

---

4 Royal Danish Ministry of Foreign Affairs and the Museum of the Danish Resistance "October, 1943; The Rescue of the Danish Jews from Annihilation," (text: Therkel Stræde, translation: Teresa Masquit), Copnehagen, 1993.

the event because the Queen was unable to do so), *was, as we all know, the grand-daughter of King Christian X, who together with his entire family, put on the Yellow Star in an act of Solidarity with his Jewish subjects."*[5]

I lived and worked in Denmark for seven years (1978-84) and was Vice-Chairman of the Danish-Israeli Friendship Society in Aarhus. On one occasion, we gave a reception for the visiting mayor of Beersheba who began his after-dinner talk in English by expressing the admiration of all ordinary Israelis for the *"heroic action of King Christian ... who put on the yellow-star to save his Jewish fellow countrymen"*. I politely informed the mayor after observing the cringing faces of the assembled Danish audience in a whisper in Hebrew that the story was a myth and got an explosive reaction (in Hebrew) ..."*Of course it's true, we all know this in Israel!"* So the BBC is certainly not alone but when I informed them of their error in a letter, what was the reaction?

In my letter, I noted the Queen's autobiography, the pamphlet in English issued by the Danish Foreign Ministry and asked that they simply contact the Danish Embassy in London for one minute to enquire about the validity of what they had just televised and broadcast around the world to an audience numbering tens of millions. Did they accept this suggestion? No!

The reply I got from their "Accountability Assistant," reads as follows....."*As this is a specialist area of knowledge, I have consulted Professor Cesarini of Manchester University* (apparently this gentleman is the ultimate authority for the BBC ...., not the Danish Embassy, but a Professor of Jewish History who has no knowledge of Danish but who has worked for the BBC in the past on research for a documentary) ... *and he has commented that it was a myth that the Danish Royal Family wore the Star of David during the occupation of their country by the Nazis......Thus, although we accept that the reference to wearing the Star of David was inaccurate we would not agree that an on-air correction would be appropriate.....I will nevertheless* (how generous !) *ensure that a copy of your letter is sent to our News Information Library for their records. Thank you for writing... Yours sincerely, Carol Deakin."*

For the BBC then and now, errors on the order of black is white, the earth is flat not round and "*King Christian X and his entire*

---

5 I have this on video if anyone doubts that the BBC could make such a colossal error and then never make an on the air correction.

family wore the Yellow Star" are simply "inaccurate", in a way similar to the statement that the atmosphere is composed of 78% nitrogen rather than the correct figure of 79%. The BBC and The New York Times use their own Newspeak for error or mistake. They publish "All the News that They see Fit to Print."

N E W S &
C U R R E N T
A F F A I R S

BRITISH BROADCASTING CORPORATION
TELEVISION CENTRE
WOOD LANE
LONDON W12 7RJ
TELEPHONE 0181 743 8000
FAX 0181 576 1721

30th November 1995

Mr Norman Berdichevsky,
69 Methuen Road,
Edgware,
Middlesex,
HA8 6EU.

Dear Mr Berdichevsky,

Thank you for your letter of 27th November, which you sent to Tony Hall, Managing Director of BBC News and Current Affairs. I am replying on his behalf.

I was interested to read your letter and enclosed paper, in particular the section concerning the actions of the Danish Royal family during the war. As this is a specialist area of knowledge I have consulted Professor Cesarani of Manchester University and he has commented that it was a myth that the Danish Royal Family wore the Star of David during the occupation of their country by the Nazis. He added, however, that the Danish government, the Royal Family and the population in general were significantly more supportive of the Jewish population of Denmark during this time than many other areas of occupied Europe and that this should be taken into consideration when reflecting on their war record.

Thus, although we accept that the reference to the wearing of the Star of David was inaccurate we would not agree that an on-air correction would be appropriate. I will, nonetheless, ensure that a copy of my letter is sent to our News information library for their records.

Thank you for writing.

Yours sincerely,

Carol Deakin,
Accountability Assistant, News & Current Affairs

6

Abraham Lincoln – Liberator of Slaves or Violator of the Constitution?

A great deal of heated discussion and debate has followed in the wake of the conflicts in Vietnam, Iraq and now Afghanistan with much criticism toward the preponderance of American military power coming from erstwhile "friends" and "allies" of the United States on the LEFT but they do not differ significantly from the views of the European social elites and ruling classes on the RIGHT of more than 150 years ago when the United States had absolutely no overseas possessions or imperialist ambitions.

"No one with his qualifications would ever become prime minister of England let alone a county court judge."

"The President is a rough Westerner of the lowest origins and little education."

"He has not shown any talents to compensate for his ignorance of everything but the village politics of his home state…you would never say that he is a gentleman."

"Neither the president nor anyone in the cabinet has a knowledge of foreign affairs."

Sound familiar?

Most friends I know who opposed the two invasions of Iraq nod approvingly - the answer is the Bushes or Ronald Reagan.

The actual answer is none of the above. All of these remarks were spoken in the heat of political debate during our Civil War or in confidential diaries against Abraham Lincoln. They appeared in the editorial comments of *The Times of London*, most of the so called establishment press of European countries, and in the private notes of many diplomats, foremost among them, Lord Lyons, Britain's ambassador to the United State, the Prime Minister, Viscount Palmerston, as well as Foreign Minister Lord John Russell. They were for the most part as ill founded then as more recent comments in the same vein against strong American leaders and policies.

Nevertheless, both Lincoln's conduct of managing the Civil War and related domestic issues as well as his foreign policy provoked considerable opposition abroad from many conservative quarters that considered him in today's terms both a radical (of the Left) and a tyrant (of the Right)

Lincoln has long been a hero of the Left lionized primarily as the author of the Emancipation Proclamation that ended slavery and as preserver of the Union. He is also the only president to have temporarily suspended habeus corpus and freedom of the press, steps taken in order to preserve the Union but criticized widely by those who believed he had violated his oath of office. This right grants relief from unlawful imprisonment unless just cause can be demonstrated in court. Article One, Section 9, clause 2 of the United States Constitution demands that "*The privilege of the writ of habeas corpus shall not be suspended, unless when in cases of rebellion or invasion the public safety may require it.*" Clearly, Lincoln and those in his cabinet believed that they had this expressed right to suspend this time honored privilege.

Lincoln suspended the writ of habeas corpus on April 27, 1861, only two weeks after the firing on Ft. Sumter. He did so only in Maryland and in parts of several Midwestern states in response to riots, local militia actions, and the threat that the border slave state of Maryland would secede from the Union, leaving Washington, D.C., the nation's capital surrounded by hostile territory. Lincoln imposed the suspension on those engaged in rebellion as well as on other classes of people, such as draft dodgers. Chief Justice of the Supreme Court Roger B. Taney declared Lincoln's act unconstitutional in the case of the arrest of a prominent supporter of secession in Maryland, John Merryman. Lincoln and the military refused to honor the judge's decision and on September 24, 1862, the president imposed martial law throughout the country by order.....

"Now, therefore, be it ordered, first, that during the existing insurrection and as a necessary measure for suppressing the same, all Rebels and Insurgents, their aiders and abettors within the United States, and all persons discouraging volunteer enlistments, resisting militia drafts, or guilty of any disloyal practice, affording aid and comfort to Rebels against the authority of United States, shall be subject to martial law and liable to trial and punishment by Courts Martial or Military Commission:

"Second; That the Writ of Habeas Corpus is suspended in respect to all persons arrested, or who are now, or hereafter during the rebellion shall be, imprisoned in any fort, camp, arsenal, military prison, or other place of confinement by any military authority of by the sentence of any Court Martial or Military Commission."

Lincoln was also encouraged by requests of several generals to set up military courts to suppress the "Copperheads," Southern sympathizers and "potential traitors" or the so called Peace Democrats who preferred to see the South leave rather than engage in Civil War (a view originally favored by influential editor of the *New York Herald Tribune,* Horace Greely).

Jefferson Davis, President of the Confederacy likewise suspended habeas corpus and imposed martial law to maintain order and spur economic development in the South to compensate for the losses inflicted by secession. The actions of both Lincoln and Davis are particularly noteworthy in view of the current controversy over the trial by military courts of those illegal combatants who planned the attacks on the World Trade Center on September 11, 2001. President George W. Bush was severely criticized for his policies by the political Left in the United States by those advocates of 'human rights' who have proposed civilian trials for the Jihadist conspirators.

A 20th Century Case Imitates Lincoln's Precedent

In 1942, eight German saboteurs, including two U.S. citizens, who had entered the United States to carry out sabotage were convicted by a secret military court set up by President Franklin Delano Roosevelt, the great hero of the American Left. In *Ex parte Quirin* (1942) the U.S. Supreme Court ruled that the writ of habeas corpus did not apply, and that a military tribunal had jurisdiction to try the saboteurs, due to their status as unlawful combatants. They were found guilty and executed. The eight men involved in the case were all born in Germany and all had lived in the United States. All returned to Germany between 1933 and 1941. After the declaration of war between the United States and Germany, they received training in the use of explosives and in methods of secret writing.

Four of them travelled from occupied France by submarine to Amagansett Beach, Long Island, landing on June 13, 1942 at night and the second group of four reached Ponte Vedra Beach, Florida on June 17, 1942. All eight wore full German uniforms, to ensure treatment as prisoners of war in the event that were captured before or while disembarking. As soon as they were clear of the beach they switched to civilian clothing. All had received instructions in Germany to commit acts of sabotage against American war industries. Two of the group, Dasch and Burger however had second thoughts and turned themselves over to the FBI and the remaining six were taken into custody.

All were tried by a secret military tribunal on July 2, 1942, found guilty and sentenced to death. The President later commuted Dasch's sentence to 30 years and Burger's to life in prison. Roosevelt, the Congress and the American people were never in doubt about the trials or the punishment meted out, just as the majority of public opinion in the North supported Lincoln's use of his Presidential powers. Both presidents revered by our two political parties refused to accept the notion that in wartime, illegal alien combatants out of uniform and intent on committing acts of sabotage or espionage deserved anything but a military trial and summary execution if found guilty.

Lincoln's Foreign Policy

French views of Abraham Lincoln and the ability of the Union to survive the Civil War were even more aggressive than the British. *La*

Patrie, the French newspaper on the same level as *The Times of London* editorialized with glee that ..."*The Union is completely dissolved and in our opinion can never be restored.*"

Most Americans rightly find European criticism today particularly unjust and misplaced. They regard the role of their country as a 20th century power as something which was forced upon the United States by the circumstances of European imperialist rivalries. The popular view currently enjoying a considerable degree of hypothetical speculation holds that the world would be a safer or better place with less American military power. This view would certainly have amused the German Kaiser and Hitler as well as the Japanese warlords who launched world wars on the assumption that basic isolationist sentiment and anti-militarism then prevailing in the United States would help ensure American neutrality.

The historical lesson of our country's turmoil and weakness on the international stage between 1861 and 1865 demonstrates how nations would likely behave in a world in which the United States withdraws into isolationism, is disarmed, or is faced with a grave internal crisis. It is quite illuminating in spite of the passage of time and a much changed world. In the run-up to the Civil War, anti-slavery opinions were popular with the more democratic political forces in much of Europe but were not regarded primarily as a moral issue except in Great Britain among the broad mass of the people. The upper class British view was colored by a pronounced sympathy for the South and its aristocratic traditions of great landed estates. Moreover the political realists of that day regarded American cotton in the same terms as Middle Eastern oil today.[1]

The French and Spanish governments were involved in expansion abroad, either attempting to recover lost colonies or acquiring new ones. They were pleased that the American government was weakened and its reach by naval power drastically reduced making enforcement of the anti-imperialist Monroe Doctrine impossible.

In Mexico, the French put their puppet, the ultra-conservative Austrian Archduke Maximilian on the throne and recognized Spain's maneuver to reestablish full control over Santo Domingo (the present

---

1 See Mahin, Dean "One War at a Time; The International Dimension of the American Civil War." Brassey's. Washington, D.C. 1999..

Dominican Republic), an even more blatant violation of the Monroe Doctrine. Even the normally reticent British were enlisted in a European colonial adventure in Mexico due to that country's defaulting on debts. The British, French and Spaniards were allied for several months against the democratic forces of Benito Juarez, a full-blooded Indian, Mexico's legal President, and a great friend of President Abraham Lincoln. None of these maneuvers would have been conceivable if the United States had not been torn asunder by the Civil War.

Napoleon III was aware that a Union victory would doom his project of French prestige in Mexico and was eager to recognize the Confederacy, support its navy by having French shipyards supply it with warships, and float loans on its behalf with cotton as collateral. Smaller loans were also raised in Britain by private means. The French pressed the British unsuccessfully to send a joint fleet to break the Union blockade of the Confederacy, a step that would have created an international war on a grand scale.

It was clear to Lincoln and Secretary of State Seward that the British and the French hoped that an independent and strong Confederacy would aid both European powers in their attempt to achieve a world-wide balance of power. Relations between Great Britain and the United States over Canada became very problematic. Ambitious Canadian politicians schemed with Confederate agents to embroil the U.S. and Britain in conflict. Although public opinion in Canada had been predominantly against slavery, anti-American sentiment was whipped up by Confederate agents and refugees who played on old Canadian fears of being absorbed by the United States. A Confederate raid launched against St. Albans, Vermont in October, 1864 almost brought about a hot pursuit policy and led to much stricter British supervision of Confederate agents and their Canadian sympathizers. It was made abundantly clear to Her Majesty's government that using Canada as a Confederate base would result in war with the United States.

Lincoln, backed by Secretary of State Seward, played an active role in foreign affairs, something which is almost entirely obscured today. He was no dove and realized that the survival of the union depended on the readiness to use military might as a last resort in order to prevent European aid and/or recognition of the Confederacy.

The systematic violation of the Monroe Doctrine by the European powers was not simply an act that damaged American interests. It was violently opposed by the native peoples of Latin America who had previously won their independence and honestly looked only to the United States for protection from the voracious appetite of European imperialism. A Union victory and growing local resentment against the French and Spanish adventures, the reestablishment of American military power, able to project its strength abroad, resulted in the collapse of the European interventionists like a pack of cards.

The consequences of American military weakness in 1861-65 for Mexico, the Caribbean Basin and all of Central and South America would have been entirely negative and have only enticed further European adventures. A Confederate victory and permanent division of the Union would have encouraged European conservatives everywhere to believe that America's militant democracy which promised universal white male suffrage followed by liberation of the slaves was no longer a long-term threat to their rule. Public opinion in Europe among the working classes continued to be strongly pro-Union especially after the Emancipation Proclamation and the North was looked upon as a democratic model.

The consequences of perceived American weakness today for the Middle East and the entire world would be infinitely greater. Much has changed since the mid-19th century but the experience of the last 150 years has repeatedly verified the need for the United States to exercise a leading role in world affairs backed by far reaching military power. This should not be taken to mean unlimited involvement in affairs abroad with the attendant risk of having to fight for the survival of unpopular regimes (as in Vietnam) and where vital strategic interests are not at stake.

To those who continue to wring their hands because of the religiously driven insurgencies of Al-Qaeda and the Taliban in Iraq and Afghanistan, let them look at how a weak appeasement oriented government in Spain or a model of non-belligerent European commitment to human rights like Denmark have fared in the face of Muslim hostility. Our allies today, in almost all of Europe, are aware that they face the same evil as we did on 9/11/01. Support for American policy and the realization that without us they are likely doomed has grown not only in Spain, France, Italy, Germany, Denmark, the U.K. and elsewhere in Europe but also in Canada, Australia, Argentina and Japan as well as those nations whose people have been attacked by Muslim fanatics such as Kenya, Indonesia and the Philippines. Even Russia and China are targets of Islamist fanaticism and know that they face a common enemy but are still reluctant to act like the appeasers in 1938-39 who were overwhelmingly on the political LEFT end of the spectrum, and hoped the crocodile would eat them last.

7

The Religious Left and the Senate Censure of Senator McCarthy

While the term "Religious Right" is one of the most frequently used terms in the political lexicon, notably since the rise of what is usually referred to as the Evangelical Churches, the Political Left is alive and well and a strong crutch for the Democratic Party calling for "social justice." During the first term of the Eisenhower administration, the role of American churches in politics became a major issue and helped precipitate the campaign to defame and censure Senator Joseph McCarthy of Wisconsin.

Joseph Brown Matthews was an important witness for McCarthy, testifying before Congressional committees and had the advantage of personal experience as an organizer for communist front organizations before World War II. He took pains to explain that naïve and busy people of good will including many clergymen were often duped into signing petitions and lending their names to what appeared as ostensibly good causes, but unaware that the leading personalities in these organizations were fronting for the Communist Party.

In June 1953, Matthews was appointed as McCarthy's research director and in July, published an article called "Reds in our Churches" in the conservative *American Mercury* magazine, Matthews referred to the Protestant clergy as *"The largest single group supporting the Communist apparatus in the United States."*[1] The result was a public outrage at Matthews as well as "his boss," Senator McCarthy. Time Magazine led the charge against Matthews and what it called *"This astounding and inherently uncheckable statement."*[2]

Reds in Our Churches

1 June, 1953
2 July 13, 1953

His authorship of the controversial article "Reds in Our Churches" exposed sophisticated communist manipulation to promote religious dissension in the United States. McCarthy's critics seized the opportunity to label his efforts as a "Crusade against all Protestant ministers," a view that Matthew certainly had not intended. In his *Mercury* article, he specifically pointed out that the great majority of all clergy in America were loyal but that a highly visible minority operating under the guise of "social justice" lent the support of the Religious Left to a variety of Liberal causes. Exaggerated and inaccurate commentaries of his intentions were used to forge a coalition among the Democrats in Congress and Republican advisors close to Eisenhower who feared McCarthy's appeal and possible candidacy in a future primary against Eisenhower lent support to censure of McCarthy as an extremist.

J. B. Matthews was born in Hopkinsville, Kentucky in 1894 and attended Asbury College. He became a Methodist missionary in Java after which he returned to the United States and studied in several different seminaries. He then joined the faculty of Scarritt, a Methodist training college in Nashville Tennessee where he became the center of a "scandal" due to the fact that he had held an interracial party at his home where Whites and Negroes had danced together. He was a brilliant linguist, but as a missionary, his sympathy for Indonesian nationalists made him unpopular with the Dutch administration in the islands and the executives of his own mission. In spite of this background which would certainly label him as a "liberal" today, Matthews was pilloried in the press as "a McCarthyite" following his article in *Mercury.*

After his tour of missionary work, Matthews settled in New York City where he became an "avowed Socialist" and the executive secretary of the pacifist Fellowship of Reconciliation. He wrote that the policy of a united front with Communism was the way to end the war, and due to the popularity of these views with the Roosevelt administration he was chosen as the first head of the American League Against War and Fascism.

He later would label this organization and his own participation in it as *"probably the most successful 'front' ever organized by the American Communists."* He wrote a book, *Partners in Plunder,* in which he attacked several of the main- line Protestant Churches – notably the

Episcopal and Presbyterian denominations as being in the pocket of millionaires J. Pierpont Morgan and Andrew Mellon respectively.

Matthews was regarded by many in the clergy at the end of World War II as "the Communists No. 1 fellow traveler." A major change in his political outlook occurred soon afterward as a result of an industrial dispute and strike at Consumer's Research, an organization where he had become a Director and Vice-President. Employees of the firm went on strike defying Matthews who had called upon them to reach a settlement. He became embittered and convinced that the workers' demands had been fomented by the Communist Party.

For Matthews, the workers grievances were a front and that morally "they were mutineers." He also was particularly aggrieved at what he regarded as the automatic liberal reactions of some of the same mainline churches he had previously attacked for being subservient to the very wealthy. Matthews then regarded himself as the victim of a Communist plot and went on to become the chief investigator for Martin Dies' new House Committee on Un-American Activities.

If one wants to understand the censure motion against McCarthy in the Senate, much of it has to do with a backlash of influential politicians, predominantly belonging to the mainline Protestant churches that were stung by what they perceived to be a wholly irresponsible and demagogic charge that these churches harbored potential traitors. White House operatives close to Eisenhower jumped on an opportunity to eliminate McCarthy for his embarrassing revelations about upper class appointees inherited from the previous Democratic administrations with dubious links to the USSR and the Communist Party that Eisenhower had seen fit to retain.

McCarthy, Falsely Accused by the Left of Antisemitism

McCarthy, falsely accused by the Left of antisemitism, had taken the lead in demanding to know why the Voice of America had cancelled its Hebrew language broadcasts at precisely the time when antisemitism was at the top of Stalin's agenda and the 'doctor's plot' in the USSR and the Slansky trial (see Chapters 2 and 15) in Czechoslovakia had pointed the finger at 'subversive cosmopolitan Jews' within

the Communist bloc who had been charged with links to American imperialism. McCarthy argued correctly that Soviet antisemitism should
be exposed and made crystal clear to the public both in Israel as well
as America. The reason for the cancellation of the Hebrew language
broadcasts was an embarrassing allegation never properly answered by
the Head of the Voice of America who used budgetary considerations
as an excuse. The revelations of the Slansky trial in Israel resulted in
a profound reaction against Ben-Gurion's leftwing partners, especially
the MAPAM party (the extreme Left of the Zionist movement) that
had generally followed the Kremlin line. Nevertheless for most American Jews, the Prague trials did not shake their deep attachment to anti-
anti-Communism

It is necessary to take a brief detour into the increasingly leftward
tilt of the Religious Left among Mainline Protestant denominations,[3]
and the career of Senator Joe McCarthy to really understand the ir-
rational behavior of so many American Jews who court their enemies
(the left wing of the Democratic Party) and spurn their friends (conservatives in general and Evangelical Christians in particular) and has
been passed on from one generation to the next since 1932.

Contrary to almost universal opinion among the so called
"enlightened" supporters of the Left, Senator McCarthy evinced no
anti-Semitism throughout his career although many Jews and those
on the Left were understandably upset and even outraged at McCarthy's role in the investigation of German S.S. soldiers who had been
accused of massacring American captive G.I.s in a POW camp near
the Belgian town of Malmedy, on December 17, 1944. The vilification
of McCarthy is a classic example of "guilt by association," but doubly
ironic because in his first term as a Junior Senator, McCarthy appeared
under the guise of an "advocate of human rights" in much the same
vein as those on the Left (who traditionally glorify John Adams as the
defender of the British redcoats who were accused of the massacre of
American patriots on Boston Common before the American Revolution) defamed American troops for "human rights violations" of Iraqi
prisoners at Abu-Ghraib. After the Malmedy verdict, the way in which
the court had functioned was criticized, first in Germany and then later

---

3 "The Death of Protestant America" by Joseph Botturn in *First Things*, August, September
2008.

in the United States by Congressmen from heavily German-American areas of the Midwest including McCarthy. The case was appealed to the Supreme Court which refused to deal with it. It came under investigation of a Senate sub-Committee in where McCarthy used it an opportunity to raise his political profile. He stated that the Court had not tried the defendants fairly.

Among Irish-American Catholics who were profoundly anti-Communist and therefore supporters of McCarthy and his role in the Army hearings, there were undoubtedly some anti-Semites incensed at what seemed to them as the preponderant presence of many Jews among Democrats and those who espoused a militant anti-anti-Communism. The American Jewish liberal establishment fell prey to this guilt by association and in 1954 the Conference of American Jewish Rabbis condemned McCarthy and "unanimously" called for him to be stripped of his committee chairmanship. Over the past half century, almost nothing has changed.

McCarthy's close associates and advisers were Jewish – Roy Cohn, G. David Schine, Alfred Kohlberg and columnist George Sokolsky. The Senator's investigation aimed toward exposing communists and their sympathizers did not single out Jews. No antisemitic statement or act has ever been alleged to have been committed by Senator McCarthy. Much of the anti-McCarthy sentiment that resulted in his being censored by the Senate and President Eisenhower had to do with his revelation that among the most prominent subversives his research correctly uncovered, was a high percentage of major figures who were appointees of the Roosevelt and Truman administration and were arch WASPS – with Ivy League educations and representing some of the most elite families at the top end of American society including several notable Protestant clergy of the Mainline churches.

McCarthy's attack on Leftwing activists

Jews were not directly involved at all in this controversy but many had been upset at the sight of Jewish writers, film producers and directors who had also appeared before the House un-American Activities Committee and easily believed that McCarthy's anti-Communism had run amuck and defamed American Jews as a group as well as the Protestant clergy. It is simply impossible for many liberal Jews today to accept that there was more than a grain of truth in McCarthy's attack on Leftwing activists (in the same vein as Reverends Wright, Jackson and Sharpton, and Father Pfleger today) who hid behind their clerical collars, nor can many of these same Jews believe that there was considerable prejudice against McCarthy by refined, wealthy and polished Ivy League types in Congress and the White House for his Catholicism, Irish-Midwestern background, frequent grandstanding, boorish behavior and hard drinking.

International Research Associates, a respected research body, measured the extent of antisemitism in 1954 among McCarthy's supporters. Only non-Jews were questioned. The poll certified that 38% of ANTI-McCarthy people would be likely to "vote against a Jew" compared to only 12% of pro McCarthy supporters.[4] Additional research confirmed that much more hostility existed against Jews by anti-McCarthyites than among his supporters. This too so violently upsets the Woody Allen view of the world among many Liberal Jews, it is rejected out of hand. They prefer to "know" what they believe rather than subject their biases to any re-evaluation.

McCarthy is often lumped together with racists and antisemites by Liberals who are fond of guilt by association. They assume some kind of relationship with a leading ultra-reactionary Democrat member of the House Un-American Activities Committee, John Rankin of Mississippi, who belittled Blacks and Jews in the House. Rankin used the epithets "kike" (against columnist Walter Winchell) and "nigger" on the floor of the House, prompting congressman Adam Clayton Powell of Harlem to call for his impeachment. The moment was referred to in the 1947 Academy Award winning film, *Gentlemen's Agreement,* which focuses on the topic of antisemitism. Rankin claimed that the Immigration and Nationality Act with quotas based on national origin was opposed solely by American Jews. None of his remarks, conduct and appeal in Mississippi had anything to do with McCarthy.

Many liberals like to point to those Democrats, like John F. Kennedy and Scoop Jackson, to assure their conscience that authentic

---

4 Weyl Nathaniel, *The Jew in American Politics* (Arlington House, New York. 1968) p.131.

liberals also opposed Communism and were therefore free from what they called the demagoguery of Senator McCarthy or his excesses yet much is known today through the revelations of the Venona documents that were not known by those in Congress at the peak of public interest in February 1954 during the Army-McCarthy hearings. Senator Kennedy and his brothers were staunch defenders of McCarthy at the time, a fact almost never mentioned today.

McCarthy was a showman and his popularity made him a threat to the moderate wing of the Republican Party dominated by an Old Guard of Ivy League aristocrats, but they needn't have worried. Televising the Army-McCarthy hearings led to a steep decline in McCarthy's popularity.[5] He came across as a bully and irresponsible. Nevertheless, in the most overplayed televised excerpt involving the supposedly befuddled witness with a slow southern drawl working for the army as a code clerk with a security clearance; the black woman, Annie Lee Moss whose claim that she had never been a member of the Communist Party or even heard of Karl Marx (Carl Who?), made McCarthy into the image of a medieval Spanish Inquisitor (he was not even present when she testified).

Senators Jackson and Symington simply took her word that there were three women with this same name in the Washington, D.C. phone book. Anyone could have checked this simple fact which was wrong but no one did. FBI documents and informers corroborated in closed session with Jackson that she was the one and only Annie Lee Moss living at the same address for years, a member on the Communist Party rolls and a subscriber to the *Daily Worker* delivered to her home. Senator Jackson was informed of this only two weeks after the famous questioning session but preferred to keep silent. Yet her 'innocence' remains part of the Liberal Canon as untouchable.

The aftermath of the Matthews incident still casts a long shadow over American politics. The Religious Left today, as then, is so determined to support what it perceives as the pursuit of 'social justice'

---

5 A Gallup Poll registered a decline in support for McCarthy from 50% to 30% from April to June 1954 during which the hearings were televised. Nevertheless, public opinion had been aroused against communism to the point that members of Congress voted to outlaw the Communist Party in the Communist Control Act signed by President Eisenhower in August, 1954. See Lichtman, Allan J. White Protestant Nation; The Rise of the American Conservative Movement. Atlantic Monthly Press. 2008. pg.191.

that it has often lent support to those whom it automatically regards as the "oppressed and downtrodden" – whether illegal immigrants who defy the law and even pro-Jihadi Muslims anxious to win additional privileges and special considerations under the guise of tolerance.

8

The Uncritical Support of the Left for 'Freedom of Religion' to Protect a Militant Islam

President Obama and scores of academics and ultra-liberals among inane/insane politicians such as Mayor Bloomberg and radio/television "journalists" do not, cannot acknowledge and prefer to remain willfully deaf, dumb and blind with regard to the Middle East, "allies" like our "friends" in Afghanistan and Iraq and so MUST accuse ordinary, decent, law-abiding and patriotic Americans with charges of Islamophobia, and worse, bigotry of every sort that includes racism, homophobia, greed, and of course, INTOLERANCE and IGNORANCE.

The sad truth is that the shoe is on the other foot. Not one of these paragons of virtue who claim sophistication and Ivy League degrees can even explain that the American Constitution does NOT ABSOLUTELY guarantee Freedom of Religion and that both Federal and State Law have taken action against the practices (not the beliefs) and consequences of dangerous and immoral behavior. This was the issue that forced the confrontation of the government against Brigham Young and the elders of the Church of Jesus Christ of Latter Day Saints (Mormons) to alter their "religion" and accept that American law and citizenship were not congruent with plural marriage or the exploitation of young teenage girls. The Utah territory would not have entered the Union without this confrontation when state power forced a "religion" to change its practices.

The same has been true in many Appalachian states, especially Tennessee, Kentucky, Georgia, Arkansas, West Virginia and North Carolina where state authorities forbade the practice of the so-called serpent churches, among several Pentecostal denominations, after the deaths of numerous individuals resulted from their handling venomous snakes. The states forced churches and church members to accept that

89

the state had a priority to safeguard individuals from reckless behavior and protect human life in spite of the claims of "religious freedom."

Had the government moved earlier, another incident in which the absurd and grotesque suicidal deaths of more than 900 people occured, most of whom were American citizens, might have been prevented. These naïve followers of the Reverend James Jones ended their lives in the greatest act of mass suicide in American history. This occurred on Oct. 18, 1978 in Georgetown, capital of Guyana. His "Peoples Temple" was a Church – i.e. a Religion, whom these same Leftwing and Liberal advocates of tolerance for Islam believe is protected by the Constitution ABSOLUTELY without any qualifications. His "religion" led to the greatest SINGLE LOSS of AMERICAN CIVILIAN LIFE IN A NON-NATURAL DISASTER BEFORE 9/11. The fact that it happened in Guyana was due to the real fear of Jones that he would not be able to continue his church in the United States because he knew that his cult was not permitted ABSOLUTELY by the Constitution to practice acts that could endanger human life.

Yet, the self appointed Liberal, tolerant intellectuals who are shedding tears over the possible need to move the Islamic Cultural Center/mosque from Ground Zero have undoubtedly never read any part of the Koran or any part of the Sira and Sunnah or done any research on the use of Jihad to expand the Dar al-Islam, yet stridently label anyone as a bigot or intolerant who has, and is aware of the potential danger.

Politicians such as Mayor Bloomberg and radio/television "journalists" do not, cannot acknowledge that the Freedom of Religion they imagine as unlimited has been curtailed by the Federal Government and the States before, acting under the Constitution and upheld by the Supreme Court. They nevertheless MUST accuse us – ordinary, decent, law-abiding and patriotic Americans of diverse religious creeds and also who are secular but who have legitimate concerns about those promoting the Ground Zero Mosque.

Supreme Court Decision, 1940

In the *Minersville School District vs. Gobitis* case (1940), the Supreme Court upheld a local Pennsylvania ordinance ordering school-children to salute the flag of the United States in the daily morning pledge of allegiance. Two Jehovah's Witness school children, 10 (William) and 12 (Lillian) years old, were suspended from school because of their refusal to salute the American flag. Consequently, their father had to pay for them to enroll in a private school. The parents alleged that their children's due process rights had been violated by the school and sued.

In an 8-1 Court Decision with Justice Frankfurter writing the majority opinion, the Supreme Court ruled that the school district had a strong interest in creating national unity that was sufficient to permit them to force students to salute the flag. This case required the Court to balance the religious interests of the Jehovah's Witness children with the secular interests of the school district. Obedience to a general law not aimed at the promotion or restriction of religious beliefs such as the pledge of allegiance was held to outweigh the "religious convictions" which contradict the relevant concerns of a political society. According to Felix Frankfurter, a prominent "liberal" Supreme Court Justice, the nation needed loyalty and the unity of all the people and saluting the flag was a primary means of achieving this legitimate goal, an issue of national importance. It is hard today to imagine that a Supreme Court with a "liberal majority" in the Roosevelt administration in 1940 agreed that the state had a right that overrode religious convictions, supposedly regarded by many as an "absolute right."

New Decision, 1943

Justice Harlan Stone, the only one who voted in favor of the right of the Jehovah's Witnesses in 1940 wrote a strongly worded objection to the decision and only three years later, the Court did reverse its decision in the case of the *West Virginia State Board of Education vs. Barnette* in 1943. With Justice Jackson writing the majority opinion, the Supreme Court ruled 6-3 that the school district violated the rights of several students whose families were Jehovah's Witnesses by forcing them to salute the American flag. The reason for the reversal many observers believe was due to the fact that the 1940 case provoked bullying against the children involved and caused hardship on the families who had to take their children out of the public schools. In the new decision, the Court argued that the fact that some students refused to recite the Pledge of Allegiance in no way infringed on the rights of other students who did participate and that the pledge indeed did force students to declare a belief that might be contrary to their faith thereby constituting a violation of their rights.

In his lone dissent, Justice Frankfurter, often looked on as a fierce supporter of the New Deal and President Roosevelt, argued that the law in question was not discriminatory because it required all children to pledge allegiance to the flag, not just some and that Freedom of Religion was not ABSOLUTE; it did not entitle members of religious groups to ignore a law when they didn't like it. Religious liberty means freedom from conformity to the religious dogmas of others, not freedom from conformity to the law because of their own religious dogmas.

NOW

The difference between past issues involving such clear principles as the protection and the wellbeing, health and safety of women and children in the case of the Mormons, and of all members of the Serpent Churches should be clearly enunciated and brought to public attention in the matter TODAY of those mosques (not all but certainly more than a few) where sedition and identification with the principles of Jihad are openly preached. Many such mosques with these values exist throughout the West and not only in the United States.[1] It should be in the fundamental interests of all Muslims who are loyal citizens to extirpate these institutions that act in their name. The background of those behind the plan of the "Cordova Project" to build a community Center/Mosque in Lower Manhattan at Ground Zero raises such doubts.

---

1 For the extent of Muslim Brotherhood Activity, CAIR and other front groups, see *Muslim Mafia: Inside the Secret Underworld That's Conspiring to Islamize America* by P. David Graubatz and Paul Sperry; *America Alone* by Mark Steyn and *Cruel and Usual Punishment* by Nonie Darwish.

The existing partially-free press in Lebanon, Turkey, Saudi Arabia, Bahrain, Qatar, Morocco, Jordan, Tunisia, Pakistan and Egypt and the Arabic press in Great Britain admitted in numerous editorials that the conflict in Iraq following the overthrow of Saddam Hussein has not been a civil war but that Jihadi terrorists have flocked there from as far away as Indonesia and Chechnia to sow death, destruction and mayhem to intimidate all those who oppose the extremist Islamist view of the world.

If we are to learn anything at all from history, it is that the Islamist concept of jihad was unequivocally understood as "violent holy war" against the infidels and not subject to interpretation. It remains a political weapon that has been used quite similarly by the last Ottoman Caliph, the Taliban, the Iranian mullahs, Al-Qaeda and rival extremist Sunni and Shi'ite clerics in Iraq today. It is still attractive to much extremist opinion in large parts of the Arab world, Chechniya, the Sudan, Pakistan and even in Indonesia. Its attraction throughout the 20th century for those autocratic and dictatorial European leaders who sought to become "Protectors of Islam" and "borrow" it, was to exploit its violent and evil appeal for their own purposes. (see Chapter 22)

The editorial in the April 15th, 2007 issue of the London based *Al-Sharq Al-Awsat*, the leading Arabic International Daily Newspaper, repeated essentially the same message and had this to say:

> "To make the picture clearer... This religious war has nothing to do even with the major issues, slogans related to which are raised in the terrorists' literature itself, like Palestine, Iraq, the U.S., etc. These are people who want martyrdom, that is, they want to fight war, anywhere in the world, and for any cause that has a religious angle.

> "They are not fighting for money, public reform, or for... the environment, and they are not nationalists, pan-Arabists, or communists... They are not jokers, hippies, or oppositionists. They are seekers of martyrdom, meaning that they are in a hurry to go to Paradise. They are not interested in the life of this world, and they want to take with them to the grave the greatest number of people possible.

"I know that this is an issue that is difficult for the Western-
er to understand. It is also difficult for many of the Muslims
themselves to accept this, and they always try to justify it with
issues that they consider legitimate and comprehensible. But
the truth is that these terrorists want death for the sake of Allah… That is, even if the Americans left Iraq tonight, and the
Jews fled Palestine, and extremist religious governments were
established in Morocco, Algeria, and Egypt - this would not
satisfy them… They want Paradise, and for this they will travel
to the ends of the earth, to the North Pole and the South Pole,
"to fight the infidels.""

It is incumbent on all of us to make certain that no connection
whatsoever exists between this view of Islam and requests to establish a
mosque in Manhattan or Tennessee or elsewhere in the United States.

9

The Stalinist and Daniel Webster

As a resident of Florida's 8th Congressional District in the Greater Orlando area, and a former New Yorker who grew up in the Bronx a few blocks away from the childhood home of Congressman, Alan Grayson, I cast my ballot in the 2010 Congressional elections in early voting to help defeat a man who rightly deserved the title of "America's Would Be Stalinist Congressman."

Grayson's attack on Republican candidate Daniel Webster whom he labeled "Taliban Dan" includes the now infamous video that follows the technique perfected by Stalin's henchmen and lackeys of splicing, editing, wiping out, skipping and superimposing images and words to convey the polar opposite of reality and historical truth.[1]

No other political ad in American history has sunk to this level and Grayson revels in it proclaiming at the end that "I am Alan Grayson and I approved this ad." Sixty years ago in my youth, Jews felt a deserved pride that "our politicians" and jurists such as Governor Herbert Lehman, Mayor La Guardia, Senator Jacob Javits and Justices Brandeis and Frankfurter were models of honesty, integrity and decorum. In today's political scene, we have descended into the gutter with the likes of former disgraced New York Governor Elliot Spitzer, political "activists" Rahm Emanuel and David Axelrod (advisor to disgraced former Senator John Edwards) and Connecticut Attorney General Richard Blumenthal (who dishonestly claimed to have served in Vietnam). All of these have been put into the shade by Grayson.

This growing leftward tilt of the Democrats was earlier the reason for the defections of Zell Miller (author of *A National Party No More*, and former Senator and Governor of Georgia), who delivered the keynote speech at the Republican convention in 2000, Joe Lieber-

---

1 To see how it was done, take a look at *The Commissar Vanishes; Falsification of Photographs and Art in Stalin's Russia* by David King, Metropolitan Books, Henry Holt & Co. Inc., 1997, and to see how Grayson perfected it, just go on the internet.

man, the former Democrat candidate for Vice-President in 2000 who also endorsed President George W. Bush in 2004 and Dick Morris, trusted political advisor of President Bill Clinton. This leftward tilt was also responsible for the worst political defeats in the Electoral College – Walter Mondale in 1984 and George McGovern in 1968 but most Democrats have very short memories.

Grayson's autobiography on his website makes Obama look like a Jesus model of humility and would make P.T. Barnum (a sucker born every minute") green with envy—yes, President Lincoln, you CAN fool some of the people all of the time. I feel a special anti-affinity for Grayson having come from a similar background in probably the most Jewish section of the Bronx in one of America's most liberal districts in the Melrose-Morrisania and Grand Concourse-Tremont sections.

On Grayson's official website, you can read what must be the most self promoting unabashed, breath-taking self-glorification of any politician now in the Congress...

> "Alan grew up in "the projects" in the Bronx. He heard the squeal of the wheels of the elevated trains, every five minutes, all day and all night. At the age of 12, he took the subway to school, by himself. At the age of 11, a bully threw him under a moving bus. He lived. Six years later, he took the standard test for 12th graders in New York. Almost 50,000 students in the Bronx took that same test. Alan received the highest score. Alan was accepted to Harvard College. He cleaned toilets there, and worked as a night watchman. He graduated in three years, with high honors. Then he went to graduate school at Harvard. In only four years, he received a law degree (with honors), he earned a master's degree in Government, and he finished the course work and passed the general examinations for a Ph.D."

I kid you not. Read it and weep. There is so much B.S. in this autobiography, it is difficult to know where to begin. I know the neighborhood where Grayson grew up very well. It was where I grew up. I also know very well the kind of economic and social status of someone like him, both of whose parents were tenured and members of the teachers' union (VERY well paid and well pensioned) in the New York City school system. His background was VERY AFFLUENT compared to mine and any of my friends on Morris Avenue five blocks away from the regal apartment buildings with doormen on the Grand Concourse, described by Grayson as "projects." To say that he scored the highest grade of 50,000 students taking the SAT College Entrance Examinations or the exam for Bronx High School of Science is nonsense.

In either case, the claim is bogus. There is no way this can be documented. With a total of 50,000 students taking the exam, many would have achieved "the highest score." His story of cleaning toilets to get through Harvard is grotesque (perhaps he is already planning whom to cast in the role for a future Hollywood blockbuster). I too took the subway to go to school by myself. The story of being thrown under a bus by a bully, yet "he lived," sounds like a messianic achievement but we are given no details.

Grayson did make a name for himself and acquired some deserved praise for combating the war profiteering of Iraq contracting firms that had defrauded the government but his megalomania is a contributing factor and symptom of the ever increasing leftward (and suicidal) drift of the Democratic Party that capitalized on sentiment against the war in Iraq but has since gone viral in its defamation of all those who oppose the Obama-Reid-Pelosi Agenda.

His autobiography goes on to refer to him in these terms…

"..And so Alan found his calling—like an Avenging Angel for the taxpayers and soldiers, he has sued the war profiteers in the name of whistleblowers, and forced them to disgorge their ill-gotten gains."

The Avenging Angel continued to pull the reputation of Congress down into the muck with the most partisan remarks ever made within its halls since Reconstruction. He warned Americans that *"Republicans want you to die quickly"* during an after-hours House floor speech in September 2009. Even many Democrats were appalled by this language but felt obligated to remain silent, as they did, even after his disgraceful, manipulated video on Republican opponent Daniel Webster, whose name he even ridiculed as a throwback to the 19th Century.

Veteran Tennessee Republicans Jimmy Duncan and Marsha Blackburn abandoned customary reticence to criticize Grayson. ...."*That is about the most mean-spirited partisan statement that I've ever heard made on this floor, and I, for one, don't appreciate it,*" Duncan said. "*It's fully appropriate that the gentleman return to the floor and apologize,*" seconded Rep. Marsha Blackburn, another Tennessee Republican.

Grayson also contributed significantly to exacerbating tensions between Jews and Christians. He is a notable JINO (Jew in name only). His Bronx born appeal and manufactured rags to riches from the tenements story is tailor made for elderly Jewish voters who moved to Florida to enjoy their retirement years. It is full of invective against Evangelical Christians (identified with opponent Daniel Webster). Clearly, Grayson was counting on a combination of the young, university crowd, Liberal transplantees/carpetbaggers and the elderly, especially among Jews to help him edge out Webster in the November 2010 election.

When Republicans demanded an apology for his remarks, Grayson used the classic JINO tactic of pulling on Jewish heartstrings by stating that "*I would like to apologize. I apologize to the dead and their families that we haven't voted sooner to end this Holocaust in America.*" Grayson's statement of a "Holocaust in America" on Sept. 30 was a response to criticism of his comments the previous day that the GOP position on health care. Ah, the Holocaust!; yes, voting against Obamacare is the equivalent of the Holocaust! His sarcasm drew a swift rebuke from the National Republican Congressional Committee. "*This is an unstable man who has come unhinged,*" NRCC spokesman Andy Sere said. "*The depths to which Alan Grayson will sink to defend his indefensible comments know no bounds.*"[2]

This had no effect, but when finally censured by Andrew Rosenkrantz, the Florida regional Director of The Anti-Defamation League (ADL), Grayson fell back on the standard pose of a JINO to express his Jewish identity—and was finally forced to issue an apology. "*I am Jewish and have relatives who died in the Holocaust. In no way did I mean to minimize the Holocaust. I regret the choice of words, and I will not repeat it.*" Rosenkrantz stated that Grayson's quip was ... "*more than*

---

2 Comment following Grayson appearance on the 'Hardball' television program, December 9, 2009..

a 'poor choice of words' and using the Holocaust as an analogy for flaws in the current health care system is inappropriate and serves only to trivialize the murder of 6 million Jews and millions of others."[3]

Apart from the claim that he had relatives who died in the Holocaust (this proves he's Jewish), I cannot find any strong defense of specifically Jewish interests and Israel in Grayson's record. Of course, he and other JINOS would have you believe that Liberalism and its agenda a la Obama (abortion, a bigger and bigger government and national debt, timidity in foreign affairs and a wholesale retreat of support for Israel) are specifically Jewish interests.

Grayson has told reporters he's not worried at all about a backlash from the voters and believes on the contrary that his chances for re-election have been boosted. *"It improves them,"* he said.... *"People like elected officials with guts who say what they mean. I stand by what I said. I didn't violate any House rules. I didn't do anything inappropriate. I'm not under any pressure at all."*

Even one of the Democratic Party leaders, Caucus Chairman John B. Larson of Connecticut, at one point publicly called on him to apologize for his Republicans Want You to Die Speech. *"I wouldn't have used the words that Mr. Grayson has,"* Larson said. *"I would encourage Alan to apologize"* but Grayson later queried whether Larson really meant what he said. *"I spoke to him and he did not ask me to apologize,"* Grayson explained. He stated he hadn't used *"exactly those words"* (also old Stalinist technique) until a reporter read his words back to him. Republican Study Committee Chairman Tom Price of Georgia drafted, but withheld from a vote, a resolution that would have expressed the House's disapproval of Grayson's remarks. Fortunately, the 2010 election put an end to Grayson's career (at least for the moment) in the House of Representatives.

---

3 Letter and phone conversation between Rosenkrantz and Grayson leading to Grayson's letter of apology on Oct. 2, 2009..

10

The Anachronistic American Jewish Affection for the Left

Time and time again, I read in websites and blogs around the internet the question and puzzling paradox posed by Gentiles who strongly support Israel; how can it be that so many Jews continue to blindly vote for ultra-liberal causes that are inherently ultra-critical of Israel and even subliminally of Jews? One of my favorite songs taken from the Hollywood musical *South Pacific* has the hero sing the haunting refrain "Some Enchanted Evening" and plaintively pose the question…"*Who can explain it; Who can tell me why? Fools give you answers; Wise men never try!*" At the risk of playing the fool, I shall try to explain it and tell you why.

The reason I dare to, is that among those who voted for Senator McCain and opposed Obama from the very start are Jews, like myself, who grew up in families and amidst environments where Jewish espousal of liberal and Left Wing causes was inherited. We have, however, demonstrated by now that, although Jewish Liberalism is an inherited disease, it is not incurable. Former White House Secretary Ari Fleischer likes to tell the story that when his parents became aware of his involvement in Republican activities in college, they commiserated with their neighbors and friends by exclaiming that "*at least he is not a drug-addict.*"

Most American Liberal Jews, whose identity has been stamped three generations ago by their grandparents under FDR, continue to picture themselves as enlightened and the true inheritors of the mantle of Jewish concerns for "social justice," followed the Pied Piper of Chicago wherever he led, oblivious to all the evidence amassed and catalogued and shouted from the roof tops in 2008. He sat in Reverend Wright's church for 20 years and couldn't hear what anybody could determine from a few minutes listening to the same old antisemitic rhetoric used by the country's most well known antisemite, Louis Far-rakhan.

Some prominent American Jews, particularly among those who cannot escape the narcotic-like trance they have inherited as "progressives," are essentially secular and ultra-critical of capitalism and American society with its underlying Christian values, have developed a new kind of psychological self-hatred to exhibit a disassociation from the State of Israel and their religious heritage. They are upset over the close Israeli-American friendship and wish to be absolved from the heinous charge that they once may have actually subscribed to a sense of Jewish solidarity when that meant only solidarity with victimhood – the Jews as eternal martyrs.

Now that Jewish solidarity is politically incorrect and Israel is so resented as a successful and prosperous society by so many among the world's poor and "oppressed," they must seek compensation and expiation from their fellow "progressives" by identifying with the prevailing winds of anti-Semitism disguised as anti-Zionism. What has changed over the past 40 years is that many prosperous and decadent Europeans and Americans feel embarrassed by the Israelis' gallant defense of their homeland against great odds.

The Diaspora Jewish critics of Israel easily see its many flaws (both real and imagined) among which, the worst is that Israel, like America is a "privileged" society, enjoying wealth amidst a world of misery. Why should American Liberal Jews renounce their previous worship of the Hollywood Celebrity Cult of "cool," proclaimed in dozens of Woody Allen movies? This fitting idol of the Jewish Cultural Left (there is a statue in his honor in the Spanish city of Oviedo) granted an interview to the Spanish newspaper, Vanguardia, on May 17, 2010 in which he stated "*I am pleased with Obama. I think he's brilliant. The Republican Party should get out of his way and stop trying to hurt him. It would be good……if he could be a dictator for a few years because he could do a lot of good things quickly.*" This from the man who is a major critic of Israel which he has never visited, made a career out of ridiculing Jewish tradition, mocked his parents, changed his name, and married his former wife's adopted daughter.

Some Jews in the Diaspora whose parents and grandparents rejoiced at the rebirth of Israel in 1948 and regarded it mystically as partial compensation for the Holocaust, have been psychologically intimidated by the constant anti-Israel line of the media and of the torrent of bloody confrontations picturing enraged Muslim mobs ready for constant mayhem to avenge what they regard as the worst injustice in human history (i.e. the creation of the Jewish State rather than the failure to establish an Arab Palestinian state).

A considerable number of American Jews who opposed the Vietnam War became alienated from America's role in the world. Many of them and their children grew estranged from the Israel their grandparents had hoped for in the sentimental image of old radicals transplanted from Europe who were delighted with the impoverished Jewish society in Palestine based on the egalitarian kibbutz and socialism but the powerful, prosperous, dynamic and successful capitalistic Israeli society, a world leader in sophisticated advanced technologies and a close ally of the United States embodied a double disappointment for them.

J-Street and Z-Street

The anti-Israel mantra they hear on all sides from the political Left and their fellow "progressives" has become a substitute for historical truth. They are the organizers and members of the newly founded J-Street, describing itself on the internet as ….*"Mainstream American Jews and other supporters of Israel who, informed by their progressive and Jewish values, believe that a two-state solution to the Israeli-Palestinian conflict is essential to Israel's survival as the national home of the Jewish people and as a vibrant democracy."*

It accepts hook, line and sinker the Obama Party Line that people like the Palestinian Authority President Mahmoud Abbas, whose Ph.D. dissertation essentially denies the Holocaust and refuses to acknowledge that Israel can define itself as a Jewish State is a "partner," and calls on the Treasury department to investigate any Jewish or Christian charity that in any way aids Jews who live in any part of "Palestine" across the Cease Fire Lines of 1949. Its two-faced approach is all the more grotesque given its concerns and hand-wringing over the lack of progress towards the creation of a 23rd independent Arab state while pooh-poohing an existential threat to Israel from Iran, its thugocracy and repeated vows to wipe the country off the face of the map. It has sparked the formation of Z-Street by those Jews who realize that J-Street are bagmen for the Democratic Party and that Obama has been a colossal fraud with the Jewish vote in his pocket.

The Jewish martyr complex of J-Street is drawn primarily from the deeply felt need to imitate both Christ and the ultra-Orthodox in their search for perfection and as proof of their superior role as a "Light unto the Gentiles." It is the reverse of the Muslim one that seeks death as a vindication of beliefs that Islam must subdue and dominate all non-Muslims. This is what leads the inane Jewish Mayor, Michael Bloomberg of New York, to support the building of a Muslim "community center/mosque" near ground zero of the Twin Towers in Manhattan or Job Cohen, Amsterdam's Jewish mayor, (his first name could not be more apt), to dismiss a need for Muslim immigrants in the Netherlands to learn Dutch and make serious efforts to integrate into the host society.

Mayor Michael Bloomberg, the chief guru of Jewish Liberalism was forced to apologize after having the gall (chutzpah) to tell an audience of the American Irish Historical Society in a speech on Feb. 11, 2011 to honor St. Partick's Day and the Irish American community, that he was used to seeing drunks hanging out the windows of the building's offices during St. Patrick's Day parades. He said, "*Normally, when I walk by this building, there are a bunch of people that are totally inebriated hanging out the window. I know that's a stereotype about the Irish, but nevertheless, 'We Jews' around the corner think this.*" The mayor's "joke" was met with boos and groans from the audience, but typifies more than any single event how J-Street spokesmen and leading members of the Democratic Party with the Jewish vote in their pocket, look down with contempt on lesser lights like the Irish and with total confidence that they speak for all Jews like themselves who must be "progessive and liberal."

J-Street's leading figures delight in proclaiming the very large Jewish majority that voted for Obama but are deluded with the sad fact of American politics that support for Obama is strongest among so called "intellectuals" (particularly among Ivy League graduates including many Jews, Hollywood celebrities, so-called journalists, young single women, Hispanics, Muslims, Blacks and the impoverished welfare dependent poor), all of which reinforces their allegiance to the liberal "cause" while ignoring the other side of the coin that this support rules out just about everyone else.

The Democratic Party was widely regarded for the first 150 years of its existence on the national scene as the party of slavery and segregation. Most American Jews including new immigrants looked askance on the mistreatment of blacks and segregation that was so much an ingrained aspect of life in the South, and many parts of the rural Midwest, identified in the minds of Catholics and Jews as the White Anglo-Saxon and Protestant heartland. The lynching victims included a Jew, Leo Frank, in one-party Democratic Georgia in 1916, sending shock waves through the community. President Wilson, who had originally attracted considerable Jewish support for his idealism, was later revealed as a racist, entirely sympathetic to the Ku Klux Klan[1] (see the film "Birth of a Nation"). His wholesale violation of the civil rights of any opponents to American entry into World War I in April, 1917 as an ally of Russia was offensive to many Jews. It is no wonder that in the 1920 elections to Congress, ten Jews were elected on the Republican ticket, one from the Socialist Party while the only two veteran Jewish Democratic Congressmen were both defeated.

Nevertheless, the Democratic Party machines in the big cities, especially New York (Tammany Hall), Boston, Chicago and Philadelphia among others were successful in providing services, jobs and patronage to new immigrants establishing their upward social mobility. They successfully posed as the protectors of immigrants from a Republican Party, demonized as the bastion of nativist sentiment, ultra-conservative social mores such as Prohibition and Sunday Blue Laws that discriminated against Jewish merchants. The Democrats also ridiculed the Republicans as supporters of an "elitist" Anglophile foreign policy, historically identified with the upper class. The last charge helped cement Irish Catholic loyalty for the Democrats both before, and especially during the early years of World War I, prior to American entry into the conflict.

Foreign policy added enormously to the reasons most Jews

---

1 See Goldberg, Jonah *Liberal Fascism*, Doubleday 2007, pp. 254-256..

eventually came to support the Democrats overwhelmingly since the election of Franklin Delano Roosevelt, who quickly became identified with an activist line to help support Great Britain and express opposition to the Nazi plans for German expansionism. Following Krystallnacht on November 10, 1938, the President's strong criticism of German conduct (our ambassador to Germany was recalled) towards its Jewish population made his support among Jews unshakeable although the following should be remembered...

1. In the 1932 election against Herbert Hoover, foreign policy played no significant role for Jewish voters. The Nazis had not yet seized power in Germany. In 1936, the Republican candidate Alf Landon, selected by the isolationist wing of the Republican Party was an outspoken supporter of NO European entanglements and "America First" making it seem that he would not be as outspoken as FDR regarding German antisemitism.

2. Neither Roosevelt nor his Secretary of State, Cordell Hull, had expressed any official policy criticizing Germany's internal affairs until Krystallnacht and expressed no opinion whatsoever on a proposed boycott of the 1936 Olympic Games held in Munich.

3. In 1940, Jewish votes were also captured by FDR even though the Republican candidate, Wendell Wilkie, represented the most internationalist and activist wing of the party, who shared much the same sentiment as FDR regarding the need to aid Britain and eventually have to come to terms with confronting Nazi Germany and Japan.

It deeply discomforts many Jews today that once again, as in the period just before the Holocaust, "they" (The Israelis and by implication, all "the Jews") are in the world's headlines and constantly viewed by "world opinion" as a source of aggravation stemming from the deep seated grievances of the Palestinians (and by extension, all the Arabs and to all the Muslims and by further extension to all the "colored peoples" of the "Third World"). This confrontation spills over what should have been a squabble over Middle Eastern borders to a world-wide confrontation between civilizations, one in which many Jews are profoundly disturbed by being cast in the image (no matter how unrealistic and false) of the "white oppressor" (the canard of the Reverend Wright and Louis Farrakhan).

What makes this all the more absurd is that American Jews and are probably 97% of Ashkenazi (East European) descent and are apparently unaware or unmoved by the fact that a majority of Israel's Jewish population are of Afro-Asian-Sephardi descent and in many cases, as dark-skinned as Obama. Nevertheless, many Liberal Jews argue that their understanding of Judaism (or what they perceive as their ethical heritage) requires a commitment to "social justice" and are fond of the expression "Tikkun Olam" (Repairing the World), that has become the byword and title of the Jewish Far Left and their journal of the same name.

As argued cogently by biblical scholars not in the thrall of apologizing for the Democratic Party and author Hillel Halkin in his article "How Not to Repair the World,"[2] the expression "Tikkun Olam" is not the automatic Liberal agenda on social and economic policy so fondly embraced by a majority of the Jewish electorate – including abortion, feminism, pacifism, opposition to gun rights, affirmative action, environmental conservation, etc. On almost all these issues, observant Jews are fundamentally at odds with the Secular/Liberal Jewish majority. Basically, the thrust of Tikkun Olam is in the opposite direction.... "For the Sake of the Public Interest," rather than "Repairing the World." It was this concept that was cited by many rabbis in the Middle Ages when they ruled that Jewish communities should not rescue Jewish captives taken by pirates if it meant paying an excessive ransom. To do so would actually encourage more attempts at kidnapping and put the entire community at greater risk.

Indeed, several varying concepts are embraced under the terms "Tikkun Olam" but the predominant one that emerged from the two great failed revolts of Judea against Roman rule in 70 and 135 A.D. that ended Jewish independence for almost two thousand years, was the fundamental need NOT for prophetic utopian visions but the necessity for laws, authority, routines, and organization to prevent future wild

---

2 *Commentary*, July-August, 2008.

and unrealistic messianic fervor. It is also this dichotomy that exists in the two visions that captured Jewish imagination in the 19th Century before mass immigration to America – Socialism and Zionism; the former being an end of days vision of a utopian universalist future to lead the rest of the world by example and the latter, a realistic attempt to live as much as possible a normal existence as a free people charged with the full responsibility of achieving an autonomous community responsible for its own order and progress.

Sixty years after its founding, Israel has become an outcast among the nations and the Jews a pariah people once again. How did this occur? From Darling of the Left to Pariah State, subject to continual venomous attacks coming from those who consider themselves "progressive" and "morally sensitive," i.e. the mainline churches, university faculties clamoring to boycott and "disinvest" from Israeli owned companies, the media elite and those on the Left side of the political spectrum.

Whatever the differences between secular and religious Israelis, they pale before the monumental differences that separate life in the State of Israel with all its inherent promises, risks and dangers from the Diaspora's ultra idealized concerns and sensibilities. The Jewish paragons of "enlightened thought" whose byword is "tolerance at any price" as they understand it, can rely on numerous naïve Reform Rabbis who have appeared on the History Channel and other documentary programs, proclaiming in all their feeble and feigned piety, innocence and assumed mantle of linguistic scholarship, that ISLAM (meaning SUBJUGATION) really means PEACE.

What is so shocking when it comes to the issue of foreign policy affairs, is that hardly any "progressive" critic of Israel is ready to admit the impeccable credentials Israel earned in 1948 in a struggle against the most reactionary elements in the Arab world and endorsed by the entirety of what was then called "enlightened public opinion," above all by the political Left[3] (see Chapter 21)

They have been seduced by the onslaught of falsified and selective history that has been so frequently transmitted by the media. Two recent works of superb scholarship that directly deal with the full range

---

3 See 'The Most Widely Believed Political Myth, What America Did for Israel in 1948 -NOTHING" *New English Review*, December, 2007.

of contemporary PRIMARY SOURCES of the Arab Central Committee in Arabic, the Jewish Agency Executive in Hebrew and the British Mandate authorities reveal a very nuanced picture of the Arab reaction to Zionism and cooperation with Jewish neighboring settlements that challenges the accepted conventional wisdom of total hostility towards the Zionist enterprise.[4]

Nevertheless, the myth persists, and is constantly reinforced and has even hypnotized many American Liberals including Jews, that the "poor wretched Palestinians" are victims and that Israel owes its existence and military superiority to the United States which unlike the Europeans has never followed an "even-handed" policy in the Middle East. Obama, oblivious to the historical truth, endorsed this simplistic and misleading view in his Cairo speech.

Most American Jews have little or no fluency in Hebrew and are remote from the achievements of modern Hebrew literature or the patriotic themes of deep and abiding affection expressed in popular Israeli song for the landscape and all that has been achieved by four generations of pioneer effort. Instead of a sense of close comradeship with Israelis that one might expect from American Jews with a distinct ethnic heritage that is shared abroad, there is primarily a lingering nostalgia for the Yiddish culture destroyed in Europe.

In the 2008 campaign, the voices of Jewish conservative intellectuals, writers and politicians was shouted down by a chorus of reform rabbis, Hollywood "stars," academics and establishment organizations who equated any criticism of Obama as a betrayal of what they call the great liberal tradition that has made them politically deaf, dumb and blind since FDR. Fox News commentator Charles Krauthammer, former White House Press secretary Ari Fleischer, Scholar at the American Enterprise Institute, Joshua Muravchik, columnist and editor of the *Weekly Standard* Bill Kristol, political analyst and former campaign advisor to President Bill Clinton, Dick Morris, Editor of *Frontpage Magazine*, David Horowitz, *National Review* columnist Jonah Goldberg, (author of *Liberal Fascism*) Senator Joe Lieberman,

---

4 See my book review of "Army of Shadows; Palestinian Collaboration with Zionism, 1917-1948" by Hillel Cohen; Translated by Haim Watzman, (University of California Press, Berkeley, 2008) reviewed in *New English Review*, February, 2009 and the just published *Palestine Betrayed* by Ephraim Karsh, Yale University Press, New Haven, 2010.

author and columnist Dennis Prager, writer Monah Charen, author of *Useful Idiots,* Dianna West, author of *The Death of the Grown-Up,* editor of *Commentary,* Norman Podhoretz, author Hillel Halkin who now resides in Israel, journalist and writer Bernie Goldberg, Ronald Radosh, author (*Divided They Fell: The Demise of the Democratic Party,* 1964 New York: Free Press, 1996), film producer David Zucker and comedian Jackie Mason among many others warned everyone in the Jewish community not to ignore the most critical evidence that all of Obama's close associates, especially Blacks, among radicals and Arabs or Muslims were overtly hostile to Israel. Among those prominent Jews who argued strongly for Barack Obama in 2008 were former Mayor of New York City, Ed Koch, the country's most well known (or infamous) trial lawyer Alan Dershowitz, trendy media-star Rabbi Shmuely Boteach, Mortimer Zuckerman, owner and publisher of the *New York Daily News* and editor of *U.S. News & World Report,* and many others who have since removed the Obama stickers from their cars and are now pleading ignorance or betrayal.

A majority of Jewish voters are either unconcerned with the increasingly low moral image of the Party's politicians and candidates and party hacks (John Edwards, David Axelrod, Rahm Emanuel, Elliot Spitzer, Richard Blumenthal). Collectively these five represent the worst in American politics. The defection of the many Jews who were formerly so proud of Senator Joe Lieberman (when he was nominated as the Vice-Presidential candidate of the party), has apparently not bothered them or caused them to rethink. Both Lieberman and former Democratic governor/senator of Georgia, Zell Miller[5] told the party faithful the same message when they supported George Bush and John McCain - the Democratic Party is a national party no longer! For many Jews, still in a time warp of the 1930s, the message is only slowly beginning to penetrate.

Democrat politician Scott Stringer, the Manhattan Borough President, boasted to Laura Ingraham on the O'Reilly Factor (Aug. 25, 2010) that he, a Jew, was elected "overwhelmingly" by Jewish voters and that he fully endorses Mayor Bloomberg's position on the mosque at ground zero. Not being satisfied with that, he then threw out absurd

---

5 Miller, Zell *A National Party No More, The Conscience of a Conservative Democrat,* Stround and Hall, 2003..

charges of antisemitism against Sarah Palin and the Tea Party. This is the ultimate example of how degraded, disgusting and demented some Liberal Jewish politicians are and how far they will go to demean themselves and exploit their naive, supporters to keep the Jewish vote in the pocket of the Democratic Party and ignore the ninth commandment (Thou Shalt Not Bear False Witness).

It used to be said of scoundrels on the political Right that their last refuge was patriotism. For the Jewish scoundrels of the Liberal Left like Scott Stringer, Democratic Representative Steve Cohen of Tennessee (comparing Republican opposition to Obamacare to the Nazis and Goebbels), and TIME editor Joe Klein, their last refuge is the Wolf's cry of 'antisemitism from the Right' as they contemplate the impending collapse of the Obama administration and its Jewish apologists

Frantic attacks on Glen Beck portraying him as another Father Coughlin from the 1930s, a racist, antisemite or mentally ill are an example of unparalleled viciousness and blatant lies. The same has been the fate of Sarah Palin whose use of the term 'blood libel' for being attacked as if she bore any responsibility for the mass murder in Tucson, Arizona in January 2011 was illegitimate and reprehensible for Jewish opinion. To his credit, Alan Dershowitz, long identified as one of the most prominent spokesmen for Liberal causes favored by the Democrats spoke out in Sarah Palin's defense and attacked the hard Left anti-Israeli propaganda of J-Street and the absurd remarks of Congressman Steve Cohen. Dershowitz said,

> "I am one of the few liberal Democrats who, while criticizing her use of crosshairs in indentifying contested congressional seats, found nothing objectionable in her use of 'blood libel' as a metaphor to describe what she regarded as a false accusation of complicity in the bloodletting in Tucson. I have heard little from the left regarding Congressman Cohen's more extreme statements. The irony, of course, is that many of the same people on the left who criticized Palin for insensitivity to Jewish suffering, have themselves contributed to Jewish suffering by unfairly demonizing the Jewish state and trivializing the increase in global anti-Semitism. They have also given a pass to those on the hard left who have used Holocaust and Nazi refer-

ences in mischaracterizing Israeli self defense actions."[6]

More than twenty years ago, Lucy Dawidowicz, one of the most respected and prominent historians of the twentieth century and author of the aptly named "What is the Use of Jewish History?"[7] lamented the lopsided and continued illogical and self destructive political support of a large majority of American Jews for the Democratic Party. She, of course, was not the first. The old joke that Jews earn like Episcopalians but vote like Puerto Ricans is no longer funny. It is indicative of a malaise that has become a compulsion with the behavior of the Jewish electorate in 2008 in disregarding the blatant antisemitic views and rants of the Reverend Wright, apologetics over radical Islam, the institutionalization of quotas (passing as "Diversity" and "Affirmative Action"), and the radical Left politics of close Obama associates. She wrote this on explaining Jewish political behavior in the U.S:

> "The answer, it seems to me, has to do with the powerful residual hold of the universalist mind set, a hold so encompassing that it has led to the alienation of the Jews as a political group from their rightful place in the American consensus…..
> No doubt most Jews who voted Democratic (in the 1984 election) believed they were voting for the age-old liberal agenda, for the extension of civil rights to those still deprived of them. But the current agenda of those who call themselves liberals is less a matter of rights and more a matter of social and economic redistribution…..Quotas threaten America with the fate of the Hapsburg Empire….Whether the democratic United States could survive institutional quotas we do not know, but it certain that, politically Jews, could not." (pp. 264;267)

The result so far of record high Jewish support for 2008 Democratic standard bearer Barack Hussein Obama (the subject of considerable pride and boasting by ultra-Liberal Jews and reform rabbis) is markedly worse racial tension, the most dismal economic situation in the country since the depression, abandonment of Israel to its fate

---

6 Dershowitz, Alan in *FrontPageMag* website, Jan. 24, 2011..
7 *What is the Use of Jewish History?* Schocken. 1994.

(probably a good thing for Israelis to know once again they must depend wholly upon themselves), worse relations with our most important European NATO allies and most likely a steep rise in anti-Semitism on the part of those who see the highly visible Jewish advisors who surround Obama (just as the Far Left saw the Jewish "neo-con" advisors to President Bush as responsible for the Iraq war).

It bears repeating the final paragraph in Lucy Davidowicz's book *What is the Use of Jewish History?*....."*If Jews need to know their own interests as well as the interests of others, they also need to know the art of politics as well as the books of the Torah. They need, in short, to live in this world, not in the world of the politically utopian or the religiously messianic.*"

11

Collective vs. Individual Rights: How The Constitution Has Been Assaulted by Multiculturalism/Affirmative Action

For more than a generation now, one of the most powerful weapons used by the Liberal-Left in American politics is to justify differential treatment of citizens, referred to by the euphemism of "affirmative action." The overriding consideration used to expound on the need for such differential treatment in hiring for jobs in teaching, government, and large areas of the private sector has been the acquisition of DIVERSITY. Three times, this was the answer I received from an "insider" involved in the decision to hire someone else when explaining that, although I was indeed the most "qualified candidate" for the position (two academic teaching jobs and one as the editor of a periodical), the body involved in making the decision was under pressure to conform to government guidelines (as opposed to "rigid quotas," they were quick to add). They explained one of their chief considerations was 'seeking diversity' which meant that the candidate hired (a woman and two members of "racial minorities") would more adequately reflect the student population at a community college, a university and the readership of the periodical and/or the "commitment" to demonstrate DIVERSITY. This "desirable characteristic" of the ideal candidate was however, not part of the original job description.

Why? How did this issue become the touchstone of hundreds of legal cases? How is it that this holy mantra of DIVERSITY was so conspicuously absent in the debate over the nomination of Elena Kagan for Supreme Court Justice?

Affirmative action in the US began as a "tool" to redress, reduce and "eventually eliminate persisting inequalities" (of results) for African Americans in the 1960s. The term "affirmative action" has a convoluted ancestry. It can be traced to US government policy in 1961

113

by the executive order issued by President John F. Kennedy mandating (Order 10925) how applicants are employed, and that employees are treated during employment, without regard to their race, creed, color, or national origin. At the time, this could hardly be construed as the first step on the legal road that has transformed our society from one in which our Constitution and form of government evolved from the guarantees promised to individual citizens to one in which group identity is a guiding principle, but so it was.

The Johnson administration adopted the policy known as "Affirmative Action" in 1965, by issuing U.S Executive order 11246, later amended by Executive order 11375 aiming *"to correct the effects of past and present discrimination."* It prohibits federal contractors and subcontractors from discriminating against any employee or applicant for employment because of race, skin color, religion, gender, or national origin.

But it is not meant to refer to individuals. The order requires that contractors take affirmative action to ensure that "protected class, underutilized applicants" are to be employed when available, and that employees are to be treated without "negative discriminatory regard to their protected-class status." What carries weight is therefore not the rights of citizens, but the rights of groups that enjoy or do not enjoy this status.

It was President Lyndon B. Johnson, the classic White Southern politician with a guilt complex, struggling to wear/inherit the cape of the great fallen leader/martyr, who turned Kennedy's order on its head by elaborating on the importance of affirmative action in achieving true freedom for African Americans when he stated:

> "...But freedom is not enough. You do not wipe away the scars of centuries by saying: Now you are free to go where you want, and do as you desire, and choose the leaders you please. You do not take a person who, for years, has been hobbled by chains and liberate him, bring him up to the starting line of a race and then say, 'you are free to compete with all the others,' and still justly believe that you have been completely fair...This is the next and the more profound stage of the battle for civil rights. We seek not just freedom but opportunity. We seek not just

legal equity but human ability, not just equality as a right and a theory but equality as a fact and equality as a result...To this end equal opportunity is essential, but not enough, not enough."[1]

In 1971, the Supreme Court ruled unanimously that employment tests have to be job-related to ensure that "extraneous criteria" are not used intentionally or unintentionally to screen out applicants because of their race, gender or ethnicity. We have reached a stage when the government could interfere with employment so as to regard intelligence as an "extraneous criteria." Is it any wonder that American society has arrived at a point, where teenagers today, operate with less than half the vocabulary they had in 1950?

A height requirement that screens out many Hispanics and women, even if it can be demonstrated that height is an important job related consideration, may be held to be invalid today. The laws relating to affirmative action currently state that if a test for merit disproportionately eliminates one racial or gender group and some equally good merit test does not, then the employer has to use the latter test. The door is thus open to endless variations of "equally good merit tests" (until you find the one that works).

Universities, hospitals, government agencies, fire and police forces were deemed to be in need of justifying that their racial, ethnic or gender make-up reflected the composition of the populations they served. The most recent case of using affirmative action tested by the Supreme Court involved the New Haven Fire Department in Connecticut that gave an exam for promotions to lieutenant and captain. Scores for Hispanics and for African-Americans ranged from 34 to 59 percent of the scores for whites. As a result, no African-American and "only one Hispanic" had won any of the 15 promotions. The question then became whether the Civil Service Board would validate the test results.

After five days of hearings, the board decided the exam was flawed. "The measured thing to do was to decide not to promote based on that exam," according to the then Acting Corporation Counsel Victor Bolden. Karen Torre, the lawyer for the whites and one Hispanic

---

1 June 4, 1965 speech asserting Affirmative Action as a legal and moral concept for government concern.

firefighter, stated that her clients had been the victims of reverse racial discrimination, pure and simple. *"There's no question that their race and skin color were the driving motivation behind the decision not to promote them,"*[2] and her claim was upheld by the U.S. Supreme Court in a 5-4 decision. Frank Ricci, the lead plaintiff in this case, was not a naturally gifted test taker. As someone with a clear disability, he could have taken a stand with those who opposed a qualifying test for promotion. Nevertheless, in an affidavit, he stated that in spite of his dyslexia, he studied as much as 13 hours a day for the firefighter promotional exam, that he paid someone to read the textbooks onto audiotapes, prepared flashcards and worked with a study group, and thus he passed in spite of multiple handicaps and as a result of extra individual effort. In effect, the board concluded Ricci was wrong to have made any extra effort to pass the test.

The most recently appointed Justices, Sonia Sotomayor and Elena Kagan, would undoubtedly have voted and will most likely vote with the minority of four judges who wished to invalidate the exam and reject the promotion of the firefighters in any similar future case involving "affirmative action." The government's policies and actions since 1964, primarily in Democratic administrations have been in the direction of promoting "groups' rights."

The absurd requirement demanding that individuals fill out the census forms to indicate their group racial and ethnic identity serves no other purposes than to document which group deserves more protection and "equality." This has the unintended consequence of often promoting racial discrimination. Although realtors are forbidden by law to inform prospective buyers of a home anything about the racial makeup of the neighborhood where the house is located, the buyers can simply go online and look up the racial composition of each area based on the most recent census data (and avoid buying where they don't like the profile).

What made the appointment of nominee Kagan all the more grotesque was that the principle of DIVERSITY is so absent in appointing her to a Supreme Court which will not have a single member "representing" the WASP (White Anglo-Saxon Protestant) group, no

---

2 Talk given to the media following case in New Haven on June 29, 2009.

longer a majority, but still the largest single identifiable ethnic or religious component of the American population. In fact, there is no Protestant of any ethnic origin, or denomination, neither Fundamentalist, Evangelical or Mainline on the current court.

With her appointment, Kagan replaced Justice Stevens (born in Chicago) and joined her mirror image counterpart on the court, Ruth Bader Ginsburg, another white Jewish ultra-liberal female from New York City. Since Kagan grew up in Manhattan and Ginsburg is from Brooklyn, and Sotomayor comes from the Bronx, "diversity" under Obama should dictate finding the next candidate in Queens. The new Supreme Court with Kagan has a composition that is 33% women and 55% Greater New York-New Jersey (Justices Scalia and Alio were both born in Trenton).

If we were still a nation of individual citizens with equal rights and opportunities and with merit the only consideration for appointment to high office, none of the above would matter, but it is the selective use of DIVERSITY, like so much else, that is part of the Obama/Left/Liberal agenda that stands out for its hypocrisy. Ironically, the leading Ivy League schools who today push the Liberal/Left agenda in the country, used "geographical diversity" as a subterfuge in the 1930s to severely limit the admission of Jewish students.

There is indeed one and only one good argument for "diversity," built into our Constitution, and that is the Electoral College, designed to prevent manipulation of specific blocks of voters in large states and afford representation to the small states and rural areas. From the very beginning, it wisely prescribed the limitation that Electors must cast at least one ballot for an individual who *"shall not be an inhabitant of the same state with themselves."*[3] This makes it virtually certain that the President and Vice-Presidential candidates will always be from different states (and preferably from different regions to win the widest support nationally).

Obama's list of nominations wholly ignored this kind of diversity and pandered to three large blocks of minority voters that gave him huge majorities, Jews, Blacks and Latinos. It is equally galling that his frequently stated objective to nominate justices "who are in touch with

---

3 Constitution Article 2, Section 1

ordinary Americans" (justification used in the selection of Sonia So-tomayor) resulted in the choice of Elena Kagan, who attended a prep school, Oxford, elite Ivy League Colleges Princeton and Harvard (like Obama) and was an adviser to Goldman Sachs (the second largest contributor to Obama's campaign; Harvard was third).

Does any real sports fan object to the fact that an overwhelming percentage of professional players in the NBA are African-American?; or that so few are professional ice hockey players in the NHL? Undoubtedly there are some but they are rightly regarded as cranks. Nevertheless, there were expressions of regret on a recent "This Week in Baseball" television program that African-Americans, who represent roughly only 13% of the general population, *used to constitute more than 25% of professional baseball players in the major leagues but now account for only 14%.* We will never escape this colossal waste of time until we return to the premise that only individuals, not groups, deserve rights and must be judged on their individual merit.

Chief Justice John Roberts has rightly expressed his firm opposition to the "whole sordid business" of dividing the American population by race and ethnicity but the prospects are dim that we can escape the fate of all of us being forced into statistical boxes. My wife was born in Argentina and her first language is Spanish. Does she qualify as a Hispanic? Her parents were Yiddish speaking Jews who immigrated to Argentina in 1920. When she asked an official at the American Embassy if she should identify herself on a form to get a green card as Hispanic, his reply was – *"I haven't got a clue."*

A first page newspaper story recently featured a story on page one entitled "Hispanic License Plate Could Sail to Approval."[4] A Hispanic Achievers plate design has been incorporated into a bill submitted to Governor Crist. The original design simply stated "Hispanics Discovered Florida" but the public relations team behind the proposal had to tone down the message to simply put the organization's name on the design Hispanic Achievers with a Spanish galleon in the center and the word UNIDOS in large print. Profits from the $25 tag fee would go to fund the group's "administrative costs" and benefit a fund to aid Hispanic achievers. The group claims a network of 14,000 sub-

---

4 Orlando Sentinel on May 12, 2010.

scribers, a drop in the bucket of the state's more than three and a half million Hispanics.

Of course, the absurd irony that no one bothers to pay attention to, is that the same mentality of group pride and a balkanized identity of hyphenated-Americans originally led most politicians on both the state and local level to go along with cancelling "Columbus Day" to satisfy American Indian groups angry at the Spanish "discovery and conquest of the Americas" as "racial genocide." Columbus Day was originally declared a federal holiday back in 1934 as an act by the Roosevelt administration to help assuage the feelings of many American Catholics, organized by the Knights of Columbus, especially of Italian origin (who claim Columbus as their own), that there was no national holiday that recognized an achievement by Catholics (and Italians). We have come full circle.

Our national motto "*E Pluribus Unum*" is out of date (as most certainly is "*In God We Trust*"). The reality of the last two generations of affirmative action policies could be summarized by what Aristotle said more than 2,300 years ago …. "*The worst form of inequality is to try and make unequal things equal.*"

Since the end of the Sixties, the political Left in the United States has strengthened its dominant position among ethnic and racial minorities, women, and gays by cultivating an all embracing sense of "victimhood." On the basis of her own experience as the head of the National Organization of Women (NOW), devoted to "freedom of choice" and a liberal agenda, author Tammy Bruce, has catalogued her own experience as to how an elite of malignant narcissists and a friendly media exert an entrenched control over the "victims" (see her book, *The Death of Right and Wrong*, 2004). Whenever a gay (like Bruce), black (Thomas Sowell), "Hispanic" (newly elected Senator Marco Rubio of Florida), or ""minority" Bobby Jindal (parents from India), the Governor of Louisiana, embraces an agenda of liberty, individual responsibility, ambition, and entrepreneurship, they are immediately condemned as "traitors." The same was the fate of three outstanding women writers and journalists in Europe who had been heroines of the political LEFT but whose integrity inevitably led them to a confrontation in which they too were cast out and condemned for thinking out of the box. (see chapter 25).

12

Fascist Italy and Austria Hand Hitler His First Defeat

T he story of how Hitler's only major diplomatic defeat prior to World War II was handed to him by the close alliance between two fascist leaders, Mussolini and Dollfuss, sheds further light on how shallow the Right/Left model of politics is. When the Austro-Hungarian Empire was shattered as a result of World War I and the Versailles Peace Treaty, most observers believed that the tiny new Austrian Republic could hardly survive. With the establishment of Austrian independence in 1919, it was often referred to as "the state nobody wants" and expressly forbidden by treaty to unite with Germany.

Adolf Hitler, born in Austria, was a "stranger" in Germany. Like Napoleon, who was born in Corsica, and regarded as a rough "foreigner," Hitler had to prove himself as a pan-German nationalist. On the very first page of *Mein Kampf* he proclaimed the necessity of union (*Anschluss*) between Germany and Austria, and immediately after his election as Chancellor in 1933, listed the annexation of the land of his birth as his number one priority in foreign policy.

The world economic crisis of the 1930s convinced many Austrians that the country was doomed to financial ruin unless it became part of a larger German state. Nevertheless, a minority of dedicated patriotic Austrians became aware that the nationalist mirage and siren call of a Greater Germany would only plunge Austria into another disastrous world war. Today, many people are unaware that Austria's conservative leaders, often labeled as "clerico-fascists" in the 1930s, opposed the local Nazi attempts at a coup and more actively combated the threat of German expansionism than anywhere else in Europe, certainly more than the "liberal democracies" that had already decided on following a policy of appeasement.

The Nazis were handed their first major political defeat by the resistance of Austrian Christian and Social Democrats, who together accounted for 77 percent of the popular vote in the national elections of 1930. Both parties stood unequivocally for national independence and against Nazi-inspired racial antisemitism. Chancellor Engelbert Dollfuss outlawed the Austrian Nazi Party and confiscated all its assets in June 1933. Dollfuss admired Mussolini, and imitated various aspects of the Italian fascist system yet both these fascist leaders were those who initially adamantly refused to be bullied by Hitler and the Nazis.

It was Mussolini who most clearly recognized the value of Austrian independence, its important economic and cultural links with the Mediterranean and Catholic Church, and correctly argued and predicted in 1934 that:

1. Austria is politically essential to the preservation of Europe.

2. The day Austria perishes and is swallowed up by Germany, the break-up of Europe begins.

3. Austria must survive culturally too, because it is a bastion of Mediterranean culture.

By this, he meant that Austria's Catholic traditions and strong links with the Vatican had made it a more humanized Germanic state than the Prussian militarist heritage that Hitler appealed to in fomenting his nationalist doctrines. Mussolini originally considered Nazi racism and antisemitism both repugnant and primitive. He had a Jewish mistress (Margherita Sarfatti) who for thirteen years guided him both intellectually and in foreign affairs urging a pro-British line until early 1933. She had been one of the planners of the "march on Rome" that enabled Mussolini to gain power and was even nicknamed by many observers as "The uncrowned Queen of Italy." Italian Jews were equal members of the Fascist Party, in fact they were proportionally over represented in the higher echelons of the party. Sarfatti's son Roberto died in action in World War I, only eighteen years old in 1918 and posthumously awarded Italy's highest decoration for valor.

Both Mussolini and his Foreign Minister Ciano made numerous mentions in their diaries of opposition to introducing antisemitic laws in Italy until forced in July 1938 under extreme pressure to do so by Hitler as part of the price of an alliance of the two Axis powers. The view that "Right-wing" or conservative or nationalist parties are necessarily antisemitic or that the liberal Left is necessarily philo-Semitic (or at least anti-antisemitic) is contradicted by the experience of Italy, several other European nations, and in the history of the various "populist" and antisemitic movements in the United States but persists as a self-evident, unchallenged cardinal point in the arguments of many American (especially Jewish) liberals.

According to their unchallenged conventional wisdom, only the Left can oppose antisemitism. If confronted with facts that two Axis "Right-Wing" allies of the Germans, Finnish Field Marshall Carl Gustaf Emil Mannerheim and Bulgarian King Boris III successfully and bravely resisted Nazi pressure to deport or humiliate the Jewish citizens of their countries (see chapters 12, 14, 17) or that the Danish resistance against the Nazis was initiated by the "Far Right" Dansk Samling political party (also labeled as "Fascist" -see chapter 16), or that General Franco allowed the passage of more than 30,000 Jews through Spain to escape occupied Europe (chapter 13) they are stunned.

Extremist elements on the political Left among the Austrian socialists (Social Democrat Party) organized into their own armed militia (The Schutzbund) threatening armed insurrection in Vienna's working class housing projects in February 1934. Dollfuss put down the revolt at the cost of critically weakening the ability of Austrians to later stand united against the Nazis. Stalin welcomed the orphans of those Austrian workers in the Schutzbund who had been killed in the insurrection and Pravda described Dollfuss and his government as "Christian Fascists" (referred to in the foreign communist press as "Clerico-Fascists").

Although Dollfuss later successfully employed Austrian troops against militant Nazis in a putsch attempt (July 1934), which also cost him his life, the country eventually lost the promise of Italian support as a result of the policies of the British and French. Their governments later felt it necessary to condemn Italy's invasion of Abyssinia in 1935 and expel it from the League of Nations while doing nothing to stop German aggression and expansionism.

Dollfuss was killed while his wife was a guest of the Italian dictator, an event that horrified Mussolini. Italian troops were rushed to the border in the summer of 1934 and full support given to the government by the Heimwehr, a national militia more reliable than the tiny Austrian army and led by the patriotic Prince Starhemberg. The Nazis were crushed and Hitler totally abandoned his proclaimed *Anschluss* policy for a time until Austrian resistance and Italian backing could be worn down or outmaneuvered.

In September 1934, a joint British-French-Italian declaration "guaranteed" the independence and integrity of Austria. This was followed by a meeting at the Italian resort city of Stresa in April 1935, condemning any violation of the Versailles Treaty. The Christian Democrats who originally had inherited an antisemitic policy from the days of the old Austrian Empire evolved under Dollfuss to reject the Nazis' open racism, street violence, hostility towards the Catholic Church and attempts to subvert Austria's independence.

Both Nazis and the Communists were outlawed and the Christian Democrats and other conservative groups were transformed into the "Fatherland Front" pledged to Austria's continued independence and rejection of *Anschluss*. For the next four years, Dolfuss's successor, Kurt von Schuschnigg, withstood Hitler's personal appeals and threats and defended the humanistic strain that Austria had long contributed to German culture. Schuschnigg was an arch-conservative, devout Catholic with a Jesuit education and had always favored a restoration of the Hapsburg dynasty.

His proposal for a referendum in February or March, 1938, a last hour attempt to demonstrate the will of the Austrian people to defend their national independence, was frustrated by German threats, street violence, sabotage and invasion. Schuschnigg was forced to resign and was sent to prison by the Nazis for 17 months where he was tortured. After losing 85 pounds, he was subsequently sent to the Dachau and Sachsenhausen concentration camps. He was rescued and liberated by American troops on May 5, 1945. After World War II, he emigrated to the United States where he taught political science at Saint Louis University from 1948 to 1967 and wrote *Austrian Requiem*.[1]

---

1 Von Schuschnigg, Kurt *Austrian Requiem* Putnams Sons, 1946.

When Austria finally fell victim to extreme pan-German nationalism, the country had been weakened internally. The events of
1938 contributed to the mistaken view that union with Germany had
been "inevitable," and minimized the willpower, pride and patriotism
of many Austrians and the prospects of it ever regaining its independence.

Catholic-Aristocratic-Monarchist-Conservative Opposition to the Nazis

Schuschnigg inevitably caved in with the growth of Hitler's
power and influence following Munich in 1938, the willingness of
the British and the French to continue to appease German power and
Mussolini's about-face. The Italian dictator abandoned what principles
he had and accepted Austria's demise when assured by Hitler that the
Nazis would not use their pan-German nationalism to demand a revision of the Austrian-Italian border. Hitler willingly abandoned the
cause of the German speaking minority in the South Tyrol region to
cement the Axis alliance with his Italian co-part.

According to the "Liberal Bible," all those who oppose fascism
are naturally drawn from the political Left, i.e. liberals, socialists and
communists. The Austrian case provides more evidence that this is
much too simple an explanation and that several varieties of Austrian
"Fascism," "Socialism," and "Conservatism" existed that, at one time
or another, opposed *Anschluss* (annexation by Germany) and a common front with the Nazis.[2] The tragedy of the never realized anti-Nazi
Front was the inability to overcome the disaster felt by them all that the
Republic was a forlorn and economically hopeless fragment. Pre-war
Austria-Hungary had been an Empire and leading power in Central
and Eastern Europe unifying the huge hinterland of the Danube Basin.
It was Catholic, conservative, multi-ethnic and multi-lingual with an
identity quite distinct from Germany. Hitler offered a new radical departure. Himself, an Austrian, he held out the triple promise of a solid

---

2 See *Fascism in Europe* by S.J. Wolf (ed.), Methuen. London and New York, 1968, especially
Chapter 5, Austria by K.R. Stader..

Germanic nationhood, economic recovery and a radical departure from the conservative and Catholic past that he detested.

Americans who have seen *The Sound of Music* were offered a sugar coated, romanticized and typically exaggerated Hollywood version of the country's crisis but it did contain a grain of truth – that the reali-life hero, Captain Von Trapp, a conservative, aristocratic, devout Catholic retired naval officer, is symbolic of those among the country's social elite who held the Nazis in utter contempt as gutter rabble. The same people whom Stalin had referred to as "Christian Fascists" (Dollfuss, the Heimwehr and Prince Starhemberg) who had crushed the working class Social Democrats' Schutzbund uprising in Vienna in 1934, were the ones who tried vainly to oppose the Nazis' repeated sabotage and coup attempts to force union with Germany.

Even those Christian Democrats with previous antisemitic leanings had met Catholic refugees from Nazi Germany and become painfully aware of the pagan and anti-Christian elements of Nazi doctrine. For a brief time, these groups tried to formulate an alternative to the tiny beleaguered Austrian rump state. This would be part of a Greater Catholic Union of the Danube region in alliance with Mussolini that might ultimately embrace Bavaria, Austria, Hungary and the Czech-Slovak and Italian areas of the old Hapsburg Empire. Such a vision however held out no attraction whatsoever for the Austrian Nazis or the working class supporters of the Socialists and Communists.

What is indeed accurate about *The Sound of Music* is not the tearful rendition of "Edelweiss" that rouses the Austrian patriotism of Captain Von Trapp's neighbors (the song was composed by American Jewish composer Oscar Hammerstein), but the teenage working class neighborhood boy Rolf, in love with the captain's eldest daughter, Liesl. He becomes the most enthusiastic Nazi and turns the family in, out of his sense of duty and loyalty to Hitler. This has its counterpart in the other great musical film about the 1930s political situation, – *Cabaret*, where the only individual seated in a park who does not rise to join in the enthusiastic singing of a Nazi anthem, "The Future Belongs To Us" (just as our 60s radicals believed), is an elderly man who had been through World War I.

Post-War Austria

Many Austrians left the country rather than submit to the new Nazi regime following incorporation of their homeland into Germany. The country, like Germany, was conquered and divided into four zones of occupation by the victorious Allied powers in 1945. Furthermore, the Soviets insisted on severe reparations mostly in the form of forced deliveries of oil. In addition, the "Iron Curtain" reinforced imposed limitations on free trade with Austria's Eastern neighbors under Soviet domination.

Austrian neutrality was thus insured in advance of the final victory over Nazi Germany. This ruled out any plans to include Austria in NATO. In private, some military strategists argued that this "neutral wedge" of Austria and Switzerland gave the Russians a tactical advantage in the heart of Europe. (West Germany and Italy became members of NATO and were hindered in the movements of NATO troops by this geographical situation).

How then has Austria managed since 1955 when it regained full sovereignty to develop its economy so successfully?

There is no doubt that today its level of prosperity and low unemployment considerably exceed that of the much larger reunited German state. The secret does not lie in raw material resources or economic aid from abroad. It is due to the hard work, devotion and the patriotism of Austrians who made up their minds to uphold a stable democratic society with full human rights for all citizens and unanimous support for permanent neutrality.

Without the temptation to look abroad for either economic assistance or the old pan-German myths of extreme nationalism, Austria has thrived. The Austrians like the Swiss, are not German in national feeling and have centuries of different history and traditions. Nazi demands to swallow up first the Saar territory, remilitarize the Rhineland and then annex Austria and the Czech Sudetenland won support from naïve liberals in the West who could not resist the arguments of "self-determination."

The results of Austria regaining its independence have turned things around. Instead of being regarded by most Germans as our "poor Austrian cousins," many Austrians have taken to calling themselves "the best Germany," a slogan that has aroused some resentment. What the Austrian model shows is that "small" is not necessarily bad. The human factors that make a country strong and its citizens patriotic and willing to work hard in a common sense of unity, favor progress. The country has benefited from being ethnically homogeneous and is proud of the reassertion of its national identity, Catholic traditions and historical heritage.

Great Britain, the U.S.S.R., and the United States agreed in the Joint Four-Nation Declaration on November 1, 1943, "*Austria, the first country to fall victim to Hitlerite aggression, shall be liberated from German domination.*" This document signified that Austria was not to be considered a defeated enemy country but an occupied one. The United States even issued a special postage stamp in 1943 with a prominent display of the Austrian flag. Had Britain and France tried to appease Mussolini rather than Hitler, the course of history would have been entirely different.

From the standpoint of today's hindsight, what is indisputable is that Italy and Austria, authoritative dictatorships of the conservative "Right," nevertheless were the first to defend their interests against Hitler and the Nazis aggressive designs on Europe.

13

Franco, Fascism and the Falange: All the Far Right, but Not One and the Same Thing

The Spanish Civil War has frequently been portrayed as an epic struggle between the forces of the LEFT (variously identified as progressive, liberal, socialist, internationalist, democratic and "anti-Fascist") and the RIGHT (labeled reactionary, conservative, religious, fascist and "anti-democratic").

In American political discourse, "Fascist!" is the ultimate epithet bandied about and frequently hung around the neck of those who value constitutional safeguards, parliamentary traditions, have deep seated religious convictions or believe in a strong military stance to defend the United States or RESOLUTELY oppose Communism. and Islamic extremism.

Of course, the only reluctance to use the term "Fascist" by a large segment of Left-Liberal opinion in America today is where it is most strikingly accurate – Islamo-Fascism, a term that describes the enemies we, Western civilization, Israel, Spain, Denmark and democracies from India to Australia and even moderate Arab/Muslim states such as Turkey, Algeria, Tunisia and Lebanon currently face. China and Russia face this same threat as well, but prefer to ignore it and pretend that it is only directed against Israel or the Western and capitalist societies.

During the latter part of General Franco's long 35-year rule, more and more speculation revolved around the question of who or exactly what type of regime would succeed him. Unlike Hitler and Mussolini, Franco survived World War II as well as the isolation of his country by the Allies, who at first considered him a remnant of the Fascist states aligned with the Axis powers. Franco, however, was a military man whose career in the army and arch-conservative views propelled him to lead the uprising against the Republic, but he did not establish a political party nor did he express open support for any of the various Catholic, conservative, monarchist and fascist parties who rallied to his cause. In order to understand both what happened during and after the Spanish Civil War, it is necessary to distinguish between the coalition of forces that supported both sides in the conflict.[1]

Franco's supporters were divided between those who hoped for a return to the monarchy, rival wings of the Bourbon dynasty, moderates, conservatives and the Fascists. The Fascist but anti-monarchist forces of the Falange Española (Spanish Phalanx), had been founded by the extremely popular (and handsome) "martyred leader" (executed by the Republican forces) Jose Antonio Primo de Rivera (son of the dictator who ruled the country following World War I), who wanted a republic modeled after Mussolini's Fascist Italy, and claimed to be the hero of Spain's poor and dispossessed. He appealed to the working class and stressed that they had his full sympathy and understanding of the oppressive role played by the monarchy and landed aristocracy.

Many conservative supporters of the church, military and monarchy were concerned as much by the leader of the Falange, Jose Antonio, (always referred to by his admirers and followers by his first names only) as by the Marxists and their myriad anarchist and socialist parties. The moderate conservative right, monarchist and centrist parties that opposed the Leftist "Popular Front" in the elections in 1936 refused to enter into an electoral alliance with the Falange which stood isolated.

Jose Antonio had stepped on too many toes by his justifiable criticism of scandal and corruption among parties of all shades. His calls for social justice for the Spanish working class, small farmers and agricultural workers led to charges by the Catholic and conservative Right Wing Press that he was a "Bolshevik" to which he responded that all those wealthy Spaniards who valued luxuries and their petty whims more than the hunger of the people were the real Bolsheviks –"The Bolshevism of the Privileged" and added oil to the fire by proclaiming *"In the depths of our souls there vibrates a sympathy toward many people of the Left who have arrived at hatred by the same path which has led us to love*

---

1 For a thorough analysis of the Falange and its different basis of support than Franco's see Stanley G. Payne *Falange A History of Spanish Fascism* Stanford University Press, 1961.

– *criticism of a sad mediocre, miserable and melancholy Spain.*"[2] Instead, he called for a '*happier Spain in a mini-skirt*.' Following his only visit to Nazi Germany, Jose Antonio wrote in his memoires that he found the country rancorous and depressing and that his high estimation of National Socialism had been badly damaged.

Mussolini had been a Socialist in his youth and demonstrated anti-Catholic sentiments during the first ten years of Fascist rule. Similarly in Spain, the Catholic Church was suspicious of the Falange and its street violence and the populist appeals of Jose Antonio. The ultra-reactionary Carlist movement that was still popular in much of the Basque Country, Aragon and elsewhere in the Northern part of the country, and had supported a return to an absolute monarchy, ridiculed the Falange, its ultra-modernism and its "intellectuals," notably Jose Antonio. The Carlists were opposed to all liberal or "modern" reforms, supported a rival wing of the Bourbon dynasty, opposed female succession to the throne and maintained its own militia known as the Requetés and a political party, the Comunión Tradicionalista. During the war, the Requetés mocked the amateurish and undisciplined nature of the Falange which they viewed with contempt. Their view was supported by the Army general staff under Franco who generally assigned the Falange units to the rear guard sectors.

Jose Antonio created a movement in cooperation with the more proletarian-based syndicalist movement known as the JONS (*Juntas de Ofensiva Nacional Sindicalista*), and appealed to the Spanish working class by attacking what he called "the social bankruptcy of capitalism." He explained that a socialist victory at the polls and a Socialist regime in Spain would be "the equivalent of a foreign invasion." To avoid this, employers and workers must be united in a system without exploitation or class struggle. The new state would draw its inspiration from traditional Spanish values, morality, the guiding spirit of the Church (to which he paid lip service), but most of all, strive to regain Spain's imperial destiny and its old "soul" - heroic, sober, austere yet generous, knightly (but not aristocratic!) and Castilian.

Neither Jose Antonio nor Franco used any antisemitic rhetoric in their propaganda, although some of their followers did, as the Na-

---

2 ABC newspaper July 31, 1935.

tionalist forces came to rely more and more on military aid from Nazi Germany and a Mussolini who had forced himself to go along with the racist anti-Jewish ideology of Hitler in order to cement the Axis alliance. The Falange had successes too during the war. They succeeded in welcoming into the party ranks tens of thousands of Spanish workers from the factories, shipyards and mines of the industrial areas of the country that had previously been the major centers of Communist and Socialist strength. Nothing better illustrates the appeal of the Falange to the same working class electorate as the Far Left.

The young dynamic leader of the Falange was, like his father, a great admirer of Great Britain and spoke fluent English. He had been repelled by Hitler on his one visit to Nazi Germany in the Spring of 1934. Had he lived, a major struggle between him and Franco would probably have been inevitable. Unlike the dour Franco, Jose Antonio was an accomplished orator, intellectual and parliamentarian. His execution by Republican forces in 1936 was a grave mistake.

The realization that their movement was beginning to wither away, caused some would-be leaders of the Falange to scheme at outflanking or deposing Franco and pushing Spain into joining Nazi Germany in World War II. By the end of the war however, the movement had been deprived of any real power in the state and Franco had come to regard them as an impediment to improving his image abroad.

Jose Antonio represented the more human face of the Spanish "Right" and had come to deeply regret the scourge of Civil War that was tearing Spanish society apart. He had supported the coup of the generals to replace what he believed was a failed chaotic Republic but he had begun to weigh more and more the possibility that only a compromise with the forces of the Left would save Spain from savagery and destruction. Even before the Civil War, he had toyed with the idea of somehow forming a coalition with the Socialists. Among his last papers written in prison before his execution was a proposal to form a unity government of pacification and reconciliation in which Socialist leader, Indelicio Prieto, would be given the portfolio of Minister of Public Works.

In the last interview conducted with him by an American reporter, Jay Allen, Jose Antonio responded to the charge that Falangist troops had committed atrocities against Republican soldiers and civilians.[3] He was shocked by this news and replied that he would like to believe that it was not true, but if it were, it meant that his followers were leaderless and had been misled under great provocation. He declared that if indeed General Franco was "a reactionary," he would withdraw the Falange from the conflict. After the Civil War, Franco had a great Monument to the Fallen constructed in the Valle de los Caídos outside of Madrid. He had Jose Antonio's body interred there as a way of capitalizing on the Falange leader's popularity and obscuring the conflict between them. Today, one may still view the funeral vaults of Franco and Jose Antonio that glare at each other across a wide hall.

During the Spanish Civil War, Franco assumed the status of Commander-in-Chief (Generalisimo), and adopted the title of Caudillo (leader). He merged the rival groups of the Nationalist coalition into a "National Movement" with the title of *Falange Española Tradicionalista y de las Juntas de Ofensiva Nacional Sindicalista* (abbreviated as La FET de la JONS), or simply *El Movimiento Nacional*. The National Movement became the only legal political entity in Spain during the remainder of Franco's rule until his death in 1975. The Falange had a major influence in the movement at its inception but its leaders were gradually reduced to a mere token presence and then almost thoroughly eliminated by the time of Franco's death.

All the constituent groups of Franco's "National Movement" maintained their identity, however, but unreservedly supported the slogans of *España Una, Grande y Libre* (One Great and Free Spain) opposed to any divisive separatism by the recalcitrant "regional nationalists" of Catalonia, the Basque Country and Galicia. Franco tiptoed among the elements of the National Movement, assigning them influence and posts in his cabinet according to his mood at the time, with the intention of balancing them so as to have everyone in doubt where he stood on a successor to the regime.

The Falangists caused concern to supporters of Franco and those who hoped for a return to the monarchy. They believed that much of Jose Antonio's rhetoric about tradition and the Church were a mask to hide his ambition. The Falange had modeled itself as a popular Fascist movement, complete with a uniform (blue shirts) and a penchant

---

3 Payne, Stanley ibid p.137.

for street demonstrations. Its youth movement taught respect for all the traditional virtues and values of Spanish civilization. It aspired to a return of Spain's glorious status as a world power. Readers of Spanish are referred to the memoirs of Luis Olero, whose book, *Al Paso Alegre de la Paz*, (On the Happy Road Of Peace), is a satirical tragic-comical look at the pedagogical "truths" and heroic, almost supernatural, virtues and austere morality of General Franco and Jose Antonio, inculcated by the Falangist youth movement.

The Franco regime endured thanks in part to food supplied by Argentina's General Perón, and managed to get through the extremely difficult first post-war years. To diminish Spain's Fascist image, the Falange was accorded less and less influence in the government, but its economic policies prevailed for a long time, with priority given to rural development and self-sufficiency, coupled with the stern morality of a nineteenth century and ultra-Catholic view of parent-child and male-female relationships. In spite of a "tight-lid" on morals kept by the Franco regime, conventional attitudes were weakened by a growing flood of migrants from rural Spain to its big cities that continued unabated from the mid-1950s.

Economic realities, continued urbanization, a growing realization that a Fascist Spain would be totally out of place in Western Europe and that Spain would benefit enormously from membership in NATO and the European Community, led Franco to further moderation of his tight political, economic and social controls. Real prosperity resulting from amazing economic growth throughout the 1960s and 1970s led to increasing unrest and further pressure to remove Spain from its self-imposed isolation and to change the unreal view of itself as a great power with a noble imperial past.

Are Franco, Francoism and the Falange just history now? Judging from the changes in many street names and the removal or neglect of statues and monuments to the Generalíssimo, Jose Antonio and the Falange symbol of the ox yoke and bundle of arrows, the answer is: Yes! However, the Falange remains a political party, actually divided today into three factions: *Falange Espanola y de las JONS* (Spanish Falange of the Juntas and of the Nationalist Trade Union Offensive), *Falange Española Auténtica* (FEA, Spanish Authentic Falange) and the *Falange Española Independiente* (FEI, Spanish Independent Falange), each of which claims to be the "authentic" movement and the true successor to the legacy of Jose Antonio Primo de Rivera. All of them ran unsuccessfully without winning a single seat in the parliamentary elections of 2004 and 2008 and together accounted for one percent of the vote.

Nevertheless, the inability of successive governments to halt the campaign of terror carried on by ETA (the Basque separatist movement) and the friction with Morocco over a host of political, economic and social issues as well as the presence in the country of almost 750,000 Muslims, some of whom are sympathetic to Al Qaeda, have led to a reaction that may ultimately benefit the Falange in spite of the movement's present moribund status. Older Spaniards who grew up in the Franco era may not look back with nostalgia on many aspects of the regime, but are certainly growing increasingly uneasy over what appears to be Spain's humiliation by the use of appeasement and the continually spiraling crime rate.

There is a National Association to Preserve the Legacy of General Franco that publishes a bulletin and tries to influence public policy by emphasizing his many achievements. It stresses his anti-Communism, active alliance within NATO, aid to refugees including many Jews fleeing Nazism, his social policies on behalf of the poor such as *el menú del día* (requirement in many restaurants to offer a four course lunch meal including beverage at a specially reduced price), providing government subsidized housing, price controls and "wise leadership in the transition towards democracy." Most critics would dispute all of these claims and believe that the previous non-Socialist governments have not accepted responsibility for the crimes of the 1936 uprising, Civil War and the entire Franco period.

The successful transition to democracy that followed Franco's death in 1975 was based partially on what has become known as "The Pact of Forgetting." Both Left and Right agreed not to open old wounds from the Civil War and Franco period by seeking "revenge" or "justice."

The parties on the Left are well aware that Republican forces also committed occasional atrocities and that there was mob violence against the Church. Nevertheless, a recent spate of revelations depicting the brutality of the Franco regime towards Republican prisoners has whipped up emotions again.

The Falange splinter groups all reject any "apologies" for the Civil War and Franco period. Their positions on many issues of public policy are indistinguishable from the far LEFT in Spain. They regard themselves as representing "The Workers," demand worker participation in the economy, celebrate the First of May and were all critical of the pro-American government of Popular Party leader Jose Maria Aznar for its "arrogance" and support of American policy in Iraq. They called for the immediate withdrawal of Spanish troops in Iraq. Like other conservative parties, they reject homosexuality and abortion and what they call "pornography" in the arts. They are in favor of strict controls on immigration and are against any measure to grant more autonomy to Spain's distinctive regions.

They would even rescind the rights obtained to use the regional languages in any public forum. They would fight Islamic terrorists, but not "as part of an American war," and call for the cession of Gibraltar by Britain to Spain. No less than the parties of the Left, they regard the Franco regime of 1936-1975 as having committed crimes, (by perverting the Falange program and suppressing the original high ideals of Jose Antonio).

They have little sympathy left for the contemporary modern "liberal" Catholic Church in Spain and all are dubious or unhappy about the monarchy.

The leveling and simplistic tendencies of modern journalism and many historians continue to speak of Franco, Fascism and the Falange and conservative Catholic traditionalists in one breath as "The RIGHT" as if they were the same thing and easy to differentiate from their "enemies" on the idealized "democratic," egalitarian, collectivist, Marxist and communitarian "LEFT" of the Popular Front. Nevertheless, in Spain, as many places elsewhere, the two "opposites" frequently met in adopting views and policies and issuing appeals competing for the same "mass audience" that were remarkably similar and equally contemptuous and dismissive of middle class "bourgeois" values, and democratic institutions based on limited government and parliamentary order.

14

How the "Reactionary Right-Wing" King Boris III Helped Save the Bulgarian Jews in World War II

Under Bulgaria's communist regime, the efforts of both King Boris III and the Bulgarian Orthodox Church, resulting in the salvation of the country's entire Jewish populaiton of 50,000, were targets of constant invective, slander and "revisionism" so that the very real role of the king in the rescue of Bulgaria's Jews has been erased or minimized. Why such revisionism and willful amnesia about the actions of King Boris?

The answers are a product of the Cold War, cultural biases, ignorance of geography and perhaps unconscious prejudices. Documents revealing the role of the monarchy and the Church in saving the country's Jews were suppressed by the Communist Party while the role of the Party and its leaders at the time were elevated to the role of heroic saviors. In this regard, hard core Jewish communists including the editors of the Sofia based Jewish communist newspaper *Evreiski Vesti* loyally repeated the Party line. The great majority of Bulgarian Jews (almost 95%) were allowed to emigrate to Israel in 1948-51 and were aware of the truth.

Michael Bar-Zohar is an Israeli historian of Bulgarian origin. He arrived in Israel in 1948 with his family, was a member of the Israeli Knesset and has told the full story of the Bulgarian rescue and the role of King Boris III in his gripping book.[1] His conclusion regarding the king needs to be shouted from the rooftops to shake up Jewish ignorance in America...."THE FINAL RESPONSIBILTY WAS THE KING'S AND HIS DECISON SAVED THE JEWS OF BULGARIA. THE BULGARIAN JEWS BECAME THE ONLY JEWISH COM-

---

1 Michael Bar-Zohar *Beyond Hitler's Grasp; The Heroic Rescue of Bulgaria's Jews* (Adams Media Corporation), Holbrooke Massachusetts. 1998.

MUNITY IN THE NAZI SPHERE OF INFLUENCE WHOSE NUMBER INCREASED DURING WORLD WAR II." (p. 268)

In contrast to the Danish yellow star armband myth, Bulgarian Jews in their thousands did actually wear armbands with the portraits of King Boris and the royal family as a sign of loyalty, devotion and gratitude. The Bulgarian authorities, as allies of the German government, required Bulgarian Jews to wear armbands with tiny Jewish stars, but most did not bother to wear them and suffered no repercussions. Those who did wear them were frequently assured by their fellow Christian Bulgarians of sympathy and support.

The *"numerus clausus"* introduced to ensure that Jews constitute only a limited participation in business and medicine was set at a higher proportion than that of the Jews in the general overall population. It reflected the much higher Jewish urban population rate. "Conversions" to Christianity were accepted by the Orthodox authorities with a minimum of embarrassment and no matter how perfunctory were guaranteed by the Church as "authentic."

The King and Bulgarian cabinet ministers (excluding the representatives of an antisemitic party eager to demonstrate complete loyalty to the Nazi racial ideology) all informed the German representatives in their country that the measures undertaken, as limited as they were, "completely solved" the Jewish problem and that deportation was out of the question. The Chief Rabbi of Sofia was hidden by one of the leaders of the Bulgarian Orthodox church, the Metropolitan Stephan who declared publicly that *"God had determined the Jewish fate and men had no right to torture Jews or persecute them."*

The Metropolitan made it clear to all of those in the church that everything possible should be done to assist Jews in thwarting the Germans and their Bulgarian collaborators including mass "christening" ceremonies (purely for the sole intention to remove their names from deportation lists). For this purpose, Stefan had prepared extensive documentation of christening certificates that didn't bear any date but could be filled in at the last moment. When the pro-German puppet government's "Commissariat of Jewish Affairs" announced its intention to deport Jewish citizens in spite of their formal new status as 'Christians,' Stefan publicly denounced the government's obstruction of "the Mission of our Holy Church." This resulted in the Minister of the Interior taking the unprecedented step of closing all the churches in Sofia to "prevent excesses in connection with the mass christening of the Jews." Stefan responded by firing back that *"I shall not obey such an order and I shall order the Sofia churches to hold services as usual."* Only in Bulgaria and Denmark did the highest leadership of national churches openly confront the government's cooperation with the antisemitic policies of their German allies or occupiers.

Nor were the church and the monarchy alone. Numerous prominent Bulgarians from every walk of life and the leaders of various civic organizations openly protested any future deportation plans for the country's Jewish citizens. Bulgaria's most distinguished writer, Ellin Pellin, a close personal friend of the king, the most prominent member of the Writers Union and known for his disinterest in politics before the war, met with King Boris and expressed his full support for protecting the Jews and preventing their deportation. It was shortly after this meeting that the King directly called on his Minister of the Interior and ordered the cancellation of deportation plans.[2]

Boris delayed and misled the Germans and acted to revoke deportation orders. Queen Giovanna (a daughter of Italian King Victor Emanuel) persuaded the Italian ambassador to issue Italian passports and transit visas to Jews of foreign nationality or those stranded in Bulgaria. German documents and the personal memoirs of Monsignor Angelo Roncalli (later Pope John XXIII) reveal the role of the king and the Bulgarian Orthodox Church in protecting his Jewish subjects. King Boris also managed to help Jewish refugees from Slovakia to be sent throughout Bulgaria and receive transit visas to Palestine.

The King failed only in extending his protection over areas temporarily occupied by Bulgaria (Greek Thrace and Yugoslav Macedonia), but not under his direct authority. Bulgaria had been maneuvered into the war as an ally of Nazi Germany primarily to recover these regions, Bulgarian before World War I and a cause of great resentment among Bulgarian nationalists. The Jews of Thrace and Macedonia were deported to Auschwitz and murdered, a fact that became known in Bulgaria and caused revulsion.

Boris died under mysterious circumstances on August 28,

---

2 Michael Bar-Zohar, pp. 242-244.

1943 and was likely murdered by agents of the Gestapo. This occurred shortly after his return from a meeting with Hitler in Berlin when he adamantly refused to change his policies on the Jewish question and join the war against the USSR. In many Jewish circles, there is a profound distrust and antipathy toward the peoples of Eastern Europe for their virulent antisemitism and extreme nationalism as well as their state churches. The considerable degree of collaboration among many Poles, Ukrainians, Lithuanians and Romanians with the German occupation forces has resulted in Eastern Europe long being regarded as a single bloc. The inclusion of all Eastern Europe into the Communist East bloc under Soviet leadership during the Cold War reinforced this perception. The fact that the Bulgarian experience was so totally different confounds those who find it easier to maintain stereotypes.

On the other hand, the stereotype of handsome, fair haired, blue-eyed Danes who appear more "Aryan" than the Germans or the Slavic Bulgarians apparently lends them a special distinction and appeal especially when it comes to having rejected the savage doctrines of antisemitism.

The overwhelming majority of Bulgaria's 50,000 Jews emigrated to Israel during the crucial years 1948-49 when the country was in the throes of its War of Independence and in crucial need of manpower at the front and in the factories and fields. They have been called the "The Most Zionist Community in Europe"[3] In October 1996, the Jewish National Fund dedicated several memorial plaques in a newly inaugurated forest named BULGARIA as both a deep sense of gratitude to the Bulgarian people and an expression of love by Bulgarian Jews for their former homeland. The plaques recalled King Boris and Queen Giovanna and Metropolitan Stefan, the head of the Bulgarian Orthodox Church.

While the real story of Bulgaria's rescue of its entire Jewish population has been lost amid the absurd denial of the Holocaust, a wholly mythical legend regarding King Christian X of Denmark has grown to astonishing acceptance due largely to Hollywood, Leon Uris (author of the best-selling novel *Exodus*), minor Danish diplomatic personnel, wishful thinking, the BBC's research methods as well as to

---

3 Michael Bar-Zohar, p. 257.

several prominent historians who have written widely about the Holocaust. It is the story of the rescue of the Danish Jews and their safe passage to Sweden in October, 1943.[4]

Only a handful of Bulgarian volunteers aided the Axis cause by serving with the German forces in the campaign against the USSR and Bulgaria, like Finland, switched sides late in the war. The Danish myth of the yellow star armband detracts from the vital participation of thousands of Danes from every walk of life who did help their Jewish countrymen at a moment's notice to assemble and flee, guarded their property and welcomed them back at the end of the war. The real story is much more inspiring and a tribute to traditional Danish values of concern for human rights than the myth of the King.

The Danish and Bulgarian peoples and their churches both have a right to take pride in their wartime record. The actions of both also stand in contrast to the generally dismal record of other European peoples, nationalist regimes and state churches. With respect to the "Tale of Two Kings," Boris III was a martyr whose personal example influenced history. Christian X was a decent man and a patriot but a weak king whom history and circumstances cast in a heroic mold because he wore the crown.

---

4 See Chapter 16 and Berdichevsky, Norman *An Introduciton to Danish Culture* (MacFarland Publishing, 2011)

15

The Nazi-Soviet Honeymoon: 22 Months of Bliss

I recently came across the full text on the internet of Molotov's speech to the Supreme Soviet following the Ribbentrop-Molotov Non-Aggression Pact of August 1939 and found one redeeming point in it. I, like so many others despair at the current unrelenting vilification of America and Israel by the current Political Left in much of Europe, Latin America and the United States. Many Americans who are subject to the unremitting hostility of the Arab world have an important ally in the impatience of "world opinion," the "desire" for peace (at any price) and often question whether cheaper oil isn't worth changing our stance.

When it comes to world history, we have the benefit of hindsight. I find it relevant and important to understand how the 22 months of Soviet-Nazi cooperation equals the absurd sympathy of the Left for Jihadi terrorism.

The Pact lasted from August 1939 to June 1941 and for a time "made a case" appealing to those who called themselves "progressives" and "anti-war activists." During this time, the Communist Party totally abandoned the boycott of German goods that had been organized by many anti-Nazi organizations in the United States. *The Daily Worker* called the pact…"*A triumph in the fight against antisemitism*" and Communist leader Earl Browder in his pamphlet "*The Jewish People and the War*" argued that… "*It makes no difference at all whether the Germans or the Allies win the war!*"

Of course, Molotov's speech below, justifying the pact may look absurd and insane today but it is worth remembering especially the lines that those who opposed Nazism in the West "….*were waging an ideological war reminiscent of the religious wars and that the principal victims of such a conflict were …the working class.*" (Sound familiar?)

On the Foreign Policy of the Soviet Union

Report of Comrade V.M Molotov, Chairman of the Council of People's Commissars and People's Commissar of Foreign Affairs, at Sitting of Supreme Soviet of USSR on Oct. 31, 1939.

Comrade deputies!

There have been important changes in the international situation during the past two months. This applies above all to Europe, but also to countries far beyond the confines of Europe. In this connection, mention should be made of three principal circumstances which are of decisive importance.

Firstly, mention should be made of the changes that have taken place in the relations between the Soviet Union and Germany. Since the conclusion of the Soviet-German Non-Aggression Pact on August 23, an end has been put to the abnormal relations that existed between the Soviet Union and Germany for a number of years. Instead of enmity, which was fostered in every way by certain European powers, we now have rapprochement and the establishment of friendly relations between the USSR and Germany. A further improvement in these new, good relations found its reflection in the German-Soviet Treaty on Amity and the Frontier Between the USSR and Germany signed in Moscow on September 28. This radical change in the relations between the Soviet Union and Germany, the two biggest states in Europe, was bound to have its effect on the entire international situation. Furthermore, events have entirely confirmed the estimation of the political significance of the Soviet-German rapprochement given at the last session of the Supreme Soviet.

Secondly, mention must be made of such a fact as the defeat of Poland in the war and the collapse of the Polish state. The ruling circles of Poland boasted quite a lot about the "stability" of their state and the "might" of their army. However, one swift blow at Poland, first by the German army and then by the Red Army, and nothing was left of this ugly offspring of the Versailles Treaty, which had existed by oppressing the non-Polish nationalities. The "traditional policy" of unprincipled maneuvering between Germany and the USSR and of playing off one against the other has proved unsound and has suffered complete bankruptcy.

Thirdly, it must be admitted that the big war that has flared up in Europe has caused radical changes in the entire international situation. This war began as a war between Germany and Poland and turned into a war between Germany, on the one hand, and Great Britain and France, on the other. The war between Germany and Poland ended quickly owing to the utter bankruptcy of the Polish leaders. As we know, neither British nor French guarantees were of help to Poland. To this day, in fact, nobody knows what these "guarantees" were. (General laughter.) The war between Germany and the Anglo-French bloc is only in its first stage and has not yet been really developed. It is, nevertheless, clear that a war like this was bound to cause radical changes in the situation in Europe, and not only in Europe.

In connection with these important changes in the international situation certain old formulas - formulas which we employed but recently and to which many people are so accustomed - are now obviously out of data and inapplicable. We must be quite clear on this point, so as to avoid making gross errors in judging the new political situation that has developed in Europe.

We know, for example, that in the past few months such concepts as "aggression" and "aggressor" have acquired a new, concrete connotation, a new meaning. It is not hard to understand that we can no longer employ these concepts in the sense we did, say, three or four months ago. Today, as far as the European great powers are concerned, **Germany is in the position of a state which is striving for the earliest termination of the war and for peace, while Great Britain and France,**

which but yesterday were declaiming against aggression, are in favor of continuing the war and are opposed to the conclusion of peace. The roles, as you see, are changing.

The efforts of the British and French Governments to justify this new position of theirs on the grounds of their undertakings to Poland are, of course, obviously unsound. Everybody realizes that there can be no question of restoring the old Poland. It is, therefore, absurd to continue the present war under the flag of the restoration of the former Polish state. Although the Governments of Great Britain and France understand this, they do not want the war stopped and peace restored but are seeking new excuses for continuing the war with Germany.

The ruling circles of Great Britain and France have of late been attempting to depict themselves as champions of the democratic rights of nations against Hitlerism, and the British Government has announced that its aim in the war with Germany is nothing more nor less than the "destruction of Hitlerism."

It amounts to this, that the British and, with them, the French supporters of the war have declared something in the nature of an "ideological" war on Germany, reminiscent of the religious wars of the olden times. In fact religious wars against heretics and religious dissenters were once the fashion. As we know, they led to the direst results for the masses, to economic ruin and the cultural deterioration of nations. These wars could have no other outcome.

But they were wars of the Middle Ages. Is it back to the Middle Ages, to the days of religious wars, superstition and cultural deterioration that the ruling classes of Great Britain and France want to drag us? In any case, under the "ideological" flag has now been started a war of even greater dimensions and fraught with even greater danger for the peoples of Europe and of the whole world. But there is absolutely no justification for a war of this kind.

One may accept or reject the ideology of Hitlerism, as well as any other ideological system; that is a matter of political views. But everybody will understand that ideology cannot be destroyed by force, that it cannot be eliminated by war. It is, therefore, not only senseless but criminal to wage such a war as a war for the "destruction of Hitlerism," camouflaged as a fight for "democracy." And indeed, you cannot give the name of a fight for democracy to such actions as the banning of the Communist Party in France, the arrests of Communist deputies to the French parliament, or the curtailing of political liberties in England or unremitting national oppression in India, etc.

Is it not clear that the aim of the present war in Europe is not what it is proclaimed to be in official statements intended for the broad public in France and England. That is, it is not a fight for democracy but something else, of which these gentlemen do not speak openly.

The real cause of the Anglo-French war with Germany was not that Great Britain and France had vowed to restore the old Poland and not, of course, that they decided to undertake a fight for democracy. The ruling circles of Great Britain and France have, of course, other and more actual motives for going to war with Germany. These motives do not lie in any ideology but in their profoundly material interests as mighty colonial powers.

Great Britain, with a population of 47 million, possesses colonies with a population of 480 million. France, whose population does not exceed 42 million, is a colonial empire embracing a population of 70 million in the French colonies. The possession of these colonies, which makes possible the exploitation of hundreds of millions of people, is the foundation of the world supremacy of Great Britain and France. It is fear of Germany's claims to these colonial possessions that is at the bottom of the present war of Great Britain and France with Germany, who has grown substantially stronger of late as a result of the collapse of the Versailles Treaty. It is fear of losing world supremacy that dictates to the ruling circles of Great Britain and France the policy of fomenting war with Germany.

Thus, the imperialist character of this war is obvious to anyone who wants to face realities and does not close his eyes to facts.

One can see from all this who is interested in this war, which is being waged for world supremacy. Certainly not the working class. This war promises nothing to the working class but bloody sacrifice and hardships.

Now judge for yourselves whether the meaning of such concepts as "aggression" and "aggressor" has changed recently or not. It is not difficult to see that the use of these words in their old meaning, that is, the meaning attached to them before the recent decisive turn in the political relations between the Soviet Union and Germany and before the outbreak of the great imperialist war in Europe, can only create confusion in people's minds and must inevitably lead to erroneous conclusions. To avoid this, we must not allow an uncritical attitude toward old concepts which are no longer applicable in the new international situation.

The relations between Germany and the other West European bourgeois states have in the past two decades been determined primarily by Germany's efforts to break the fetters of the Versailles Treaty, whose authors were Great Britain and France, with the active participation of the United States of America. This was what in the long run led to the present war in Europe. (STORMY APPLAUSE)

The Pact and Its Interpretation Today

At the outbreak of war on September 1st 1939, the Royal Navy launched a blockade of Germany hoping to repeat its success in World War I. One major difference was already apparent, whereas in 1914-17,

Czarist Russia was one of the allies on Britain's side, the USSR under Stalin immediately became Germany's most important supplier of strategic materials especially oil. This amounted to a virtual alliance until June 22, 1941. The Soviets effectively cooperated in the joint invasion of Poland beginning on Sept. 17th thereby ending the possibility of any further Polish resistance against the Germans.

Commercial agreements between the two countries were discussed by Reich Minister for Foreign Affairs and the Chairman of the Council of People's Commissars, Molotov (September 28, 1939) and a final agreement was reached a few months later, resulting in the Memorandum on the German-Soviet Commercial Agreement (February 11, 1940). This included a schedule of Soviet deliveries of war materials. The Soviets agreed to immediately begin to exchange strategic materials including grains, cotton, phosphates, chrome ores, iron ore, platinum, manganese ore, and lumber for German industrial goods that would be delivered over a longer time frame. The Soviets even provided cover for German imports of vital raw materials such as tin and rubber forbidden by the British and Dutch in their Southeast Asian possessions of Malaysia and Indonesia. The Soviets had them shipped to their ports in Odessa and Murmansk and from there reshipped or sent them overland by rail to Germany.

Hitler agreed to the evacuation of all ethnic Germans in the Baltic States as these were recognized to be within the Soviet sphere of influence and were annexed soon afterward. So convinced was Stalin as to the obviously mutual benefit of the pact that he obstinately refused to listen to dire warnings of true German intentions and as a result, Soviet forces were caught completely unprepared for the offensive of the June 22, 1941, an attack in which three million German troops participated.[1] During the period of the pact, the Communist parties of Great Britain and France opposed their nations' war effort and the Communist Party of the USA (CPUSA) campaigned strongly against President Roosevelt's efforts to win congressional support for war aid to Britain and against his third term candidacy in the 1940 presidential election.

The CPUSA did not simply drop its boycott of German goods;

---

1 For a full reliable and impartial account of the full extent of the close Soviet-Nazi cooperation during the 22 months of the pact, see Anthony Read and David Fisher *The Deadly Embrace; Hitler, Stalin and the Nazi-Soviet Pact 1939-1941* (W. W. Norton & Company) 1988.

it spread the slogans "The Yanks Are Not Coming" and "Hands Off." Its activists picketed the White House and set up a "perpetual peace vigil" calling Roosevelt, *"The head of the war party of the American bourgeoisie."* By April 1940, the *Daily Worker* and Communist pamphlets stated the Jews had just as much to fear from Britain and France as they did Germany. In August 1940, after NKVD agent Ramon Mercader killed Leon Trotsky in Mexico, American Communist Party leader, Earl Browder, repeated Moscow's line that the killer, who had been dating one of Trotsky's secretaries, was a disillusioned suitor and follower.

The Nazi-Soviet Non-Aggression Pact signed by Foreign Ministers Von Ribbentrop and Molotov was reached on August 23, 1939 at the very time when the British and French delegations in Moscow were vainly trying to reach an agreement with Stalin. He was convinced, however, that they were conspiring to draw him into a war with Hitler. The two countries which until that time had been bitter foes, pledged not to attack each other. Any problems developing between the two countries were to be dealt with "amicably" and the duration of the pact was for 10 years. It shocked the world but what was not known at the time was that there was a secret protocol to the pact which in effect divided Eastern Europe between the two countries.

This protocol was discovered after the end of the World War II in 1945 and its existence was denied by the USSR until 1989. The original German language copy of the protocol on a secret division of Soviet and Nazi spheres of influence in the Baltic and along their common frontier (after the 'disappearance of Poland') was seized by Soviet troops and brought to Moscow.

The official Party Line in Moscow had always been that the pact was a brilliant defensive move that in effect prevented an alliance between Hitler and the Western capitalist states to destroy the USSR and communism. In 1989, the first semi-democratic parliament just prior to the complete dissolution of the USSR passed a resolution condemning the pact but recently there have been interpretations by government and polling agencies offering the explanation that the measure was designed to protect the population of those parts of Eastern Poland (now part of Belarus and the Ukraine) and that there was 'nothing reprehensible' about it.

In early July, 2009, the Parliamentary Assembly of the Organization for Security and Co-operation in Europe passed a resolution proposed by Lithuania and Slovenia that equated Nazism with Stalinism. Almost all historians outside of Russia would agree with this view and that the pact made possible the firm German decision to launch its war of aggression against Poland with its back secure. The Assembly proposed the date of the pact, August 23rd, a Day of Remembrance for the victims of the two totalitarian systems which provoked the Russian delegation to storm out, and promise a "harsh response." For them and those who continually feel obliged to deny the equivalence of the Far Left and the Far Right, August 23rd must be forgotten or rationalized away by absurdity.

The wretched opportunism of the American Communist Party was revealed in the attempts to wrest control of the anti-Nazi German-American League for Culture and use it as a front organization as they had similarly done with many Jewish organizations. As soon as news of the infamous, Ribbentrop-Molotov Non-Aggression Pact was proclaimed, the Communist front groups ceased their cooperation with Jewish opposition to Nazi activities in the U.S., making them an object of derision among Jews everywhere.

Two months after the division of Poland between Germany and the USSR, the powerful French Communist Party had turned into a vociferous critic of French participation as an ally of Great Britain, arguing for withdrawal from the war. Thirty-five of the forty-six Communist deputies in the National Assembly were arrested on October 9, 1939 and the remainder fled to Moscow.[2]

For more than forty years after the event, the USSR and communist parties around the world denied Soviet guilt in the Katyn massacre of April 9, 1940 in which Stalin's henchmen murdered in cold blood approximately 22,000 Polish officers and intellectuals in what ranks as the worst and most flagrant violation of the rights of prisoners of war in modern times (see chapter 2).

The infamous alliance between Hitler and Stalin did more to mobilize general American support among Gentiles against antisemitism than any other factor. It had become abundantly clear that in spite of a noisy and all too visible Jewish presence in the American Com-

---

2 Read & Fisher *The Deadly Embrace* p. 359.

munist party, it represented only a tiny fraction of the community. The communists' patient and persistent efforts to penetrate anti-Fascist organizations, as well as their activities on behalf of the Spanish Republic, in favor of boycotting German goods and protests against Nazi antisemitism had all been tactical maneuvers.

The publicity provoked by the resistance, anti-Nazi organizations helped focus Congressional investigations spearheaded by New York Congressman Samuel Dickstein (Chairman of the House Un-American Activities Committee known as HUAC) who relentlessly pursued leads that uncovered the financial assistance provided by the Nazi German government to both the Friends of the New Germany and its more powerful successor organization, The German-American Bund.

The Last Straw

For many, the Von Ribbentrop-Molotov Non-Aggression Pact of August 23, 1939 was the last straw and the ultimate betrayal which led them to commit an act they had foreworn in the long years of deliberation of considering renouncing their communist beliefs. For Whittaker Chambers, who had reached the pinnacle of influence and prestige for a Soviet agent as Senior Editor of Time Magazine, "... *To be an informer ... ..Men shrink from that word and what it stands for as from something lurking and poisonous. It was worse than being a spy, it was betraying the confidence of many friends and their families yet there could be no other act of expiation.*" For anyone NOT deaf, dumb and blind, the pact was simply Stalin's seal of approval for Hitler's decision to attack and destroy Poland and unleash world war.

Chamber's book *Witness* says it better than anyone has.

"I had to hurry from my office at Time magazine to the airport to catch the six o clock flight to Washington. [*in order to volunteer his services and lay the facts of Communist subversion before Adolf F. Berle, the Assistant Secretary of State in charge of security.*] I fastened my safety belt, chewed my gum lay back and closed my eyes. The great plane took off into the serene evening sky of September 2, 1939 On the plains of Poland, at the same moment, a new day was awakening the Polish nation to terror and insane distress as its cavalry tried to turn back, with lance and rifle, a new force in the history of war and men – The German panzer divisions.

"In Moscow, a few days before, Stalin, with a tigerish smile and a more reserved Ribbentrop, had signed the pact that made Nazism and Communism allies. By the same scratch of the pen, Stalin had unleashed upon mankind, for the second time in two decades, the horror of world war. Soon the Stukas would be screaming above the screaming babies, pushed or carried by long lines of frantic women, along roads jammed by the clutter of soldiers and civilians fleeing the collapse of armies, cities, nations, order, civilization. This was the war that for as long as I had been a Communist, every Communist had foreseen and dedicated himself to struggle against. That a Communist had unleashed it upon mankind was a fact so monstrous that it absolved every man from the bonds of common humanity with that breed and made it a pious act to raise his hand in any way against them."[3]

A Postscript:
Postwar Stalinist Antisemitism Fails to Arouse the Hard Left

In spite of the infamous record of the USSR during the 'brief' period of the Hitler-Stalin Pact of 1939-40, the International Hard Left of 'fellow travelers' including its Jewish component remained unconvinced of the essential similarities between the Soviet and Nazi regimes and their obsession with antisemitism as a useful propaganda weapon.

The Slansky trials in Czechoslovakia in 1952-53 (see Chapters 2 and 7) failed to arouse the revulsion and worldwide condemnation caused by the 1956 suppression of the Hungarian uprising and Khruschev's famous 20th Party Congress speech on the "excesses of Stalin-

---

3 Chambers, Whittaker *Witness* Regnery Gateway. By arrangement with Random House. Lake Bluff Il. 1952.

ism'" The trials presented the 11 Jewish defendants (out of a total of 14) as entirely "alien to the Czechoslovak People." Their "origins" had prevented them from assimilating into the national society and "incapable of understanding the workers' plight." The Anti-Defamation League of Bnai Brith (The Protocols and the Purge Trial, 1953) reached the inevitable conclusion that *"Antisemitism is the distinguishing feature that sets off the Prague affairs from all previous purge trials. The prosecutor's indictment and the robot-like testimony of the defendants made clear that neither 'bourgeois nationalists' nor 'Zionists' alone but Jews – are the target of the most vicious antisemitic attack by a major power since Nazi Germany."*

16

The "Far-Right" Danish Unity Party
Begins Anti-Nazi Resistance 1940-41

It continues to rankle some historians and "pundits" that it was the "anti-democratic" Dansk Samling (Danish Unity) on "The Far Right" of the political spectrum that took the lead as early as the Spring of 1941 to call for active resistance against the German occupation. For all those without ideological blinkers, it is not difficult to understand. Dansk Samling's stand was based on Danish nationalism, anti-Nazism and a continued mistrust of the established parties' politicians for appealing to small and divided constituencies primarily about immediate bread and butter issues that ignored larger national questions and the ethical and moral standards derived from Christian principles.

Just before the outbreak of World War II, liberal "Left" Social-Democratic/Labor dominated governments in Britain, France, Belgium, the Netherlands, and Denmark were all reluctant to oppose German expansionism and aggressive Nazi designs. Under the German occupation, collaborators were found to offer a façade of home rule under German protection. In Denmark, Christian X was a puppet king. He did not choose as did other monarchs such as Queen Wilhelmina of Holland and King Haakon of Norway to flee to England and help in the establishment of a government in exile.

During the first three years of the occupation and in full agreement with the Danish government, the king warned his fellow countrymen not to participate in acts of sabotage against the German occupation forces. This was the government line that he adhered to and which also guaranteed Denmark a special relatively mild status, including no discriminatory measures against the Danish Jews until the planned deportation in October, 1943.

During the "honeymoon" between Stalin and Hitler from August 1939 to the invasion of the USSR on June 22, 1941 (see Chapter

15), the puppet governments and Communist Parties in the occupied countries more than just acquiesced in the occupation. They opposed any resistance against the occupation, renewal of the war effort and discouraged attempts at sabotage of any active kind.

The Wikipedia entry on the internet under the title "Danish Resistance" has nothing to say about Dansk Samling or Arne Sørensen, in its list of prominent members of the Freedom Council. The Holocaust Research Project, a Jewish website called HEART (Holocaust Education and Archive Research Team) mentions both the "BOPA" coalition and the Holger Danske group but is silent about Dansk Samling and Arne Sørensen.

These sites and others proudly give full credit to the Danish Communist Party as the leading element in the Danish Resistance. This is the same hard line Stalinist party that endorsed the Soviet invasion of Finland in December 1939 and called the outbreak of World War II on September 1st "a war between European imperialist powers" that meant nothing for the international working class except needless bloodshed. On the same day that Denmark was invaded by the German army (April 9th, 1940), Stalin's henchmen were busy murdering thousands of Polish army officers in the Katyn Forest, an unprecedented atrocity of the most gruesome proportions, an event denied by the Soviet and Danish Communist parties from 1943 onwards until admitted by them during the last days of the existence of the USSR.

The idea that the wartime resistance to the Nazis anywhere could have been initiated by a right-wing or "Fascist Party" (as they were labeled by the political Left in Denmark before the war) is supposed to be an oxymoron. In general, a very large proportion of Liberals and many Jews accept the thesis that to be "Right Wing" is ipso facto to be "Fascist" and antisemitic or, the contrary, that to be a Liberal means you necessarily must be anti-antisemitic. Neither is necessarily true.

The first steps calling for active resistance in occupied Denmark were taken by "Dansk Samling" (Danish Unity) and its charismatic founder, Arne Sørensen (1906-1978). The party was founded in 1936 and contested elections in 1939, 1943, 1945, 1947, 1953 and then once more in 1964. Based on a form of Christian nationalism, it presented itself as a "Third Way" between socialism and liberalism.

Its rejection of Denmark's parliamentary system of multiple political parties, each catering to selected interest groups led to accusations of Fascism, although it clearly rejected antisemitism and denounced Nazi doctrines as evil, pagan and a threat to Western civilization.

Arne Sørensen, The Founder of Danish Unity

Arne Sørensen was born in 1906 in the Northwestern Himmerland region of Jutland. He was originally educated in business administration but became a teacher, journalist and author taking part in the debate over Denmark's social, economic and political future. He attracted attention by criticizing the traditional parties of both the Right and the Left. Sørensen expressed support for "dynamic" leaders who were not bound by catering to divisive and selfish interests, a view that initially was understood by many as support for a Mussolini or Hitler in Danish politics. What he meant was a leader who could rally a large segment of the people across party, regional, confessional and class lines.

His father was a smallholder eking out an existence from farming and unable to provide support for his ambitious son. In quick succession, the young Sørensen became drawn to the capital, involved with politics, a modern poet, freelance journalist for the great liberal Copenhagen daily *Politiken* and a teacher. He gradually veered away from the radical-socialist milieu and adopted a vision of a "Third Way" in politics between with the traditional standpoints of the Labor Movement and the Conservative Free Market.

Although Sørensen was dismayed by the parliamentary form of Danish democracy, any brief attraction he may have had for European Fascism quickly faded with the growing fanaticism of Hitler's antisemitism and its anti-Christian ideology. Added to this repulsion was the growing conviction that a large part of the Danish public had failed to rally around any strong sense of national will, a conviction aided and abetted by the Social Democratic Party in power which failed to challenge the threat of German expansionism. He became strongly involved in the movement to protect Denmark's border with Germany.

Sørensen had been in touch with both ethnic Danes in German occupied South Schleswig and with refugees who were able to provide realistic and reliable information on the anti-Nazi "Confessional Church" led by Dietrich Bonhoeffer whose 700 pastors had been imprisoned by the Gestapo. In the 1939 election to the Parliament, Dansk Samling received only 8,000 votes and no seats. It had appealed unsuccessfully to all the Danish parties to present a common "Danish Front" in South Jutland, the critical border area where an aggressive German minority was increasingly being financed and encouraged to exhibit irredentist demands for a revision of the 1920 border in Germany's favor.

Sørensen's new found interest in the border issue brought him into contact with the distinguished historian, Vilhelm la Cour in the summer of 1940. La Cour's joining Dansk Samling created a stir and brought the party new prestige. By the autumn of 1941 both Sørensen and la Cour had been arrested by the government for their publication of illegal leaflets calling for a restoration of Danish pride and resistance to the German occupation.

In the Spring of 1942, British Special Operations Executive (SOE) began to infiltrate agents into Denmark by parachute to organize armed resistance. The Danish agent in charge of operations, Christian Michael Rottbøll, contacted Danish Unity's leaders as the most promising initial address with a request for assistance. They both arranged for the accommodation, identification documents, and ration coupons for the agents as well as transmission locations for the radio operators. Active members of Danish Unity (a few of them were former volunteers for Finland during the 1940 Winter War) organized the Holger Dansker resistance group that carried out sabotage against the German occupying forces and their installations.

At this juncture, the King and Government under duress and the fear of German reprisals still continued to broadcast appeals to the Danish population not to engage or help in sabotage or threaten the relations between the civilian government and the German occupying forces. The Danish Communist Party had only just begun to recover from the shock of the German invasion of the USSR in June 1941 and begun to seriously mount an effective campaign of resistance, after almost two years of having criticized the Allied war effort as "*The preservation of the British and French colonial empires.*"

Following the German invasion of the Soviet Union, the Danish Communist Party was made illegal and immediately went underground. Throughout 1942, it organized to carry out a resistance against the occupation forces but it was not involved in the first serious acts of sabotage carried out by students and former Danish volunteer veterans in the Holger Danske group. The group was originally formed in 1940 to resist Soviet aggression against the Finns. It was among the largest resistance groups and consisted of around 350 volunteers towards the end of the war. The group carried out about 100 sabotage operations and was responsible for around 200 executions of informers who had revealed the identity and/or the whereabouts of members of the resistance.

On January 25, 1943 a group of students who had previously been refused membership of the communist resistance group due to the mistrust held by its members toward what Stalinist ideology still regarded as "elitism" and the "bourgeois" character of the group set fire to a stock of German listening devices at Dansk Industrisyndikat in Hellerup (suburb of Copenhagen).

Only after this action were the students accepted into the group, and this caused a change of name from the original KOPA (Kommunistiske Partisaner, Communist Partisans) to BOPA (The "B" for Bourgeois). In the last election of the Danish parliament under German occupation in the summer of 1943, Dansk Samling was still officially regarded as a legal party and able to participate. It won three seats and a popular vote of over 40,000.

The vote was also a wakeup call for the majority party, the Social Democrats to undertake a major shift in policy and defend Danish rights even if it meant a break with the occupying German forces. Dansk Samling's participation was a bone thrown by the German occupation authorities to the Danish politicians to bolster their claim that they were not interfering with the Danes' right to manage their own affairs. This however gave the Communists added prestige as the only "illegal" (until late 1943) and "underground" political force of the Resistance. Their pre-war stand as pacifists committed to neutrality was thus largely forgotten and forgiven.

In September 1943, the Danish Freedom Council in London was created as a shadow government in exile. This move attempted to unify the many different groups that made up the Danish resistance movement. The council was made up of seven resistance representatives including Arne Sørensen and the Danish Communists and one member of SOE. The resistance movement had grown to over 20,000 by the summer of 1944 and in the lead-up to D-Day, acts of sabotage markedly increased. Though the D-Day landings were to be in Normandy, SOE believed that the more German soldiers tied up elsewhere in Europe, the less that could be present in northern France. Therefore, the more acts of sabotage in Denmark, the more German troops would be tied down there.

In 1944, the Danish Freedom Council stepped up its efforts and more than 11 million copies of underground newspapers were published. That June, following a declared state of emergency, the entire city of Copenhagen went on strike. Infuriated, German troops flooded the city, cut off water and electricity, and established a blockade. From this time, all Danes under occupation looked towards London and the Freedom Council as their legitimate government in exile.

By then, Sørensen had reached London where he was instrumental in trying to formulate a policy that would gain recognition for the Danish minority in the North Schleswig region following the collapse of Nazi Germany. He was encouraged to believe that the British would favor the internationalization of the Kiel Cal and involve Danish troops to occupy a zone North of the Canal. In the first postwar election in 1945, Dansk Samling won 64,000 votes and increased its representation to four representatives but the Communists emerged as the major force profiting from their war time resistance (however belated). It proved a major disappointment for Sørensen who saw his fears realized that the old style politics of division and cultivation of special interests would return as the standard format of Danish politics.

By the Liberation of Denmark on May 5, 1945, the Communists were widely seen as the most effective underground resistance movement. This was due in part to their greater experience in military training that included several hundred veterans of the Spanish Civil War and the rise in prestige of the Party due to the success of spectacular sabotage actions, especially the destruction of several factories in Copenhagen.

Both la Cour and Sorensen became deeply involved in the postwar effort to support the Movement of the Danish Minority in Germany (SydSlesvig Forening SSF -The South Schleswig Association) that experienced an explosive growth from 1945 to 1947. The Danish government was astounded by the renewal of sentiment for Denmark and a forty-fold growth in membership compared to the 1939 size of the Danish minority. They were however careful at making any demands for a new plebiscite and were reluctant to be swept up by emotions.

The failure of most of the traditional Danish political parties and the opposition of the Communists to any border change and a general desire to return to normalcy meant that Danish Unity had no prospects for continued growth. It has since stagnated and declined. The grandiose plans and commitment to win back part of South Schleswig formulated by Sørensen and others among nationalist circles were regarded by the majority of the Danish public as too ambitious and risky.

Former supporters of Arne Sørensen believe he made a critical mistake in joining a postwar government after the rejection of his South Schleswig policies and became "Kirkeminister" (a Danish Minister of Religious Affairs tied to the State Affiliated Danish Lutheran Church), a position without any real influence and easy to satirize and even lampoon. Opponents laughingly referred to the remnants of the party as a form of "Danish Disunity"

Danish Unity continues to be against "all isms." It unabashedly proclaims that its central point is to embrace and cultivate all that is essentially Danish and the belief that Denmark cannot just be the address of new immigrants but that the home of the Danish People and all that it has created of lasting value, the Danish language, its Christian heritage, tolerance, culture and ideals without any disrespect for other peoples.

Dansk Samling still exists today as a political organization but not a party. Many of its former supporters lost faith in its ability to present a realistic alternative to the traditional Danish multi-party system catering to special interests. It opposed Denmark's membership in the European Union and is highly critical of the large scale immigration from North Africa, the Middle East and East Asia that has created a substantial foreign population of "residents" or citizens who do not identify with Danish history, language, values and traditions. Arne Sørensen, like the Danish prince Hamlet suffered "the slings and arrows of outrageous fortune." He left a legacy that should not be forgotten.

17

The Two International Brigades: One Glorified, the Other Forgotten

Of all the memorabilia and wistful pining by the Left for its lost innocence, nothing surpasses the romantic nostalgia of the Spanish Civil War. This was supposedly "THE Good Fight" of all time pitting the good guys of the Republican Left against the evil forces of reaction in the Spanish Catholic Church, General Franco, the Spanish Falange Movement (see Chapter 13) and military aid from both Hitler and Mussolini.

This is an especially sensitive and emotional issue for the Jewish Left. It is estimated that almost 20% of all the volunteers in the International Brigades, who came to Spain to fight Fascism were Jews and in the case of the Americans, perhaps as many as 38%.[1] Their heroism and experiences have been vividly recorded. Their struggle shaped the view of Franco as a close ally of Hitler, but a more objective view would regard Franco as primarily an opportunist, a fervent anti-communist who represented conservative Spanish traditions and aspirations.

The various reactionary factions in Franco's coalition participated in an orchestrated campaign against "communists and Jews" who rallied to the cause of the Republic and identified them with separatist forces in Catalonia. Their intense dislike of Catalan separatism was linked, in the mind of many Spaniards, with what they perceived as the arrogant, ambitious, commercially oriented and politically progressive Catalans. The Fascist and part of the Catholic press railed at what they called the "Judeo-Catalan conspiracy" to destroy Spain.

---

1 Fernandez, Alberto Judíos en la Guerra de España. Tiempo de Historia. Madrid. 1975; Sugarman, Martin Against Franco, Jews Who Served in the International Brigades in the Spanish Civil War. AJEX Archives, Jewish Military Museum. Medem, Gina Judíos Luchadores de la Libertad. Madrid, 1937. Toch, Josef 'Juden im Spanischen Krieg, 1936-39. Zeitgeschichte. Vienna. 1973.

General Franco, however, did not personally employ antisemitic themes in his rhetoric, although several extreme right wing parties had labeled prominent personalities of the Republic on the political left as "secret Jews." There were also persistent rumors that Franco himself was of "new Christian" (i.e. Jewish) origin from his native Galicia in Northwestern Spain. The names Franco, as well as Castro, are common among Sephardim (Jews of Spanish and Portuguese origin). What is undeniable is the action of Spanish authorities, under Franco's direction, to rescue Jews during the Holocaust.

Less comfortable for the Left today is the fact that a considerable number of Moslems who had served with Franco when he commanded Spanish forces in Morocco, joined in the attack on the Republic in 1936. In spite of the constant propaganda put forth by the church, that the nationalists were intent on saving Christianity from the evil forces of communism, Franco's triumph would have been impossible without the participation of large numbers of well trained Muslim troops in the Spanish "Army of Africa." They were especially hated and feared by most Spaniards in the Republican areas.

The heroism and idealism of those who joined the International Brigades cannot be faulted or disparaged.

Nonetheless, their naivety and inexperience, and their ignorance of Spanish conditions allowed them to be brutally exploited and often sacrificed to protect more politically loyal hard core cadres of the Spanish Communist Party. Practically none of them had any knowledge of the complexities of Spanish politics, the rival unions and parties on the Left or the complex regional and linguistic picture in Spain in which Catalan and Basque national sentiments often ran higher than political ideologies.

Moreover, those who found themselves unwittingly serving with units belonging to the various Anarchist, Socialist or Trotskyite militias had more to fear from their Communist "allies" than from Franco and the Nationalist troops.

Two of the greatest writers of our time, George Orwell (Homage to Catalonia) and Arthur Koestler (Darkness at Noon) bore witness to this. Both writers realized soon enough that Stalin's first intention was NOT to save the Republic but establish a communist beachhead in Western Europe.

Many of these volunteers were intellectuals, writers and artists and totally inexperienced in military affairs. Even those from a working class background had never served in the military before. Among the approximately 40,000 volunteers who served in the Brigades, it is estimated that more than 10,000 were killed and many of the others seriously wounded.[2]

By Royal Decree many years later, a democratic and conservative (i.e. RIGHT-wing) government with communist support in 1996 accorded Spanish nationality to any of the veterans who solicited it. For decades, the cause of the Spanish Republic stood high on the "favorites" list of the political Left in many countries and was celebrated in the songs of the Brigade.

Many of the veterans enlisted and fought in World War II shortly after returning from Spain. Stalin turned his back even on the most loyal Communist Brigadistas and native Spaniards who had received refuge in the USSR after the end of the Spanish Republic. They were suspect due to their foreign origin and experiences.

Even more grotesque was the attitude of local orthodox Stalinist Communist Parties in Argentina, Mexico, Belgium and France that were instructed by Moscow not to give any aid or assistance to Brigade veterans who had served with the anarchist, or Trotskyite (POUM) militias. These were attacked in the communist press as agents of Franco or German or Italian spies. More galling still was Soviet refusal to recognize the Spanish Republic in exile in Mexico City because the USSR had looted Spain's gold reserves in the final days of the war and

---

2 Durgan. Andy *International Socialism Journal*, Autumn, 1989. Number 18. "Freedom Fighters or Cominterm Army? The International Brigades in Spain." This brutally honest research report cites an estimated third of all international volunteers were killed and the majority of the rest wounded; only 7 percent of the International Brigades left Spain unscathed. The death rate among different national groups appears to have differed. Those who were refugees from authoritarian regimes appear to have been considered both more expendable and more reliable. So while the fatal casualty rate of US, British and French combatants was around 30 percent, still extremely high, 40 percent of Germans were killed, along with 48 percent of Yugoslavs and 42 percent of Hungarians. The exception was the Italians, of whom 'only' 18 percent died. Other sources place the number of fatalities (all killed and missing and those who eventually died from their wounds) at close to 18,000. De Andres, Jesus *Atlas Ilustrado de la Guerra Civil Española*, Susaeta ediciones, Madrid. p.98. The International Brigades did not save Madrid, as was subsequently made out by the Communists. Both the militia and civilian population had checked the main fascist advance the day before, but their bravery and example proved an important morale booster for the beleaguered Republican forces.

refused to negotiate with the republican government for its return.

The chief organizer, original over all commander and commissar of the Brigades was the French communist leader Andre Marty. He was a veteran of World War I and had been instrumental in organizing a mutiny in 1921 in the French fleet. He was a dedicated Stalinist and one Franco-Belgian unit of the Brigades was named after him. He was by most accounts not simply brutal but mentally unstable. His paranoia led to a continual witch-hunt among Brigadistas suspected of Fascist-Trotskyite sympathies. Marty himself supposedly admitted that he had ordered the execution of "hundreds" of International Brigade volunteers.

The true figure was probably smaller but his reputation had created such distrust and low morale that the Italian Communist Party Leader Palmiro Togliatti insisted in November 1937 he "change radically his working methods" and "refrain from intervening in military and technical matters affecting the Brigades."

Hatred of Marty grew at Brigade Headquarters in the city of Albacete so much that his flight in the closing days of the war was engineered to escape the vengeance of former 'comrades' as much as from General Franco's advancing troops. Several hundred Brigadistas deserted and those who managed to returned home were thoroughly disillusioned.

The distinguished British historian of Spain, Raymond Carr, had this to say of Orwell's experience and the Stalinist Left's distortion of the truth:

> "The Spanish Civil war produced a spate of bad literature. Homage to Catalonia is one of the few exceptions and the reason is simple. Orwell was determined to set down the truth as he saw it. This was something that many writers of the Left in 1936-39 could not bring themselves to do.

> "Orwell comes back time and time again in his writings on Spain to those political conditions in the late thirties which fostered intellectual dishonesty: the subservience of the intellectuals of the European Left to the Communist 'line', especially in the case of the Popular Front in Spain where, in his

view, the party line could not conceivably be supported by an honest man. Only a few strong souls, ... and Orwell among them, could summon up the courage to fight the whole tone of the literary establishment and the influence of Communists within it.

"Arthur Koestler quoted to an audience of Communist sympathizers Thomas Mann's phrase, 'In the long run a harmful truth is better than a useful lie'. The non-Communists applauded; the Communists and their sympathizers remained icily silent....It is precisely the immediacy of Orwell's reaction that gives the early sections of Homage its value for the historian."[3]

The 'Other' International Brigade: In Defense of Finland[4]

At the end of 1939, as the remnant of the International Brigade sought to reintegrate into national life back in their homelands, another spontaneous movement of idealistic and dedicated volunteers from many countries vainly strove to join another cause, one of a thoroughly democratic state and proud people who had been brutally invaded by the Soviet Union after failing to surrender sufficient territory to satisfy Stalin's desire for a major "border revision" to protect Leningrad in the event of a European war.

These young men, unlike the volunteers for Spain enjoyed no support or subsidies and travel aid from an international political network as did the Leftists who flocked to Spain. When the USSR invaded

---

3 Carr, Sir Raymond, "Orwell and the Spanish War," essay in *The World of George Orwell* by Miriam Gross. London. 1971

4 For detailed information on foreign volunteers who came to Finland's aid, see this study of Swedish military volunteers in the 19th and 20th centuries. Justin Brooke: *Talvisodan kanari-alinnut* -a study of British volunteers written by a volunteer. Jorma Mutanen: *Jalkaväkirykmentti 200* -a study of Estonian volunteers in Finland during WWII. Antti Juutilainen: "Talvisodan ulkomaiset vapaaehtoiset" -an article on foreign volunteers in the Winter War *Talvisodan historia*, volume 4 -an "official" Finnish history of the Winter War by the Department of Military Science. Lauri Haataja: *Kun kansa kokosi itsensä* -a one-volume history of the Winter War from other than purely military perspective. Gabor Richly: "Unkari ja Suomen talvisota" -an article on Hungary and the Winter War, published in the 1996 issue of the *Finnish Military Historical Journal*

Finland at the end of November, 1939 the assault was condemned widely. Although public opinion was entirely favorable to Finland outside the communist parties' apparatus, none of the western democratic governments was ready to provide military aid or send regular troops to intervene in the conflict. Nevertheless, Churchill briefly considered it.[5] There was no time even to design beautiful recruitment posters as in the case of the cause of International Brigades fighting in Spain.[6]

In December, 1939 the Finnish government decided that volunteers would be accepted only from those countries definitely friendly to the Finnish cause such as the neighboring Scandinavian states, Britain, France, and Hungary (distantly related by language to the Finns). No German or exile Russian volunteers were permitted. Only a few months earlier as a result of the Molotov-Ribbentrop Non-Aggression Pact, Hitler and Stalin were close allies and had already cooperated in the field in attacking Poland and dividing its territory between them.

Owing to the shortage of military equipment, the volunteers were required to come with their own arms and basic military gear. They were also to come as organized, trained units with their own officers. In January 1940, after heavy losses among Finnish troops, this decision was modified so that all able-bodied men were henceforth to be accepted at the discretion of Finnish embassies.

Both the French and the British made contingent plans to come to the aid of Finland although this risked enlarging the conflict they faced in Europe in order to ensure that Germany be denied the supplies of Swedish iron ore crossing Finnish territory. The planned expeditionary force did not materialize as the conflict ended too soon in April, 1940 just before the great offensive of the German Army in the West that defeated France in May-June.

The French even discouraged any potential volunteers for Finland from among the Polish troops who had been able to reach France after their defeat in September, 1939 since it was thought that all able-bodied men were needed in the French army. Official German policy

---

5 Trotter, William R. *Frozen Hell, The Russo-Finnish War of 1939-40.* Algonquin Books of Chapel Hill. 2000, pp. 236-237.
6 Berdichevsky, Norman *Spanish Vignettes, An Offbeat Look Into Spain's Culture, Society and History* Santana Books, Fuengirola (Malagala,) Spain. 2004 Chapter 19, The Spanish Civil War Propaganda Posters are now Art, pp.175-181.

under Hitler prevented any Germans trying to enlist as a volunteer for Finland. Mussolini, although sympathetic to the Finns had to toe the new line prescribed by his German ally. About 5000 Italian volunteers had expressed a willingness to come to Finland but their government denied them passports.

Swedish and Norwegian volunteers - The largest single nationality group was understandably Swedish. Close to 8000 men served in different formations. The most important unit was the Swedish Volunteer Corps (Svenska Frivilligkåren) with three battalions, all formed in Finland, since the Swedish government did not wish to send volunteers from Swedish territory as a unit. This also shows how careful government was in not taking an official position that could draw Soviet and/or German criticism.

The Corps' commander was General Lieutenant Linder, a Swede born in Finland. He and all three battalion commanders of the Corps and other senior officers had had experience of war in Finland when they fought as volunteers in 1918 on the anti-Communist ("White") side in the Finnish Civil War. The Volunteer Corps took over the front-line on February 28th 1940 and saw two weeks of action. Since this part of the front was generally calm, the Swedish losses were a modest 28 killed in action and about 50 wounded, and an additional 140 frostbite casualties.

Flight Regiment 19 flew with aircraft from the Swedish Air Force: Gladiators, Harts, Bulldogs and other British built planes. The unit of 25 aircraft was based in the north of Finland with the task of protecting the largest towns and communications network in the area. They were protected by Swedish anti-aircraft units in the area.

Norwegian and Danish volunteers - About 700 Norwegians volunteered, but since their government would not release any senior officers, they were enrolled together with the Swedish Volunteer Corps. When it disbanded, the Norwegians returned home and most of these men saw action against the invading Germans. About 1000 Danish volunteers reached Finland and were sent to training in Oulu in the central region, however, they were not ready for front-line duties when the war ended.

Hungarian volunteers - Only Hungary sent volunteers as an organized unit. It consisted of 346 officers and men with one month of training in Hungary. These men reached Finland on March 2nd and were stationed to Lapua for further training. Their commander was a right-wing activist with experience from the fighting that ensued when Hungary occupied parts of Slovakia in 1938

British and Estonian volunteers - When the war ended there were only 13 British volunteers in Finland but many more had volunteered, including 214 men who reached Finland and Lapua one week after the war had ended. There were an additional 750 volunteers waiting to be shipped to Finland, but the armistice came on March 13th, too late for their arrival. According to the initial British plan, the British volunteers were to fight in a single unit under the command of Colonel Kermit Roosevelt, a son of Theodore Roosevelt. Estonians, closely related by language to the Finns provided the next largest group of approximately 60 men who had volunteered although their government was under intense Soviet pressure.

American and Canadian volunteers - In spite of immense difficulties and the problems of distance and transportation as well as the cost of outfitting volunteers to serve in a European war, about 350 Americans and 250 Canadians, mainly of Finnish birth, were also sent for training in Oulu. One company reached the front on March 12th and was supposed to take charge of the trenches on the 13th, but the order was reversed when the war ended on the very same day. An early group of about 30 Americans managed to get posted at the front in December. This group saw action and suffered some casualties.

Pilots - About 60 foreign pilots volunteered and were sent to Flight Regiment 19 for training. Some pilots also flew with Finnish units. Foreign pilot casualties were three Swedes, four Danes, one Italian and one Hungarian.[7]

Due to the difficulties of logistics, this "Other" International Brigade received enormous encouragement and good will in their countries of origin. Their idealism and readiness for self-sacrifice compares favorably in every way with those who volunteered to fight in Spain but the difference lies in the simple fact that they have been forgotten, yet a look at the chronicles in American, Canadian and British newspapers reveals the tremendous enthusiasm these men evoked. They were

---

7 See Foreign Volunteers in the Winter War internet website by Tapani Kossila. AHF FORUM.

fighting for freedom against an evil tyrant as menacing as Hitler.

For the organized hard Stalinist Left, they could not be called Nazis because Germany was an ally of the Soviet Union. They could thus be labeled as adventurers, bandits, criminals, mercenaries and outcasts. While the Spanish Civil War took three and a half years, the fighting in Finland barely lasted four months. In spite of all the difficulties, 11,500 foreigners volunteered for service in Finland but not all managed to arrive, very few saw combat action and the number of killed and wounded can be counted in the dozens. This does not detract from their courage and determination.

The full extent of willingness to help the heroic Finns taxed the resources and imagination of many tens of thousands of individuals and organizations all trying to express their solidarity. Many private organizations sent medical and humanitarian aid. Thousands of workers in the Scandinavian countries volunteered to work in Finland to replace those who had been drafted but had to make their way and arrangements privately without government assistance. For the non-Communist press, this was not an issue of Left vs. Right but of Right vs. Wrong.

An Extract of News Clippings:

December 1939–March 1940[8]

> The American daily, *The Chicago News* suggests the 1940 Nobel Peace Prize be awarded to Finland. The German war correspondent Otto von Zwehl enlists as a volunteer in the Finnish Army. Hitler hears of this and strips him of his German citizenship and military rank. Swedish Nobel Prize Winner Frans Emil Sillanpää arrives in Haaparanta en route to receive his Nobel Prize for Literature and pledges to donate the award for Finnish defense.
>
> A private umbrella organization, the Finnish Centre for Nordic

---

8 From website: Navigate 3 D Forum Nyhettsblog: Vinterkrigen.

Aid, is set up to organize the evacuation of Finnish children to Sweden. The first shipment of children arrives by sea in Stockholm. Film star Greta Garbo gives 5,000 dollars to the Finnish aid fund. Despite the war, Finland is given immense publicity for continuing to repay its First World War debt to the USA. Princess Juliana and Prince Bernhard give 1,000 guilders to the Dutch Red Cross to be passed on to the Finnish Red Cross. The first 150-bed field ambulance from the Swedish Red Cross arrives in Finland. The Hungarian Pen Club awards its medal for 1939 to the Finnish poet Otto Manninen. Argentina's appeal at The League of Nations' to aid for Finland is joined by a similar response from Ecuador, Haiti, Peru, Bolivia, Venezuela and Mexico. United States. Gunnar Bärlund, the Finnish heavyweight boxer resident in the USA, beats Italo Golonello and donates part of his winnings from the fight to the Finnish Relief Fund. Pope Pius XII condemns the Soviet attack on Finland. Uruguay announces it is to send material aid to Finland. Mexico also promises to send Finland whatever assistance it can afford.

The London dailies, The Times and the Daily Telegraph praise the stalwart Finnish resistance against overwhelming odds. In Amsterdam, unknown persons raise the Finnish flag on the mast of the Soviet steamship Joseph Stalin. Ten well-known Russian émigré writers, including Nobel Prize winner Ivan Bunin, issue a communiqué in Paris condemning the Soviet Union's invasion. More than 10,000 Swedish homes have volunteered to receive Finnish mothers and children.The Canadian Red Cross sends 50,000 dollars in aid to Finland. Herbert Hoover, the former US President, sends his fifth 100,000 dollar check. In response to the appeal by the League of Nations, Argentina sends 50,000 tons of grain to Finland with no fixed date for payment.

The Nicaraguan Government launches a national appeal for aid for Finland. Germany forbids the passage of volunteers to Finland through German territory. At the Brenner Pass, Germany halts a shipment of war material en route from Italy to Finland. The Italian Ambassador has lodged a protest with the German Foreign Ministry and tension rises between the two erstwhile allies Hitler and Mussolini. Prince Ferdinand of Liechtenstein arrives in Finland and declares his wish to serve as a volunteer on the front. The Swedish novelist Selma Lagerlöf donates her gold medal from the Swedish Academy and her Nobel Gold Medal for Finnish aid. A Danish association of factory-owners is sending a railway wagonload of food aid.

United States President, Franklin D. Roosevelt says the USA can extend a non-military loan to Finland as this would in his opinion not compromise US neutrality. The Swiss Medical Association announces it is to send a group of volunteers. Hungarian professor Albert Szent-Györgyi, winner of the 1937 Nobel Prize for Medicine, contributes his Nobel Medal to Finland.

Winston Churchill, Great Britain's First Lord of the Admiralty, addresses the British nation in a broadcast speech: "All Scandinavia dwells brooding under Nazi and Bolshevik threats. Only Finland superb, nay, sublime in the jaws of peril shows what free men can do. ... They have exposed, for all the world to see, the military incapacity of the Red Army and of the Red Air Force."....

At a press conference in Washington, US President Franklin D. Roosevelt emphasizes that any American who enlists in and swears allegiance to the army of a foreign country at war will thereby lose his American citizenship. However, since there had been no official declaration of war, the United States did not consider Finland to be a country at war, and American volunteers would therefore retain their citizenship. The renowned French general Clément Grandcourt arrives in Helsinki to enlist as a volunteer in the Finnish Army.

The famous Spanish fighter pilot Nicolas Beries is on his way to Finland as a volunteer. South African wine growers donate

14,000 liters of wine and 7,000 liters of brandy. The Soviet news agency Tass claims Sweden has emptied its prisons to allow convicts to go off to Finland as volunteers. In London, prayers are said on behalf of Finland in St Paul's Cathedral. Those present include the Archbishop of Canterbury and all the Nordic ambassadors. Brazilian President Getulio Vargas announces that Brazil is to send Finland a gift of 10,000 sacks of coffee. The International Labor Office announces that the Soviet Union has been expelled from the International Labor Organization (ILO).

The great Finnish runners Paavo Nurmi and Taisto Mäki receive a hero's welcome on arrival in New York. Thousands of people and dozens of reporters come to the harbor to welcome them; they continue on to Washington where they are received by US President Franklin D. Roosevelt. A thousand Danes volunteer to go and work in Finland. In the United States, the 'one dollar collection' organized by the Finnish committee has already raised over a million dollars.

In Sweden, a collection of gold rings has raised 1,500 rings. The office of the Canadian Prime Minister announces there are no legal obstacles to Canadian volunteers participating in the war in Finland. The first batch of volunteers board ship in Ottawa. According to the *New York Herald Tribune* the Treaty of Moscow demonstrates the inability of democratic countries to help a small freedom-loving people. The paper reserves its main ire for the United States' Congress, whose inertia and hesitation hampered the sending of aid to Finland. Norwegian Nobel Prize winner in literature for 1928, Sigrid Undset denotes her award to Finnish relief. After her demonstration of support for Finland against Stalin and communist tyranny, she is forced into exile by the Nazis a few months later for her outspoken condemnation of their antisemitism and brutality.

Probably no other conflict elicited so much popular appeal from so many people from so many countries and of such diverse social and economic classes. In no other conflict was there such a recognition and revulsion of the single nature of the two extremes of Right and Left, Germany under the Nazis and Hitler, and the Communist USSR under Stalin. Never has the term "international community" been more justified than in condemnation of the attack on Finalnd in 1940.

The Finnish-Americans and Canadians

Between 1870 and 1930, many tens of thousands of Finns migrated to the United States and Canada (see chapter 23). The motivation for this migration was both economic and cultural. It attracted a large number of families who had despaired of acquiring sufficient farm land to support themselves at home and feared the growing foreign presence and threat to Finnish identity under Czarist rule in what was the Russian possession of the "Grand Duchy" of Finland.

New migrants sent letters home, describing their life in the New World in very positive terms and professional recruiters, or "agents," employed by mining and shipping companies were also active and helped provide funding for the voyage. During the period 1900-1914, 150,000 new Finnish migrants arrived in North America.

The regions preferred by most Finnish immigrants bore a similarity to the landscape they were familiar with back home, especially in the Upper Midwest although several pockets of Finnish settlement appeared in New England and the Pacific Northwest as well. The heaviest levels of Finnish Settlement were seen in an area known as the Finn Hook, which includes Northeastern Minnesota, Northern Wisconsin, and the Upper Peninsula of Michigan. Today, the region is recognized as having the highest population of Americans of Finnish Ancestry of any region in the United States. They constitute the plurality of the population in the North-Western half of the Upper Peninsula of Michigan. The immigration of Finns gave birth to a strong Finnish American culture, especially in cities such as Duluth and Detroit, and many villages were named after places in Finland.

Many Finnish immigrants retained a strong sense of affiliation with the Socialist movements and had a strong proletarian identity and limited knowledge of English. The Communist Party in both the United States and Canada successfully attracted many Finns who became the largest group of recruited members and supporters organized into a specific ethnic organization. Following the failure of the Communists to create a Soviet style Finland after the country won its independence from the new government of the USSR, a bitter Civil War took place simultaneously in the new Finland and Russia. Whereas the Reds triumphed in Russia, the "Whites" aided by German troops were victorious in Finland and provoked a new exodus of all those Left-wing Finns, some of whom managed to emigrate to the United States and Canada. In spite of the considerable amount of Leftwing and Communist activity among the North American Finns and considerable feelings of being exploited and often discriminated against in their new homelands in North America, the Soviet invasion was almost universally received with shock and disgust. Helsinki had been chosen for the site of the 1940 Olympic Games, Finnish communal organizations in North America that had organized for the games turned their attention to support Finland. Travel and enlistment for the Canadians was especially difficult because Canada, along with Great Britain, were already at war with Germany, Stalin's ally in November 1939 – March 1940.

Absurd Communist Propaganda

The campaigns run by Communist front organizations in the United States and Canada and the editorial line of the *Daily Worker* that had waxed so eloquently over the International Brigades in Spain, incensed public opinion by their support of Soviet aggression. Even among those Finns who had been communists, there was a full realization that the Mannerheim government had not provoked war, and that the "Finnish People's Republic" established by Stalin on Soviet soil and headed by communist leader, Otto Kuusinen, was a puppet regime of traitors. Kuusinen was a veteran communist who had fled Finland after the loss of the "Reds' in the Civil War and had spent the years 1921-1939 in Moscow. No sane person could accept that a nation of under four million with a long tradition of strong Christian and humane values had invaded the largest military power in the world, a brutal dictatorship and close ally of Hitler who had just divided the corpse of

Poland between them.

Many Communist Party members in the United States and around the world were still in shock from the Molotov-Ribbentrop Pact and the joint Nazi-Soviet invasion of Poland and simply ignored the propaganda. One such example was a grotesque portrait of Finland's Marshall Gustave Mannerheim posted around Detroit assembly lines with the text "Not a Dime for Mannerheim!" (at least it rhymed). It went on to read…"*What guy would be dumb enough to lay his hard earned dimes on the Mannerheim Line, when that line is backed by the Hoovers and Fords and Chryslers and the rest of the facist punks? And their stooge, Butch Mannerheim, the last of the Czar's White Guard majordomos = those who made a bloody shambles of the first worker's republic in early years. In 1918 Mannerheim massacred 30,000 Finnish workers and their wives and kids, arming his murderers with money loaned from Britain, France and the U.S.A. in the war to "make the world safe from Socialism" Today, the Finnish Big Bankers are paying the war "debt" in full – the debt of the slaughtered Finnish workers !!!*

These propaganda efforts were made all the more ridiculous as Finland had enjoyed the enviable reputation among ordinary Americans as the only European state that was not in arrears in repaying its World War I debt to the United States. The reference to "Finnish Big Bankers" was just as silly, and most of these posters were immediately ripped off the factory walls by angry American workers. Former President Herbert Hoover and New York's Mayor Fiorello La-Guardia spoke out strongly at a "Let's Help Finland" rally at Madison Square Garden they organized on December 20, 1939.

The American veterans of the Abraham Lincoln Brigade who had fought in Spain issued a statement on Christmas day 1939 in support of the Soviet Union and promising the Finns that "The Yanks Are NOT Coming" to demonstrate their total rejection of any comparison between their fight against Fascism in Spain and the idealism of international volunteers to fight Soviet aggression against Finland. The statement condemned "*people who prate about the rights of small nations and about the Soviet Union because she is wiping out an imperialist base for aggression.*"[9]

---

9 *New York Times*, Dec. 25, 1939 and *The New Republic*, Jan. 1, 1940.

The Two Brigades From Today's Perspective

Both International Brigades were the product of a noble ideal-ism, the desire of free men to defend the values of civilization against tyranny. The major difference is that for many of the Spanish Civil War Veterans, their devotion was tarnished by the excesses and lies of Sta-lin's henchmen and the Far Left that served him across the globe. For those who tried to aid Finland, there are only the fond memories of world solidarity.

2005 commemorative stamp in honor of all those who fought to secure Finland's continued independence in the Winter War.

The Finish Lilliputians strike back at the Soviet Gulliver!
A 1940 cartoon in a French poster. The text reads:
"Heroism does not pay attention to the number of armies."

Polish Stamp issued in 1947-48 to commemorate 10th anniversary of Polish volunteers for the International Brigade in Spain. The soldiers of the Jarosław Dąbrowski XIII International Brigade fought on the Republican side during the Spanish civil war. The brigade composed mostly of Polish volunteers was named in honor of General Jarosław Dąbrowski (1836-1871) who fell in defense of Paris during the Paris Commune of 1871. Translations: Pamięci walk w Hispanji Brygady Polskiej im(ienina) Jarosława Dąbrowskiego = Remember the fighting in Spain of the Polish Jarosław Dabrowski Brigade.

Za wolność waszą i naszą = For your freedom and ours.

Voluntarios Internacionales de la Libertad (Spanish) = International Volunteers of Freedom.

Por vuestra libertad y la nuestra (Spanish) = For your freedom and ours.

18

Ionnas Metaxas: The Autocrat, Monarchist, Fascist and Germanophile Who Led Greece AGAINST the Axis

Among the national leaders who roused their people to resist Hitler and Mussolini and became a heroic figure in the Allied camp was Ionnas Metxas, Prime Minister and Dictator of Greece. Although universally regarded as a firm nationalist, a monarchist, ultra-conservative, even an admirer of Italian fascism (as long as it was not a threat to Greek Independence) and a pronounced Germanophile, Metaxas is unfortunately a forgotten figure. He does not conform to the typical "Leftist" image of the Resistance or leader of democratic nations like Belgium or Denmark or Czechoslovakia who all succumbed to the Nazis in a matter of a few days or offered no resistance at all.

He probably would not have been portrayed by a "heroic" Hollywood actor such as Humphrey Bogart if producers had screened a film on the Greek resistance in World War II. Hollywood made several repetitive films on the struggle between the Free French and the Fascist Vichy regime but had only one model for the Bogart-hero role – the sentimental but tough guy crusading journalist or nightclub owner with Leftist sympathies (see chapter 2). Like other ultra-conservatives of the Right who ultimately opposed the Nazis, Metaxas was attacked in the Soviet and leftwing press throughout the 1930s as a Fascist sympathizer like Austria's Engelbert Dollfuss, (see chapter 12) as were Finland's Mannerheim, and Bulgaria' Boris III (see chapter 14)and Poland's Jozef Pilsudski.

Born on the island of Ithaca (home of the mythical hero Odysseus of Homer's The Iliad and The Odyssey), Metaxas was a career military officer who first saw action in the 1897 Greco-Turkish War. He pursued his studies in Germany and brought back valuable experience in German military techniques that were integrated into the modernization of the Greek Army. He joined the General Staff and served in the Balkan Wars (1912–1913).

Metaxas was a staunch supporter of the monarchy and opposed Greek entry into World War I. His chief opponent was the pro-Allied political figure Eletherios Venizelos the Prime Minister at the time of the Dardanelles Campaign and Gallipoli landings on the Turkish Coast by combined British-Australian-New Zealand forces. Venizelos saw this as a historic opportunity for Greece to enter the war against its arch-enemy Turkey and gain further territory. Metaxas's refusal to cooperate provoked new elections in May, 1915 in which Venizelos won and tried to mobilize the army to aid Serbia, resulting in his dismissal by King Constantine I. This move deepened the chasm between the two major political forces in Greece and the stark choice between neutrality or war. In 1916, Metaxas was promoted to the rank of Lieutenant General.

In August 1916, supporters of Venizelos in the army launched a revolt in Thessaloniki, winning control of the northern half of the country and established a separate "Government of National Defense" with Venizelos in charge. This new regime entered the war with the support of the Allies and then helped depose the King in June 1917. Metaxas was appalled. Venizelos assumed full power declaring war on behalf of the whole country on 29 June 1917.

Exile and Return

Metaxas followed the king into exile in Corsica until 1920 when the defeat of Venizelos in new elections paved the way for their return. The country continued fighting to win the fruit of victory promised by the Allies to the Greeks in Asia Minor. The conflict against the Turkish republican forces under Kemal Attatürk in 1920-22 led to major repercussions following defeat and popular discontent with the monarchy which again forced King Constantine into exile. He participated in a failed royalist coup attempt in October 1923 and had to flee the country once again. The monarchy was again abolished and a Republic proclaimed in March 1924.

After publicly stating his acceptance of the regime change,

Metaxas returned to Greece. His political ambitions as a royalist were frustrated by disunity and his political party made little headway. In the 1926 elections, his Freethinkers' Party managed to win about 16% of the vote and 52 seats in Parliament. This was approximately the equivalent of the rival monarchist party, The People's Party. Although briefly serving as Communications Minister, the fortunes of his Freethinkers Party declined to only a few seats in the elections of 1928, 1932 and 1933 but he nevertheless became Minister of the Interior, an important post in the cabinet. New elections improved his party's bargaining position in 1935 and 1936 and he was appointed Minister of War just in time for the return of the monarchy.

Metaxas Inaugurates the Fourth of August Regime

George II, son of Constantine I, returned to take the throne in 1935. Political instability was heightened by the 1936 elections ending in a stalemate and by the rise of the Greek Communist Party (KKE). The King, fearing the communists and the risk of a coup to bring back the Republic, appointed Metaxas as interim prime minister on 13 April 1936. Continued unrest and a wave of strikes in May enabled Metaxas to declare a state of emergency, indefinite suspension of the parliament including several articles of the constitution. On August 4, 1936 Metaxas declared a new authoritarian form of government (The Fourth of August Regime) that declared him to be "the First Peasant," "the First Worker" and "the National Father" of the Greeks.

Following in the footsteps of der Fuehrer and Il Duce, Metaxas adopted the title of Arkhigos, Greek for "leader" and proclaimed a "Third Hellenic Civilization" (to follow ancient Athens and Sparta and then the Byzantine Empire), banned political parties, prohibited strikes and adopted widespread censorship of the media. Critics both inside the country and abroad ridiculed Metaxas and his "Third Hellenic Civilization" as a Greek imitation of Hitler's use of the term "Third Reich" to categorize "The New Germany" under the Nazis.

Working closely with his Minister of Security, government agents infiltrated the Communist Party and effectively suppressed it. Metaxas cultivated Greek history and considered the roots of his regime to lie in Greece's classical history. He believed that Hellenic nationalism would mobilize *"the heathen values of ancient Greece, specifically those of Sparta, along with the Christian values of the Medieval Empire of Byzantium."* Although his regime was frequently compared to Mussolini, Metaxas considered the authoritarian conservative ruler of Portugal, Antonio Salazar his main inspiration. His Fourth of August regime used its own military-like uniforms, greetings, songs and rituals, including the Roman salute adopted by Hitler.

Metaxas consistently praised the traditional Greek values of "Country, Loyalty, Family and Religion," thereby winning popularity for what appeared to most Greeks as a period of stability and order. He copied some of the institutions of the authoritarian Italian and Portuguese National Labor Services including the 8-hour working day and mandatory improvements of working conditions such as maternity leave. These measures were very popular but Metaxas was universally regarded by the Left-Liberal press everywhere as a European dictator of the Far Right. He did not however establish a mass political party, preferring to rely on the power and backing of the army and support of King George II. Greece's major trading partner in the 1930s was Nazi Germany and in foreign affairs, Metaxas followed a line of strict neutrality and no alliances.

As in most other authoritarian regimes, the Fourth of August adopted a strong nationalistic program. Although Metaxas was opposed to the invasion of Asia Minor as part of the Megali Idea (a greater Greece including a large part of Anatolia), he used strong nationalist language concerning Greek minorities in Albania, Bulgaria and Turkey. How then did Metaxas, this rightwing Germanophile copycat of Italian fascism become THE national hero to oppose the Axis?

Fascist Regimes in Greece and Poland Without Antisemitism

As with many nation states at the time, Metaxas frequently used the term "race" in praising Greek culture, tradition and national identity. His regime however was relatively tolerant to the Jews, repealing the antisemitic laws of the previous republican regime. A large community of Sephardic Jews was present in the region of Thessaloniki which had been annexed by Greece in 1913, and Jews had largely been unhappy with Venizelos. Metaxas was a strong opponent of Slavic-Bulgarian speakers in Macedonia and Thrace, and repressed any manifestation of the Slavic languages both in public and in private. Nevertheless, most Slavophone Greeks and Greek Jews identified with the state and fought bravely and loyally on the Italo-Albanian front.

In many ways, Metaxas' career, policies and nationalist stance ran parallel with Poland's dynamic leader, Jozef Pilsudski, who depended more on his charismatic authority than on parliamentary support. During the period 1926–35, under Pilsudski's authoritarian rule, the situation of many Polish Jews improved and he was viewed as the only leader capable of restraining antisemitic currents in Poland and maintaining public order. His death in 1935 was rightly viewed as a tragedy for Europe's largest Jewish minority.

The Dodecanese and Conflict with Italy

In spite of confidence in Metaxas as dictator, King George and most of the country's traditional elites were staunchly anglophile. As a maritime nation made up in part of a peninsula and hundreds of islands, Greece appreciated the power of the Royal Navy. Experience in World War I with Italian expansionism and familiarity with Mussolini's ambitions to convert the Mediterranean into "Mare Nostrum" drove Greece to lean towards the Franco-British alliance, a reality that Metaxas was unable to challenge.

In World War I, Article 122 of the Treaty of Sèvres ceded all of the Dodecanese islands to Italy but on British insistence their eventual return to Greece was "guaranteed" except the island of Rhodes - to be retained by Italy for a period of fifteen years. According to a secret agreement that persuaded Italy to enter the war on the Allies' side in 1915, some of the islands had been promised to Italy in an eventual peace settlement. The population of the islands was predominantly Greek and their proximity to both the Turkish coast of Anatolia and Greek mainland argued for such an eventuality but Mussolini was hopeful of securing a submarine base from which to expand Italian influence into the Aegean Sea and secure economic advantages in the region.

The Turks had rejected the Treat of Sèvres and successfully de-feated Greek forces, occupying Smyrna and parts of the Turkish coastal region on the Aegean Sea. A revised Treaty of Lausanne in Turkey's favor enabled Greece to hold onto territorial gains in Thrace but left the mat-ter of the Dodecanese for future negotiations between the allies. This continued to be an irritant and a warning to both Britain and Greece of Italian designs. In August, 1923, an Italian officer working to establish the boundary between Greece and Albania was killed on Greek terri-tory, resulting in an Italian shelling of the island of Corfu from the sea causing civilian casualties. The matter was brought by Greece to the League of Nations. The League was confronted with a clear case of ag-gression and Mussolini threatened to withdraw Italy from membership on September 23, 1923, if condemned by the League. The Corfu inci-dent resulted in the issue being shelved and referred to a "Conference of Ambassadors," a sign of the league's ineffectiveness and the reason for its eventual demise.

Metaxas became aware that Mussolini's aggressive designs in the Eastern Aegean were Greece's greatest danger. His policy to keep Greece out of World War II was broken by the blunt ultimatum made by Mussolini on 28 October 1940 demanding occupation rights to strategic Greek sites. Metaxas' laconic reply *"Alors, c'est la guerre"* (then, it is war) has become part of Greek folklore and symbolic of Greek popular feeling expressed in the single word "No" (*Ohi*). "Ohi Day" is still celebrated in Greece each year. Within a few hours, Italy invaded Greece from Albania and started the Greco-Italian War.

Thanks to Metaxas, the Greeks were able to offer a successful defense and launch a counter offensive, forcing the Italians back into Albania and occupying large parts of Northern Epirus (Southern Al-bania). Less than two weeks after crossing the frontier, Italian troops were in flight and disarray. Only six days after the initial assault, Greek General Papagos struck into Albania outflanking the Italians and cut-ting roads.

Using mountainous terrain and aided by RAF supplies in-cluding anti-tank weapons, the Italian Julia Division was trapped and 5,000 prisoners were taken by the Greeks. On December 6, Mussolini dismissed Marshal Pietro Badoglio as Chief of the General Staff. Two days later, Greek troops captured two other towns and had reached a junction 40 miles from the Greek-Albanian border and then seized the town of Himara on December 23. At this juncture, world opinion was stunned by the first major victory on land against Axis forces by the only active ally of the British.

In January, 1941, British troops won a stunning victory against the Italians near Tobruk in Libya taking 45,000 prisoners and the Greek offensive in Albania received encouragement and praise from British Prime Minister Churchill. These were the first real convincing allied victories in the war. Churchill believed it was essential for Britain to support Greece in every possible way. On January 8, 1941, he stated that "*There was no other course open to us but to make certain that we had spared no effort to help the Greeks who had shown themselves so worthy.*" These victories enormously increased moral in Britain and humiliated Mussolini, prompting Hitler to change his plans and rush aid to the Italians to stem the Greek advance.

Metaxas was regarded as a national hero although still considered as a 'reactionary fascist and oppressor of the Greek working class' by the pro-Soviet International Left under the influence of the Hitler-Stalin Pact. Metaxas died in Athens on January 29, 1941 and thus did not live to witness the German invasion of Greece. After his death, the invading Germans met considerable difficulty with the fortifications constructed by Metaxas in Northern Greece, along the Bulgarian border and known as the Metaxas Line. Like the Mannerheim Line in Finland that stopped the Soviet invasion for several months and caused enormous casualties to the Red Army, it was regarded as a first rate example of strategic defense.

The German decision to aid their failing Italian ally resulted in turning Greece into a major theater of war. The Germans invaded across the Bulgarian border in the North on April 6, 1941. Greek and British Commonwealth forces fought back courageously but were vastly outnumbered. Athens fell on April 27, but the British managed to evacuate about 50,000 troops in what was called a "Second Dunquerque." The time and resources needed to subdue Greece and Yugoslavia, where an anti-Axis coup had deposed the pro-German heir to the throne, resulted in a postponement of "Operation Barbarossa," the invasion of the Soviet Union. Had the Germans not diverted their energy to the Balkans in the early Spring, they could have attacked the Soviet Union then, rather than in late June and with the ferocity of their forces might have reached Moscow before the onset of the very cold Russian winter of 1941-42.

Iannos Metaxas, undoubtedly a "rightwing dictator," is nevertheless still regarded with great admiration by most Greeks as a hero for his popular policies, patriotism, defiance of aggression, and the magnificent performance of the Greek army against the Italian and German invaders. It is however unlikely that Hollywood will ever make a film celebrating his life.

Metaxas, like Dollfuss and Pilsudski, was not "cool."

19

Communist Party Support for Both Castro and Batista

It is worth dwelling on the Cuban story at greater length, if for no other reason than more than any other, it is so obvious and so close at hand, both geographically in its distance from American shores and by the presence of more than a million individuals who now reside in the United States and were personally involved and aware of how the Cuban Revolution came to power. It is all the more important to reveal the stark naked truth of the Cuban episode that has for the past fifty years elevated both Fidel Castro and Che Guevara into international icons on the level of pop-stars. The number of teenagers and would-be teenagers wearing Che or Fidel T-shirts probably exceeds those wearing any other emblem with the possible exception of the cross (the latter probably worn more as a cosmetic adornment rather than a real religious symbol of faith).

Of course, all of this is a matter of simple research available in thousands of documents and first hand sources, but young people all over the world continue to sport their T-shirts in the self-induced hypnosis that opposition to the U.S. by Castro and the support given to him by the USSR and communist bloc as well as his fifty year long tenure in power and thousands of hours of speeches all vouchsafe that the Cuban regime deserves the support of The LEFT. The reason is simple. Castro opposed U.S. imperialism and overthrew a dictator and therefore, - as in Orwell's book Animal Farm (Two Legs Bad; Four Legs Good!), i.e., the Communists were/are/always have been on the side of "The People."

There were, however, many Cuban refugees in the United States before Castro came to power. They had fled the island to escape the dictatorial and corrupt rule of Fulgencio Batista and they were also fleeing the communist influence in his government and domination of many Cuban labor unions. Let today's teenagers ask their grandparents! Certainly, all of us who are 65 and older will remember how Desi Arnaz, the star-husband of Lucille Ball of the "I Love Lucy Show," explained to an American audience that the shocking tabloid newspaper headlines (LUCY BALL IN RED LINK, LUCILLE BALL LISTED AS RED) accusing his wife of communist sympathies were pure libel and a foul trick of yellow-press journalists (no doubt they would be called practitioners of "McCarthyism" today).

Lucy and her brother had registered Communist in a California primary election in 1936 at the request of their father, a long time labor activist. There was no other "red" connection to Lucy but in addition, Desi revealed in several public appearances how he had fled Cuba and been "kicked out" because of his refusal to toe the line of the Communist dominated unions. He had arrived in the U.S.A. penniless and cleaned canary cages to earn money. As for Lucy's alleged communist sympathies, Desi put it succinctly ---*"the only thing red about Lucy is her hair and even that is fake."*

Batista and several puppet presidents under his control had "earned" the support of Cuba's Communist Party because they appeared as "revolutionary" and "Anti-American." Other Latin American leaders such as Argentina's dictator, General Juan Perón and Hugo Chavez of Venezuela today, also appealed to the same electorate as populist, anti-American, charismatic figures with strong support among government controlled labor unions. The historical obedience to Moscow that typified most Latin American Communist parties since their creations in the twenties and thirties lay behind the difficult relationship between Fidel Castro's initial attitude toward Communism and the role played by the old Cuban Communist Party before he gained power in January, 1959.

Although many Afro-Americans were hoodwinked by Castro's propaganda about the Cuban Revolution bringing "racial equality" to the island's population for the first time, it was none other than dictator Fulgencio Batista, a "mixed blood," the descendant of Italian, Spanish, Chinese and African ancestors, who had been the victim of discrimination. He had not been allowed to join the Havana Yacht Club because of his mixed race, a factor he exploited because it focused attention on the elitist character of the Cuban government and its old colonial heritage of racial prejudices. These prejudices were shared by none other than Fidel Castro's father, a wealthy land and sugar plantation owner who had prospered.

The Early Party, 1920-1954

Surprisingly, the Communist Party had deep roots in Cuba going all the way back to the success of the Russian Revolution and Lenin's ascension to power. The future seeds of distrust between the old Cuban Communists and Fidel Castro were sown many years before Castro became an important figure in Cuban politics. The party was organized in Havana in August, 1920 by a few admirers of the Russian revolution and by the 1930s had become a powerful force in many labor unions, an achievement unmatched elsewhere in Latin America. Its founders were a particularly diverse group of individuals, Julio Antonia Mella, a student activist, Carlos Balino who had been a follower of Cuban nationalist hero Jose Marti and Fabio Grobart, a Jewish immigrant tailor who had been caught up in the Civil War that occurred in Poland and managed to reach Cuba.

Communists played only a very minor role in the 1933 popular revolution that deposed the dictator Gerardo Machado. It was during this episode that "strong man" Fulgencio Batista with Communist support emerged on the national political scene. Latin American Communist Party leaders in late 1934 met for a conference in Moscow chaired by Dimitri Manuilsky, for many years head of the Comintern and one of Stalin's closest friends.

The Cuban Communist party was led at that time by Blas Roca, its Secretary General. Decisions were made with Stalin's blessing to support insurrection in Brazil, a popular front in Chile, favor an extreme anti-American nationalist program in Mexico and the formation of an eventual alliance with the ruling clique headed by "radical nationalist" leader, Batista in Cuba. This coalition was named the Unión Revolucionaria.

In September 1934, Batista issued a declaration stating that *"The Communist Party in accordance with its own statutes is a democratic party which pursues its objectives within the margin of the capitalist regime and denounces violence as a means of political action, and a consequence of this, has the right to the same treatment as any other party in Cuba."*

Batista ruled the nation through a puppet president and in 1937, gave his full agreement to the creation of the Unión Revolucionaria Party. In 1938, he permitted the publication of the (then still illegal) Cuban Communist party's official newspaper Hoy, edited by Anibal Escalante. Communist leaders Blas Roca, and Joaquin Ordoquí, met with Colonel Batista and issued the resolutions to be followed that the Party had to adopt a positive attitude towards Colonel Batista "*in view that Batista was a defender of democracy.*"

By the late 1930s, Batista and the Communists worked hand in glove to allow "free elections" in order to continue their control of the government, form a constituent assembly to produce a new constitution and legitimize the power of a puppet president, Frederico Laredo Bru.

In May 1939, 937 Jewish refugees on board the German passenger ship St. Louis were denied entry to Cuba due to the revocation of their visas by President Bru. Apparently, the only motivation for this inhuman act was Bru's desire to obtain an even bigger bribe than he had been promised, a move that also garnered support from many Cubans under the guise of protecting "Cuba's Workers," fearful of more Jewish refugees receiving asylum or economic assistance during the Depression. This was the politics of envy so carefully nurtured by the Nazis and the Communists who, only a few months later, would celebrate their alliance in the Molotov-Ribbentrop Pact of Non-Aggression between the USSR and Germany.

The St. Louis affair was a terrible blot on the conscience of all those who opposed the Nazi threat and antisemitic policies. It also sits uncomfortably for the Castro regime who thus required a version of their own "Cuban history." Rather then admit that the totally corrupt Cuban government of President Bru (with Batista sitting in the wings) and actually controlling affairs with Communist support was responsible for refusing permission for the Jewish refugees of the St. Louis to seek safety, the version taught in Cuban schools today (and repeated by stooges of the Castro regime writing in to several internet sites about the St. Louis affair), is that the Roosevelt administration ordered the Bru government to reject the right of the passengers to disembark in

Havana although they were in possession of Cuban immigration visas and landing permits.

The Communist Party took no steps to demand acceptance of the refugees. This is all the more reprehensible and disgusting since an earlier generation of Jewish refugees arriving on the island in the early 1920s gave support to it out of all proportion to their miniscule representation in Cuban society. The great majority of Cuban Jews were however not Communists and had formed a committee to consult with President Bru in the hope that the refugees would be accepted elsewhere but appeals to half a dozen Latin American countries and the United States to accept the St. Louis passengers fell on deaf ears and they were ordered to return to Hamburg. At the last moment, Britain, Holland and Belgium agreed to accept the passengers. World War II began only two months later and at least 90% of them were murdered in the Holocaust.

The U.S. has nothing to be proud of in this story since U.S. Coast Guard boats shadowed the St. Louis to make sure that no attempt was made to dock and unload the "illegal immigrants" on American shores but the absurd attempt by the Cuban government to transfer the blame on the U.S. is typical of more than fifty years of Castro's regime.

Frederico Laredo Bru (a name that will "live in infamy") was driven by greed and a thorough disregard for any humanitarian concern. Although put in power by Batista, he also wanted to show that he was not just an insignificant puppet but could demonstrate his own power and pride by defying the Minister of the Interior, appointed by Batista, who had originally granted the visas to the St. Louis passengers.

In the 1940 election, although the Communists dominated most unions, anti-Batista candidates won 41 of 76 seats, receiving 225,223 votes, while Batista and the Communists won 35 seats and only 97,944 votes. In spite of this rejection of a popular mandate, the Cuban Communist Party urged continued support for Batista who, with their aid, managed to be elected president in spite of his poor parliamentary election results.

Batista resigned his military post as Chief of the Armed Forces and announced his candidacy for the 1940 Presidential elections. It was an honest one in in which he won with full Communist support, promising partial state control of the sugar, tobacco and mining industries as well as land reform. Batista also made anti-American statements to endear him to the working class which, in spite of U.S. intervention to help win Cuba's independence from Spain, still regarded the United States with distrust and envy.

Two close associates of Batista were also later to become high ranking Communist members of Fidel Castro's government, Juan Marinello (later a member of the Politburo), who lost his attempt to win the post of mayor of Havana in the 1940 elections and Carlos Rafael Rodriguez (who eventually became Castro's Vice-President).

Batista's popularity increased during the war years of his second official presidency, 1940-1944 due to the rise in prosperity caused by the Allies' demands for sugar, nickel and manganese. As 1944 approached, Batista played a charade by appearing to "step down" as a true democrat. In this way, he would win additional good will support from the United States that was anxious about his ties to the Communists.

As president, Batista was a strong, "democratic leader" but had to suppress an attempted coup by his chief of staff. He extended social welfare measures to workers in the countryside and declared war on the Axis Powers on December 9, 1941 followed by recognition of the Soviet Union in 1943. During the war, Cuba benefited from US aid and the high fixed price of sugar at 2.65¢ a pound. This helped moderate Batista's anti-American tone.

Once again however, a fairly honest election set back the Batistianos and the Communists. In 1944, Dr. Ramon San Martin Grau was an ex-University professor with substantial student backing and promises of a more honest regime. He won the popular vote in the presidential election and served until 1948. Despite his initial popularity, accusations of corruption tainted his administration's image, and a sizable number of Cubans began to distrust him.

Batista, who had garnered a fortune of twenty million dollars, the result of his being the real man in charge of Cuba since 1933, appeared to fade away yet communist leaders Carlos Rafael Rodriguez and Blas Roca wrote, in their 1945 book, *En Defensa del Pueblo*, that "the people's idol (Batista), the great man of our national politics" was not gone forever.

Although the dictator enjoyed Communist Party support for well over twenty years of despotic rule, left-wing college students and many American journalists will assure you that "America has always supported corrupt dictators like Batista." During a period of several years, Batista relocated to Florida 1945-48, and lived in Daytona Beach where there is still a museum of Cuban art with works that he had "borrowed."

Batista was a masterful politician who enjoyed the confidence and support of the propertied classes while he cultivated the Left, but the wealthy class in Cuba understood that they need not fear him. He had become quite conservative as he became wealthy. Moreover, Cuba on a few additional occasions demonstrated its "popular" anti-American line such as the vote against the partition of Palestine.

Cuba was the only non-Arab and non-Muslim state that voted against the proposal to establish a Jewish state thereby accenting its "independent" line of foreign policy. Incredibly, several Jewish Cuban communists fully supported the decision simply because it helped cement an image of the Party as "anti-imperialist." The two Latin American states that had had strong ties to the Axis with strong pro-German leanings at the beginning of the war, Chile and Argentina, abstained. Mexico also followed a "neutral" policy to show its independence of the United States.

The Latin American headquarters of the Comintern moved from Mexico to Cuba in 1940 and the Communists had a very strong presence in the Cuban Federation of Labor. There were chronic strikes and labor disputes in 1947-48. Student rioters (including Fidel Castro), urban gangsterism, roaming armed bands in the countryside and political assassinations all produced turmoil. The spark for Castro's political activism was Eduardo Chibas, who, like him, came from a well-to-do Galician family from Guantanamo, in Oriente province. Like Castro, he was educated by Jesuits, and was a member of the elite, deeply religious, but a violent anti-Communist.

In 1948, a stooge of Batista, Carlos Prío Socarrás, was elected as a minority President but the Communists lost three seats in the Senate. Ominously, and forgetting all of his previous anti-American rhetoric, Batista ran his campaign from Florida and was elected as a Senator. Castro, at this time was a prominent figure in Havana politics and a protegé of Chibas. In response to these events, the Communist Party criticized Castro and the other student adventurers for participating in anti-government street fighting during an international conference in Bogota, Colombia.

At the same time and place as the Colombian events, Argentin-ian Communist Party member, Ernesto Che Guevara, who was pres-ent at the Bogota conference, never left his boarding house during the disturbances. Eddy Chibas committed suicide in 1951 during a public address to the nation to call attention to what he believed was a cam-paign by corrupt politicians to deny him the election, thereby creating a political vacuum in Cuba, leading to the reemergence of Batista in Cuban politics. A few weeks after Chibas' suicide, Castro met with then Senator Batista and spent several hours in discussions with him at Ba-tista's ranch. What they discussed is not known but on March 10, 1952, Batista usurped control of the government in a bloodless coup thereby fulfilling Chibas' worst fear expressed before his death.

The next day, as proclaimed chief of state, Batista moved into the presidential palace. The most radical opposition to Batista's seizure of power came from the wealthy racist Cuban elite who had detested Batista as a "mixed-blood." From 1948 to 1952, the Communist Party lost control of the unions and the party was divided on whether to sup-port him again. Batista suppressed all opposition newspapers but al-lowed the Communist daily "Hoy" to remain open, an obvious ploy to win continued communist support.

When Fidel Castro founded his "Revolutionary" Movement, Communists were automatically excluded from joining it and the Party denounced Castro's attack on the Moncada Barracks of July 26, 1953, in Santiago de Cuba. The American Communist daily newspaper *The Daily Worker* described the Castro led attack as "a putschist method peculiar to all bourgeois political factions."

When Castro ultimately succeeded, he and the Communists knew they were meant for each other regardless of the past. For Fidel, it was the discipline and support of an international force directed against "American imperialism" and capable of providing massive economic, diplomatic and military support. For the Communists, it was a simple shift to another "people's idol." Find the official website in Spanish of the Cuban Communist Party, and read the section marked "History."

It contains not a word about the Party from its founding until January 1, 1959. This is how internal contradictions are typically resolved by totalitarian regimes.

Much water has passed under the bridge since then. Part of the self-delusions of those who identify themselves as "progressives," or many liberals today is their immediate and most often mistaken gut reaction that the "masses" must be right when they emotionally respond to anti-Western and especially anti-American (and even more irrationally, anti-Israel, anti-Christian and anti-Jewish) rhetoric and jargon.

For the Marxist LEFT and many of those who call themselves "Liberals" today, there is no better litmus test for political correctness than the envy of the poor and downtrodden, a powerful force that can be manipulated.

No matter how fanatical, corrupt, degenerate and blind to any humanitarian consideration of such despicable characters as Batista and Bru, or Peron, and later Castro, Nasser, Arafat, Ahmadinejad, Mao Tse Tung, the Ayatollah Khomeini or Saddam Hussein were, many on the Left assume they speak for "The People," the "Nation," the "workers," the "dispossessed," the "poor," the homeless, refugees etc. The failure to see in such leaders both a symptom and a basic cause of their nations' problems is a continued malaise.

20
Peronism in Argentina: Populism of the Right or the Left? (or does it matter?)

For most Latin Americans today and their parents, General Juan Perón of Argentina was the precursor to Fidel Castro who represented the image of a proud crusading nationalist leader rejecting the overtures of the United States and devoted to raising the standard of living of those at the bottom of the social and economic scale, i.e. the most destitute and humble citizens who had been exploited by a tiny privileged elite. This leader and his wife Eva Duarte Perón were the source of the political movement in the country that has dominated Argentine affairs for most of the past seventy years.

The movement known as '*Justicialismo*' (Justicialism embracing the ideal of social justice) but recognized more familiarly abroad as Peronism created an economic, political, and social ideology that exalts the state, nationalism and by its own description attempts to accommodate the interests first and foremost of THE POOR as well as labor, and industry. This form of government highly controls and subsidizes many labor unions, strongly supports the military, private industry, and public works. This model of a Latin American Populism was followed in Cuba by President Fulgencio Batista (see chapter 19), and 'Papa Doc' Duvalier in Haiti[1] and Hugo Chavez of Venezuela.

1 Duvalier was a populist nationalist leader emphasizing negritude on behalf of the overwhelming majority of Haiti's population that had long resented rule by a tiny elite of light skinned mulatto. He often attacked the United States for its friendly relations with Dominican dictator Rafael Trujillo. The Kennedy administration was particularly upset at his misappropriation of millions of dollars of international aid. He later claimed that Kennedy's death was the result of a voodoo curse he had placed on the American president. Everywhere outside of Latin America, Duvalier was recognized as a 'Right-wing' dictator but his populism appealed to the vast majority of Haiti's poorest population. His grip on power was cemented by a rural militia, the Milice Volontaires de la Sécurité Nationale (MVSN, English: National Security Volunteer Militia), popularly known as the Tonton Macoutes after a Creole term for the bogeyman, The Macoutes had twice the numbers of the regular army, and was personally loyal to Duvalier. In the name of Haitian nationalism, Duvalier expelled almost all of Haiti's

Is Peronism a Rightist or Leftist movement? OR, Does it make any difference to those who opposed his rule? Argentina with Perón's support was anti-American and favored the Axis powers during the early years of World War II, only reluctantly being pressured into declaring war on Germany and Japan in the closing weeks of the war. Both Juan and Eva Perón were instrumental in providing assistance to facilitate the escape of many Nazi war criminals and their establishment under hidden identities in Argentina. Nevertheless, the Perón regime was on very good terms with the Jewish community, and maintained friendly relations with the State of Israel.

Following World War II, that was extremely beneficial to Argentina, the Peronist regime's inefficiency led to the decline of the country's economy, the bankrupting of the civil services, profitless industries and further strengthening control of labor unions. Subsequent military governments, however, that followed Perón's death in 1983, were guilty of much greater and widespread abuse of human rights and led the country into ever worse difficulties and the adventurist war over the Falklands.

Perón's policies and ideas were initially popular among a wide variety of different groups across the political spectrum and led to the paradox of Peronism being classified as a "populism" of both the Left and the Right. Juan Perón could speak to the masses in the most contemporary lower class *"Lumfardo"* dialect of the Buenos Aires slums and write in classical correct Spanish. He could identify his major target as the great American oil companies in public speeches and yet sign unpublicized lucrative agreements with them. He nationalized Argentina's largest corporations and at the same time protected and won the support of major labor unions that agreed to relinquish the right to strike.

About the only certainty regarding Peronism is the identity of those elements of the population who came to regard Perón with contempt. They were the old landed aristocracy, the Roman Catholic Church and intellectuals who regarded themselves as "liberals" in the old fashioned sense of supporting individual rights and who admired the United States and Great Britain as models for a democratic society.

---

foreign-born bishops, an act that earned him excommunication from the Catholic Church.

Judging by the nature of these "enemies," most observers would brand Peronism as a form of a Leftwing fascism yet, Perón served as a military attaché in Italy and expressed great admiration for the policies and personality of Benito Mussolini. It was there that he acquired a taste for the kind of authoritarian rule and a corporate economic system he believed would propel Argentina into the ranks of a great power.

Juan Perón returned to Argentina shortly after the entry of Italy into the war in 1940. While serving in Italy he lost his first wife of thirteen years, Aurelia Tuzón, who died from uterine cancer at the age of twenty-nine. He supported the military coup of 1943 in Argentina that placed a clique of generals in power with whom he shared the same political views but realized quickly that they lacked the ambition to become a truly popular national leadership and had failed to reach the broad sections of the lower classes, especially urban workers, women, and immigrants.

He became Minister of Labor in 1944 and supported legislation to raise wages and grant special privileges to favored unions. Suspicion of his policies led to an attempt by rivals to force him from power but loyal labor leaders rallied mass demonstrations to protest his imprisonment. This support engineered his release and success in national presidential elections in 1946. Perón's appeal was also linked to policies that typified what many lower class Argentines defined as virtues such as national pride, resentment of snobs, intellectuals and aristocrats, success in football, the tango, and a contempt of homosexuality.

Opposition of the Communists, Borges and 'Liberal' Intellectuals

During World War II, the Communist Party line from Moscow was to support the Allied cause after the German invasion of the USSR, a step that led to Perón posing as the benefactor of the working class. He intervened to support striking workers, including those working for the British owned firms, a step criticized by the Communists as hurting the allied war effort. Having come to power as a candidate of the Labor Movement, Perón proclaimed a new ideology of social justice that he argued was more in line with Argentine reality than the "class struggle." In his ideology, all classes had to work in harmony for the common good. The economic prosperity resulting from Argentina's status as a neutral country and the demand for its meat and grain exports were cleverly used to increase real wages, making it appear that Perón was the true friend of the working class. This isolated the previously strong influence that Communist and Socialist parties had exercised within the unions. Perón used his influence and charisma to replace union leaders with communist or socialist sympathies with his cronies and by appealing to the workers that real bread and butter issues would be given more sympathy by a government in his hands. At the same time, he explained to employers that his policies ultimately benefitted them by ensuring fututre labor peace. His policies granted collective bargaining to the unions that increasingly became dependent on his good will. The Communist Party lost support and felt itselt outmaneuvered by Perón's success. Reluctantly, they had to support him until they saw a chance that his fall from power would allow them to again take charge of the worker'smovement. For many Argentine workers, the period 1943-53 was the "Golden Age" of Peronism.

Argentina's most renowned author, Nobel prize laureate Jorge Luis Borges, became his country's most esteemed writer and philosopher but expressed an unremitting hatred of Perón and his two wives with political ambitions – Evita and Isabella who also became President of Argentina. His dislike began in the 1940s even before Perón became President for the first time. Borges was a classical liberal who had favored the Spanish Republic and objected to Perón's fascination and approval of Mussolini and in particular to his support of Nazi Germany. When Perón became President, Borges was fired from his post as municipal librarian and offered the position of Poultry and Rabbit Inspector of the Buenos Aires Markets to humiliate him.

Perón was not content with this but even imprisoned the writer's mother and sister. After Perón's fall in 1955, Borges became Director of the National Library almost simultaneously with the onset of full blindness, to which he remarked, "*I speak of God's splendid irony in granting me at once 800,000 books and darkness.*" He became professor of English literature at the University of Buenos Aires, and taught there from 1955 to 1970.

Borges never ceased his opposition while Perón remained in office, or after the coup which deposed him, nor during all the intervening years. Shortly after the success of the Peronists in the 1973 elections, he gave an interview to a Brazilian newspaper and stated *"When I think of the cases of torture, I have the impression that my country is disintegrating morally as well as economically."* Following the death of Juan Perón, he was succeeded by his third wife Isabella who, after being deposed and exiled herself, continued in the leadership position of the Justicialismo Party. When she was overthrown in March 1976, Borges wept with joy and upon meeting the engineer of the coup, Colonel Videla, he thanked him for "*having liberated the country from the infamy which we bore.*" Borges spoke too soon however, and the Peronist influence has continued in one form or another to the present day.

Borges' hatred of Perón stemmed not simply from the principles of opposition to a demagogue and dictator who practiced torture and suppressed civil liberties. It was also part of the old struggle in Argentina between a populist appeal to the masses that downgraded the respect for education, erudition, high culture and art that Borges had grown up with and which he felt had been prostituted by Perón and his wives.

If any further proof were needed of the diverse, often contradictory nature of General Juan Perón and his bases of support in the country, it has to be his fall from power under the joint attack of The Catholic Church and a Free Press headed by the great Buenos Aires liberal journal *La Prensa*. This was followed by eighteen years of exile in the Spain of General Franco only to return and then win the presidency by a landslide victory in what all observers agree were free and honest elections. Even more remarkable was the growth of his wife Eva's status as an adored icon of the masses symbolized so effectively in the musical *Evita*.

Although Perón himself did not encourage antisemitism the Peronist legacy in Argentina has taken on this dimension with the popularity of Fidel Castro in Cuba and his pro-Soviet and pro-Arab foreign policy and the growing demonization of Israel so common now in many third world countries hungry for the attention of the oil rich Arab world.

Perón's Conflict with the Great Buenos Aires daily Newspaper *La Prensa*

The new editor of *La Prensa* following his grandfather's retirement in 1943 was Alberto Gainza Paz, son of the founder's daughter. The new military junta had placed Colonel Perón in the position of a centralized office of information on "official news" limiting the activities of the real free press. Journalists had to register with the Government or be barred from working. On April 26, 1944, Peron suspended *La Prensa* for five days as punishment. He followed this step by urging his goons to boycott it, plaster the walls of surrounding buildings with anti-*La Prensa* leaflets and setting up loudspeakers across the street to blast insults at the editors, but the newspaper refused to bow. The gauntlet had been thrown. From that moment, all those who supported Perón knew that the niceties of a liberal regime such as freedom of the press were a thing of the past.

During the war, *La Prensa* had attacked the government's sympathy for the Axis powers. On the day the war ended with a final allied victory over Japan, Perón's strong armed thugs invaded the offices of *La Prensa*, bombed it and put Paz under arrest. In the eyes of world opinion, Argentina could hardly be considered an ally.

Further actions were taken against the newspaper in 1947 and in January, 1951, the government-controlled Union of News Vendors demanded *La Prensa* allow the union to handle its circulation. The editors refused and appealed to the police, a hopeless gesture. The 1,300 loyal employees of the paper kept working in spite of intimidation and on the night of January 26-27, Perón's men blockaded the plant. When the staff tried to enter the building, armed Peronistas opened fire. One workman was killed, and 14 were wounded followed by seizure of the paper by the government. Most of its staff left Argentina. Alberto Paz escaped in a small boat over the Rio de la Plata to find refuge at his mother's ranch in Uruguay.

Following Perón's overthrow, Paz returned to Argentina in February, 1956 to take over the paper again and the first issue to appear under his control was numbered 29,476 ignoring the years Perón had controlled the paper. In a short time, it once again became the leading newspaper in the country and regained its prestige.

Eva Perón's Growing Influence and Cult Status

As First Lady of Argentina from 1945 to 1952, Eva Perón was generally regarded as the most powerful woman in the world and referred to officially as the country's "Spiritual Leader." The "Cinderella from the Pampas," was a common nickname for her idealization by many of the country's poor who identified with her humble origins. She had grown up uneducated in a small rural town, been looked down on as an illegitimate daughter and an actress who had slept her way into fame but rapidly acquired a taste for elegance and glamorous style. When she met and married General Juan Perón, she added greatly to his support among the poor both in the slums of the big cities as well as in the countryside.

Perón's Fall

Severe economic problems were not sufficient to cause a decline of popularity among Perón's most ardent supporters. It was his apparent lecherous behavior towards a 14 year old girl, Nelly Rivas, who, after several meetings as part of a Peronist girls' club to learn fencing, swimming and motorcycling, began "helping with house chores" and then moved in with him. This, of course, was also a terrible slight to the memory of the sainted "Evita."

The growing dissatisfaction of the Catholic Church that had never fully endorsed Perón's worship of the state as the source of all authority led to increased tensions with the church. This was followed by the setting up of a rival Catholic trade union to which Perón responded with verbal threats against priests "meddling in politics." Although frequently cast as a "rightwing dictator," that many observers immediately and automatically assume means support for the established church. Perón was undone by his conflict with the Church.

Several priests were arrested and imprisoned followed by Perón shutting down Catholic newspapers and banning religious processions. Followers in the street demonstrations he organized in his support chanted the slogan of "Priests NO, Perón YES!" He threw some priests in jail and closed Catholic papers. Hoping for support from liberals, he had Congress legalize divorce and remove religious instruction from the schools. Going even farther, Perón granted legitimacy to children born out of wedlock, and legalized prostitution.

The Church then incited mass demonstrations and utilized the slogan of, "Is it Christ or Perón?" The Congress under his control expelled two Argentine priests and on June 16, 1955, the Vatican excommunicated those responsible for the expulsion, without naming anyone specifically. On that same day, the Airforce and Navy launched a coup, and airplanes bombed Perón's home. He survived, but 350 civilians were killed in the assault.

His strength had always rested in the support from the Army that remained loyal to him and opposed the takeover by the Navy and Airforce. They launched a counter-attack and suppressed the coup. Perón's supporters then rioted and looted the Buenos Aires Cathedral. They destroyed the headquarters of the archdiocese and burned several Catholic churches. Perón pretended to denounce these excesses and made changes in his cabinet. In September, 1955 to show popular support, a delegation from the government controlled unions offered to provide Perón with armed workers' militias, an idea that Evita had originally proposed during a previous crisis.

This however proved to be the last straw. The Army's leaders did not want another rival military force. They were fed up with Perón and the armed forces fought each other again, for three days, a mini-civil war raged in which several thousand died. Perón took refuge in the Paraguayan embassy where he wrote a goodbye letter to Nelly Rivas, signed "Daddy" and then went into exile, first to Paraguay and then to Venezuela. Anti-Perón mobs then broke into Perón's several luxurious homes and ransacked them, an example of how fickle populism of any kind can be.

Perón's Shadow 1955-73

In spite of his humiliating fall from power, Argentina's inability to solve its major economic problems and notably the ruinous runaway inflation that had been accelerated by Perón's policies of generous welfare subsidies and protected national industries, contributed to a growing nostalgia for Peronism. Attempts to rein in these policies led to demonstrations and unstable governments with periodic military intervention. Because the government's policies had tried to reverse some of the popular measures taken by Perón, much of the opposition focused on recalling and restoring his heritage. Thus arose the phenomenon of what has been called "Leftwing Peronism" (ignoring many anti-intellectual cultural elements) and calls for his return from exile to lead the nation again. Although opposed by a broad coalition of forces that could be defined as both Left and Right, the strong street based neighborhood and union cadres of the Peronista movement had considerable organizational strength and staying power and won handily, bringing Juan Perón back in triumph.

After receiving an "invitation" from the Military Government, Perón returned to Argentina in 1973. He was elected president in free and fair elections and his third wife, the unstable Isabel de Perón, was elected as his vice-president. She succeeded him after his death on July 1, 1974. During his short term and that of his wife's, problems were exacerbated and the military found that it had no choice but to once again seize power in 1976.

The Power of Peronism Without Perón

In spite of all the instability of the Peronist era, it appears that Argenitina cannot escape his legacy. The continuing economic problems especially ruinous inflation, the weakening of the middle class, disastrous adventurism of the lost war in the Malvinas (Falklands Islands), the legendary 'good times' of Juan and Eva Perón continue to exercise a fascination and a political power that seems to defy gravity. More than any other country, Argentina's political history over the past eighty years can be framed in terms of Peronism, a philosophy uniting many elements of both the Left and the Right against the Center.

In its own words, Perón's Party, still in existence today (but divided into antagonistic competing wings) and called *El Partido Justicialista* (PJ) describes itself as an *"Argentine Political Party, a continuation of the Peronista Party, founded by General Juan Domingo Perón in 1947. Its original principal banner is The Defense of the Workers, remain-*

ing since then a deep attachment to the Working Class and the Unions."

21

Israel: From Darling of the Left to Pariah State

The belief, never challenged by the media, that the United States was wholly or largely responsible for fully supporting Israel on the ground from the very beginning of its independence in May, 1948 is wholly without any foundation in fact.

The world has been inundated with a tsunami of Arab propaganda and crocodile tears shed for the "Palestinians" who have reveled in what they refer to as their Catastrophe or Holocaust ("Nakba" in Arabic). Their plight has been accompanied by unremitting criticism that the United States was the principal architect that stood behind Israel with money, manpower and arms. The fact is that President Truman eventually decided against the pro-Arab "professional opinion" of his Secretary of State, General George Marshall and the Arabists of the State Department. He accorded diplomatic recognition to the new Jewish state but never considered active military aid.

His own memoirs recall how he felt betrayed by State Department officials and the American U.N. Ambassador, Warren Austin, who "pulled the rug out from under him" one day after he promised Zionist leader Chaim Weitzman support for partition. Truman's memoirs revealed a bitter contempt for the professional "striped-pants" boys of the eastern Ivy League Colleges who were the old-timers in the State Department. Although sometimes angered by Jewish pressure on the question of the Zionist movement's goal of a Jewish state, Truman's strong Baptist sentiments and basic human decency won out in reaching his decision against the "experts" to recognize the State of Israel and his comments that:

> "Hitler had been murdering Jews right and left. I saw it, and I dream about it even to this day. The Jews needed some place

where they could go. It is my attitude that the American government couldn't stand idly by while the victims [of] Hitler's madness are not allowed to build new lives."[1]

American Jewish voting in the 1948 Presidential election leaned heavily for President Truman but also cast a substantial number of votes for third party "Progressive" leader Henry Wallace who had spoken out even more strongly on behalf of American support for the Zionist position and aid to Israel. It was actually not until the administration of President John Kennedy in the early 1960s that American arms shipments were made.

Soviet Diplomatic Support

The struggle of the Jewish community in Palestine was endorsed completely by what was then called "enlightened public opinion," above all by the political Left. Andrei Gromyko, at the UN, asserted the right of *"the Jews of the whole world to the creation of a state of their own,"* something no official of the U.S. State Department has ever acknowledged. Soviet support in the U.N. for partition brought along an additional two votes (the Ukrainian and Bielorussian Republics within the USSR and the entire Soviet dominated bloc of East European states). Taking (as always) their lead from Moscow, the (hitherto anti-Zionist) Palestinian communist organizations merged their separate Arab and Jewish divisions in October, 1948, giving unconditional support to the Israeli war effort and urging the Israel Defense Forces to *"drive on toward the Suez Canal and hand British Imperialism a stinging defeat!"*

World Wide Support from the Left

The most famous and colorful personality of the Spanish Re-

---

1 Quoted from footage of Truman speaking, presented in the film *The 50 Years War*. A slightly different quotation appears in the book, *Harry S. Truman and the Founding of Israel*, by Michael T. Benson. 1997, p. 64.

public in exile, the Basque Communist delegate to the Cortes (Spanish Parliament), Dolores Ibarruri, also known as "La Pasionaria," who had gone to the Soviet Union following the Civil War, issued a proclamation in 1948 saluting the new State of Israel and comparing the invading Arab armies to the Fascist uprising that had destroyed the Republic. Just a few months earlier, the hero of the American Left, the great Afro-American folk singer, Paul Robeson had sung in a gala concert in Moscow and electrified the crowd with his rendition of the Yiddish Partisan Fighters Song.

Jewish Attempts to Buy Arms and Czech Approval

The major Arab armies who invaded the newly born Jewish state were British led, equipped, trained and supplied. The Syrian army was French-equipped and had taken orders from the Vichy government in resisting the British led invasion of the country assisted by Australian troops, Free French units and Palestinian-Jewish volunteer forces in 1941. In their War of Independence, the Israelis depended on smuggled weapons from the West and Soviet and Czech ams.

The leaders of the Yishuv (Jewish community in Palestine), already in the summer of 1947, intended to purchase arms and sent Dr. Moshe Sneh (the Chief of the European Branch of the Jewish Agency, a leading member of the centrist General Zionist Party who later moved far leftward and became head of the Israeli Communist Party) to Prague in order to improve Jewish defenses. He was surprised by the sympathy towards Zionism and by the interest in arms export on the side of the Czech Government. Sneh met with the Deputy Foreign Minister Vladimir Clementis, who succeeded the non-Communist and definitely pro-Zionist Prime Minister Jan Masaryk. Sneh and Clementis discussed the possibility of arms provisions for the Jewish state and the Czechs gave their approval.

In January, 1948 Jewish representatives were sent by Ben-Gurion to meet with General Ludvik Svoboda, the Minister of National Defense, and sign the first contract for Czech military aid. Four transport routes were used to ship weapons to Palestine, all via Communist countries: a) the Northern route: via Poland and the Baltic Sea, b) the

Southern route: via Hungary, Yugoslavia and the Adriatic Sea, c) via Hungary, Romania and the Black Sea, d) by air, via Yugoslavia to Palestine.

At first, a "Skymaster" plane chartered from the U.S. to help in ferrying weapons to Palestine from Europe was forced by the FBI to return to the USA. By the end of May the Israeli Army (IDF) had absorbed about 20,000 Czech rifles, 2,800 machine-guns and over 27 million rounds of ammunition. Two weeks later an additional 10,000 rifles, 1,800 machine-guns and 20 million rounds of ammunition arrived. One Czech-Israeli project that alarmed the Western intelligence was the so-called Czech Brigade, a unit composed of Jewish veterans of "Free Czechoslovakia," which fought with the British Army during WWII. The Brigade began training in August 1948 at four bases in Czechoslovakia.

Czech assistance to Israel's military strength comprised a) small arms, b) 84 airplanes - the outdated Czech built Avia S.199s, Spitfires and Messerschmidts that played a major role in the demoralization of enemy troops, and c) military training and technical maintenance. On January 7, 1949, the Israeli air-force, consisting of several Spitfires and Czech built Messerschmidt Bf-109 fighters (transferred secretly from Czech bases to Israel), shot down five British-piloted Spitfires flying for the Egyptian air-force over the Sinai desert causing a major diplomatic embarrassment for the British government. According to British reports, based on informants within the Czech Government, the total dollar income from export of arms and military services to the Middle East in 1948 was over $28 million, and Israel received 85% of this amount. As late as 1951, Czech Spitfires continued to arrive in Israel by ship from the Polish port of Gydiniya-Gdansk (Danzig). Since May, 2005 the Military Museum in Prague has displayed a special exhibition on the Czech aid to Israel in 1948.[2]

In contrast, the American State Department declared an embargo on all weapons and war material to both Jews and Arabs in Pal-

---

2 Waller, Uri *Israel Between East and West; Israel's Foreign Policy Orientation, 1948-56,* Cambridge University Press 1990. Zdroje Lederer and Vucinich, *The Soviet Union and the Middle East; The Post-WWII Era,* Stanford University, California 1974, M.Confino and Sh. Shamir, *The USSR and the Middle East, Israel,* Universities Press 1973, Susan Hattis, *Political Dictionary of the State of Israel,* Jerusalem Publishing House, 1987.

estine, a move that only had one effect in practice. There was no Arab community in North America to speak of and given the fact that a substantial and overwhelmingly sympathetic Jewish community in the United States was anxious to aid the Jewish side, the embargo simply prevented a large part of this intended aid from reaching its destination. The small trickle of supplies and arms reaching Israel from North America was accomplished by smuggling. The U.S. vote in favor of partition was only de facto reflecting the State Department's care not to unnecessarily offend the Arab states whereas the Soviet vote recognized Israel de jure.

Even with Czech weapons and Soviet aid, Israel would undoubtedly have been unable to halt the Arab invasion without a massive inflow of manpower. The United States, Canada and Europe provided no more than 3000 volunteers, many of them combat hardened veterans from both the European and Pacific theaters of war plus a few score idealistic youngsters from the Zionist movements with no combat experience or training. But their numbers were a drop in the bucket compared to more than 200,000 Jewish immigrants from the Soviet dominated countries in Eastern Europe, notably, Poland, Bulgaria (almost 95% of the entire Jewish community) Romania, Yugoslavia, Czechoslovakia, the former Baltic States and even the Soviet Union who emigrated to Israel arriving in time to reach the front lines or replenish the depleted ranks of civilian manpower. Without both the arms and manpower sent from the "Socialist Camp" to aid the nascent Israeli state, it would have been crushed.

The About-Face of The Party Line on Zionism

Jewish Marxist theoreticians the world over including several high ranking Party activists, all dedicated anti-religious and anti-Zionist communists had followed the Party Line and even praised a vicious pogrom by Muslim fanatics carried out against ultra-Orthodox Jews in the town of Hebron in Palestine in 1929. The Party Line then was that the Arabs masses were demonstrating their anti-imperialist sentiment against British rule and its sponsorship of Zionism. In 1947, when Stalin was convinced that the Zionists would evict the British from Palestine, the Party Line turned about face. Following Soviet recognition and aid to Israel in 1948-49, both the *Daily Worker* and the Yiddish language communist daily in the U.S. *Freiheit* (Freedom) outdid one another to explain the new party line that.... *"Palestine had become an important settlement of 600,000 souls, having developed a common national economy, a growing national culture and the first elements of Palestinian Jewish statehood and self-government."*

A 1947 CP-USA resolution entitled "Work Among the Jewish Masses" berated the Party's previous stand and proclaimed that "*Jewish Marxists have not always displayed a positive attitude to the rights and interests of the Jewish People, to the special needs and problems of our own American Jewish national group and to the interests and rights of the Jewish Community in Palestine.*" The new reality that had been created in Palestine was a "Hebrew nation" that deserved the right to self-determination. Remarkably, the Soviet propaganda machine even praised the "far Right" underground groups of the Irgun and "Stern Gang" for their campaign of violence against the British authorities.

Church Support in the U.S.

The Jewish cause in Palestine enjoyed the support of a large section of mainstream and liberal Protestant churches and not primarily the "lobby" of Protestant Fundamentalists as is often portrayed today by critics of Zionism. As early as February 1941 and in spite of the wholehearted desire of the American Protestant establishment not to risk involvement in World War II, Reinhold Niebhur spoke out convincingly through the journal he founded *Christianity and Crisis* and sounded a clarion call of warning about Nazism. Its final goals were not simply the eradication of the Jews but the extirpation of Christianity and the abolition of the entire heritage of Christian and humanistic culture. This is the only kind of a "World Without Zionism" that the Iranian and Arab leaders long for. Niebhur based his views not on any literal "Evangelical" interpretation of Biblical promises but on the essentials of justice for the nations and also called for some form of compensation to those Arabs in Palestine who might be displaced if their own leaders refused to make any compromise possible.

Nazi and Reactionary Support for the Arabs

There was nothing "progressive" about those who supported the Arab side. The acknowledged leader of the Palestinian Arab cause from 1931 to 1949 was the Grand Mufti of Jerusalem, Haj Amin al-Husseini, who had fled from Palestine to Iraq to exile in Berlin where he led the "Arab office," met with Hitler whom he called "the Protector of Islam," served the Germans in Bosnia where he was instrumental in raising Muslim volunteers among the Bosnians to work with the SS. At the end of the war, the Yugoslav government declared him a war criminal and sentenced him to death. Palestinian Arabs still regard him as their original supreme leader. Lending active support to the Arab war effort were Falangist volunteers from Franco's Spain, Bosnian Muslims and Nazi renegades who had escaped the Allies in Europe.

The close relationship between the Nazi movement and the German government under Hitler in courting the Arab Palestinian and Pan-Arab attempt to act as a fifth column in the Middle East has been thoroughly researched[3] by two German scholars. Their book documents the Arab sympathies for Nazism, particularly in Palestine and German attempts to mobilize and encourage the Arabs with their ideology, especially the Muslim Brotherhood, and the forces around the Grand Mufti of Jerusalem.

Nazi radio broadcasts to the Arabs between 1939 and 1945 constantly proclaimed the natural German sympathy for the Arab cause against Zionism and the Jews. German Middle East experts stressed "the natural alliance" between National Socialism and Islam. And such experts as the former German Ambassador in Cairo, Eberhard von Stohrer, reported to Hitler in 1941 that "*the Fuhrer already held an outstanding position among the Arabs because of his fight against the Jews.*"

The two German scholars Cüppers and Mallmann quote many original documents from the Nazi archives on this close relationship. From the late 1930s, the planning staffs dealing with the external affairs of the Reich in the Head Office of Reich Security (RSHA, *Reichssecu-*

---

3 Klaus-Michael Mallmann and Martin Cüppers *Halbmond und Hakenkreuz. Das "Dritte Reich", die Araber und Palästina*, (Crescent Moon and Swastika: The Third Reich, the Arabs, and Palestine) 2006.

ritathauptamt, originally under the monstrous Gestapo-chief Reinhard Heydrich), sought to engulf the Arabian Peninsula and win control of the region's oil reserves. They dreamt of a pincer movement from the north via a defeated Soviet Union, and from the south via the Near East and Persia, in order to separate Great Britain from India.

Thanks to the counteroffensive of the Red Army before Moscow in 1941/1942 and at Stalingrad in 1942/1943, and the defeat of the German Africa Corps at El Alamein, the Germans never managed to actively intervene in the Middle East militarily although they helped spark a pro-Axis coup in Baghdad in 1941.

Britain and the Abstentions

In the vote on partition in the UN, apart from the states with large Muslim minorities (like Yugoslavia and Ethiopia), the Arabs managed only to wheedle a few abstentions and one lone negative vote out of the most corrupt non-Muslim states. These included Cuba (voted against partition) and Mexico (abstained) eager to demonstrate their independence of U.S. influence and Latin American countries whose regimes had been pro-Axis until the final days of World War II such as Argentina and Chile (both abstained).

All the West European nations (except Great Britain) voted for partition as well. No other issue to come before the U.N. has had such unanimous support from the European continent or cut across the ideological divide of communist and western sectors. The Jewish state was even supported by Richard Crossman, a member of the Anglo-American Committee of Inquiry on Palestine who had been handpicked by Britain's anti-Zionist Foreign Secretary, Ernest Bevin. Crossman, taking a principled stand, refused to endorse the Labor Party Line.

He had visited the Displaced Persons camps in Germany where Jews who had sought entry into Palestine were being detained. He realized that their sense of desperation derived from a world with no place which they as Jews could truly call home. He wrote that when he started out he was ready to believe that Palestine was the "problem," but his experiences made him realize that it was the "solution."

The Arab Lobby, the Oil Companies and the Leftwing *Nation* Magazine

For more than 70 years, the most powerful oil companies have effectively supported the Arab cause and lobbied against American diplomatic, military and economic support for Israel.[4] The State Department effectively backed the claims of Arab leaders and Middle East "experts" that such support would undermine British and American cultural, political economic and commercial interests throughout the region. The State Department and oil companies' views were given considerable credence by President Roosevelt following his meeting with King Ibn Saud in February 1945 at the Suez Canal.

Both the State Department and the CIA argued on the basis of their familiarity with their military intelligence that the Jews would be incapable of resisting an invasion of Palestine by a combined force of several Arab states and that the only way to secure a Jewish state would be protection provided by U.S. troops. Warren Austin, U.S. ambassador to the United Nations on instructions from the State Department met with Zionist leader Moshe Shertok (Sharret) on May 8, 1948 only one week before the Declaration of Israeli Independence to argue for a postponement of the declaration arguing that the Jews' position was hopeless and that the Arabs held the strategic high ground, had regular armies and were much better armed and better trained than the guerilla forces of the Hagana and the Irgun.

The editor of the most prominent leftwing publication in the United States, *The Nation*, Freda Kirchwey, wrote to President Truman in May, 1948 informing him that James Terry Duce, the Vice-President of Aramco was trying to undermine his policy and had met with Azzam Pasha, Secretary General of the Arab League to discuss possible alternatives to Jewish statehood. Duce had argued that a Jewish state would become a Soviet client state because of the predominance of Leftwing political parties in the Zionist movement and a pro-Russian orientation of large numbers of East European Jews who were grateful to the Soviet Union's role in defeating the Nazis.[5]

---

4 Bard, Mitchell *The Arab Lobby; The Invisible Alliance that Undermines America's Interests in the Middle East,* Harper. New York, 2010.
5 Bard, ibid. p.30.

What Today's So Called " Progressive" Jews Have Forgotten or Ignore

Leon Uris unapologetically made a pro-Israel film, *Exodus,* only a decade after every Jewish movie producer had turned down making the film *Gentleman's Agreement* (1947, starring Gregory Peck) about polite antisemitism. It was made into a film by the great Greek-American producer, Elia Kazan who was later turned on with vengeance for cooperating with the House un-American Activities Committee revealing communist influence in Hollywood. Uris himself had been in the front lines in Guadalcanal and Tarawa island and felt an immense respect for the Israelis who defeated the invading Arab armies and defied the legion of pro-Arab diplomats in the British Foreign Office and the leadership of the Labor Party (a sin the British Left has never forgiven).

Today's crowd of "progressive" Jewish actors and entertainers outdo even the writers Uris attacked fifty years ago. Woody Allen, Barbra Streisand, Dustin Hoffman and Richard Dreyfus ("The Gang of Four") were among the most visible and acidic critics of American policy in Iraq and called for the impeachment of President Bush. They naturally proclaim themselves to be fervent supporters of Israel without realizing how convoluted their antics appear to others. (See Chapters 2 and 10.)

Many Israelis reject their elitism of supposed high moral values so out of place in the Arab Middle East and as remote from the real world as were the great majority of the victims of the Holocaust whose Jewish values prevented them from attributing such evil to the Germans. Two of these stars, Streisand and Hoffman played the lead roles in self-mocking doubly ironic roles of a liberated Jewish couple in the comedy "Meet the Fockers" (a sequel, "Little Fockers", has appeared and perhaps we can expect the spectacle of many future Fockers). This is a grotesque example of art imitating reality (or is it the other way round?).

The Jewish couple in the films have nothing but disdain for traditional American manly heroic virtues of military valor or achievement in sports nor do they demonstrate any respect whatsoever for what were classical Jewish virtues of learning, decorum and piety. They exhibit the most crass, offensive loud and vulgar behavior, constantly embarrassing their son. For them and much of the Left, the very concept of civility is regarded with contempt.

Whatever the differences between secular and religious Israelis, they pale before the monumental differences that separate life in the State of Israel with all its inherent promises, risks and dangers from the Diaspora's ultra idealized concerns and sensibilities. This is as true today was it was in 1948. The Political Left today refuses to admit (or remember) that it stood wholeheartedly behind Israel much like the exercise performed by Stalin's staff of photographers who could surgically extract and obliterate old time Bolsheviks who had fallen out of his favor.

A Brief Aside: The Discomfort of the Cosmopolitan Jewish Left with Sovereignty, Pride, Heroism and "Hadar"

We are three generations removed from Zev Jabotinsky's proud declaration of the desirability of a reborn Hebrew state sharing in the great gift of "the nations," one that still strikes many Diaspora Jews as anachronistic in spite of the Holocaust and the specter of nationalist turmoil and ethnic divisiveness almost everywhere.[6] For some Jews in positions of wealth, power and comfort who are either entirely secular in outlook or affiliated with the Reform Movement in the United States and Western Europe and far removed from any sense of a Jewish ethnic identity, Israel has become an embarrassment, one that threatens their self-image as profoundly cosmopolitan, liberal and understanding of others' grievances. For them, the Israelis, as fellow Jews, living amidst the cauldron of a strident, militant, exclusivist Islam and the legacy of repeated Arab nation-state failures, should shoulder the burden and responsibility of giving up much of their sovereignty for the delusion and illusion of rescuing the 'Palestinians' and thus, helping to ensure what they believe will be a "peaceful world order."

The animating spirit of Zionism and the nationalism of other small nations was pride and sovereign self-respect. For Jews, denied of

---

6 See Shalit, Yaakov *Jabotinsky and the Revisionist Movement, 1925-1948* (Frank Cass Publishers, London) 1988

a homeland for almost 2,000 years, it could only be obtained in the face of an immensely hostile Gentile environment. It was a revolutionary call for Jews to shoulder all the obligations of nationhood and take up the sword in self-defense. This meant doing all the dirty work of soldiers, jailers, farmers and street cleaners instead of preaching to the Gentiles on how these affairs should be properly managed.

Borrowing from the vision of Italian nationalist leader Mazzini, the Revisionist Zionist leader, Zev Jabotinsky (who had lived and studied in Italy for three years), proclaimed that each and every nation makes its own contribution to human culture within the sovereign body of nationhood in order to fulfill its task and mission. This is still foreign, and appears even "crude" to those Jews whose cosmopolitan vision of their identity, much like the ultra-Orthodox, believe they have a universal mission to bring "God's word" (in their own liberal-cosmopolitan interpretation) to other nations.

For Jabotinsky and Menachem Begin, often labeled as "Fascists" by their critics, the concept of hadar, an explicitly Hebrew concept remains fundamentally at odds with the century long attraction of many Jewish intellectuals for the illusion of socialism and their false sense of noblesse oblige for the "masses." The essence of hadar is untranslatable. Literally, it means shine or glow. It implies chivalry in conduct and life-style, a combination of "spiritual beauty, respect, self-esteem, immaculate grooming, politeness, faithfulness and integrity."

These are precisely the values that have always been mocked by the Left, their cultural icon, Woody Allen; and most regrettably by the overwhelming majority of the Reform/Reconstructionist Rabbinate. The letter addressed to Rupert Murdoch and published in *The Wall Street Journal* on January 27, 2011, "International Holocaust Remembrance Day" was signed by 400 rabbis, mostly from Reform and Reconstructionist congregations. It excoriated Glenn Beck, Fox News and Robert Ailes, President of Fox News, a media consultant for several Republican presidents.

These rabbis have slandered Glenn Beck, the most outstanding defender in the media of the State of Israel in its life and death struggle with Islamic fanaticism and more than any other media personality, whose staff has done serious research into the shared roots of totalitarian and antisemitic policies of Nazism and Soviet Communism under

Stalin. Beck's crime was to dare to criticize George Soros, one of the wealthiest men in the world, whose political activism has consistently funded Leftwing and anti-Israel causes. Soros himself has claimed the mantle of a "holocaust survivor" in the face of statements he has made regarding his own total estrangement from his Jewish origin.

Those who take Beck to task by asserting that "No one has the right to question the tactics used by a teenager in order to survive" may indeed argue a point that it is impossible to put oneself into the shoes of someone else faced with a grave threat and requiring any subterfuge to avoid detection. Their moral point is weakened however by failing to see the consistency of Soros' record and his own hypocritical use of the status as a "survivor" to escape his moral and ethical failings. Soros is someone who escaped the Holocaust by doing everything possible to reject any solidarity with an unwanted Jewish identity, then boasting about it and cynically using his father's reputation as a prominent Esperanto author to reach safety in Britain only to subsequently disassociate himself wholly from that cause as well when it no longer served his purposes.

Convenient Amnesia

Today's media never attempt (not even the History Channel) to explain how it was Soviet and East Bloc aid and not American support that was the crucial factor which brought both essential weapons and manpower to the beleaguered newborn Israeli state in 1948-49 and enabled it to turn the tide of battle and justifiably hand the Palestinian Arabs and their allies their "Nakba." Soviet hopes that they might eventually pressure the new and profoundly democratic Israeli state to side with them in the Cold War were hopelessly naïve.

The Arabs cannot admit the truth of Soviet aid to Israel as it would rob them of their psychological advantage that they are victims who have the right to continually browbeat Western and especially American public opinion as responsible for their catastrophe. Amnesia is a common malady among politicians. Democrats and others who soured on American intervention in Iraq now have great difficulty remembering Iraqi aggression against Iran, Kuwait and the atrocities committed against the Kurds, Assyrians, Marsh Arabs and all opponents of the regime. Even President Bush and his supporters suffered from this amnesia and were reluctant or incapable of setting the record straight about 1948 and is all the more regrettable in the light of the fervent support, then, of the Left for Israel.

22

The Attraction of Jihad for the Far Right and Far Left:
Connecting the Dots

The Five Pillars of Islam are: the shahada or declaration that Allah is the only God and that Muhammad is his prophet, the haj (the pilgrimage to Mecca), sala (prayer five times a day), zaka (the giving of alms), and (saum), the month long fast from sun-up to sun-down during the month of Ramadan, yet the focus of attention of Islam's political geography and role in international affairs has always been JIHAD.

In order to understand jihad as a veritable sixth essential element in the spread of Islam historically and the threat it poses today, one must understand how Islam radically differs from other faiths and functions politically and geographically.

In Medieval Spain, numerous theological debates were held to discuss the relative merits and claims of the three monotheistic religions. Even though many centuries have passed, there is still a fundamental division among them. The Jews first discovered a path towards redemption and how to live in a just society according to God's commandments. They thereby believed they were setting an example by serving God as a nation and demonstrating their way of life to other peoples. This continued to be possible even after the destruction of the Temple and loss of Jewish independence in 70 AD.

Christians, on the other hand, believed that this was possible on an individual level through the agency of God's church and could be achieved by anyone no matter what his or her nationality, race or sex.

The radical interpretation of Islam (frequently referred to as "Islamism" and now in power in Iran) that has become a threat to the traditional Western model of the state requires a continual appraisal of a chess-board like map of what part of the world has been subdued and placed under Muslim rule FOREVER (no retreats or "do-overs" are allowed). In this regard, territories such as Israel, Spain, Chechnya, Greece, Bulgaria, Kosovo, Armenia and even large regions in China, Ethiopia, and India which were once under the sway of Muslim rulers are therefore considered submitted to Allah. They cannot be allowed to return to the Camp of War.

The *"Camp of Believers who have already submitted to the will of Allah and Muhammad's message,"* is referred to as the Dar al-Islam. Its success is to be measured on the political map to the extent it has prevailed over the other camp of non-believers (the infidels in the Dar al-Harb, or "Camp of War"). More than a matter of personal submission to the will of Allah, the Camp of War requires dominion over territory.

Dar al-Harb is used by Muslim scholars to define where Muslims are not in power and therefore not able to "practice their religion without interference." A non Muslim resident of the Dar al-Harb is called a harbi as opposed to a tolerated non-Muslim subject (dhimmi) living in a land within the Dar-al-Islam. A dhimmi has no rights, not even an unconditional right to live. For centuries, if a harbi from "outside" wanted to enter the territory of Dar al-Islam, Islamic tradition required a passage of safe-conduct. Sheikh Yusuf al-Qaradawi recently stated… *"It has been determined by Islamic law that the blood and property of people of Dar Al-Harb is not protected."*[1] Who is Al-Qaradawi? He is a highly respected and popular Egyptian theologian who appears regularly on Al-Jazeera and is the founder of IslamOnline – a popular website offering opinions and religious edicts ("fatwa").

He is considered to be a favorite Islamic scholar of the extremist Muslim Brotherhood in Egypt and for many years regarded as the chief opponent of the Mubarak regime. He is also regarded as the most prominent spokesman for rejecting the Universal Declaration of Human Rights and democracy as inappropriate for Muslims to follow. He has supported Palestinian suicide bomb attacks against Israeli civilians and demanded a worldwide Muslim reaction against Denmark in the wake of the Muhammad cartoons.

No reputable Muslim cleric in a Muslim majority state has

---

1 An interview with the prominent Arabic language newspaper in London, *Asharq-al Awsat*. July 19, 2003.

openly confronted Al-Qaradawi's interpretation of Jihad (Holy War) based on ultimate political-military confrontation with Dar al-Harb. Jihad is mentioned in the Koran more than 150 times. Literally, the word means "striving" or "struggle" but it is almost always mentioned in connection with appeals to devout believers to confront, conquer, convert and kill pagan non-believers or to humiliate and subdue Christians and Jews.

Who then are "moderate Muslims" that want to live in harmony with their neighbors but have a theological sword hanging over their heads? They are of two types, both of which seek to avoid ever having to explain their views to non-Muslims.

1. Believers who are far from the centers of Muslim political power such as West Africa and India. Muslim clerics and scholars in these areas have tended to stress Jihad as an internalized exhortation to "strive in the way of God," thereby overcoming man's baser instincts.

2. Rulers, whose security in office, has depended on a close tactical alliance with non-Muslim nations and are themselves targets of the "Islamist" movement everywhere. Prominent among these are the current Saudi dynasty of Arabia, the ruling Hashemite clan in the Kingdom of Jordan, the former regime of Hosni Mubarak in Egypt, the Persian Gulf Shiekhdoms - Qatar, Abu-Dhabi, etc., and the current leadership in the North African states of Morocco, and Algeria who have been subject to more than a decade long insurgency from native Islamist extremists. Mubarak and the Tunisian regime are now gone and the others are all walking on a tightrope.

Such rulers representing Muslim states that coexist and even depend upon more powerful "unbelieving states" that are part of the Dar al-Harb, have accepted the principle adopted by the Ottoman sultans that a protracted peace may be necessary. Rather than confront powerful non-Muslim states, especially the United States and the major European nations with the inconvenient and potentially embarrassing reality that they are only useful temporary allies who will inevitably be forced to recognize the superiority of Islam and submit to Dar al-Islam, a neutral "Dar al-Ahd" (Camp of Truce) was invented to define them.

Jihad in World War I

The 20th century has witnessed examples of jihad used as incitement to commit genocide and in two world wars in which a "selective jihad" was used by Muslim and tyrannical European regimes as allies to mobilize the political and economic resources of the Muslim world against Western civilization and democracy. In 1914, the only focus of Muslim power in the world was the Turkish Ottoman Empire whose sultan still commanded the respect and obedience of most of the world's Sunni Muslims whether or not they were citizens. The Turkish Sultan, Mahomet V, was the only acknowledged "Caliph" and he and his court in alliance with the "Young Turk" movement followed a pro-German line, convinced that a victory by the Central Powers would help reverse the backward slide of the empire and enable them to recover territory lost to the hated Russians who had connived to help liberate the Christian Slavic peoples and the Greeks from Turkish rule.

In response to the call for jihad, approximately a million and a half Armenians throughout the Turkish Empire died as a result of executions, mass violence, hunger and forced expulsions during 1915-1917. Several similar genocidal crimes against Greeks in the 1890s and again in the period 1919-1924 resulted in close to a million fatalities. In both cases, civilians, many of them aged men, women and children were the victims. All of the soldiers following the orders of their superiors were Muslims (Turks, Arabs, Kurds, Druze) convinced that they were following the justified edict of jihad.

The court of the previous Ottoman Sultan, Abdul Hamid II (deposed in 1909), had welcomed and flattered Kaiser Wilhelm II on his visit to Palestine in 1898 and expressed a favorable attitude towards the construction of a German financed Berlin to Baghdad railway. German military officers were involved in the training of both the Turkish army and navy. The controlled Turkish press represented the Kaiser in the most favorable light and hinted that he was considering conversion to Islam and regarded himself as a European "Protector of Islam." In a future European conflict, the Ottoman Sultan would endeavor to promote religious extremism by calling upon Sunni Muslims everywhere to join a "selective jihad" against the British, French and Russian infidels. The Germans with no Muslim subjects and Austria with only a few in Bosnia could be regarded as allies in spite of their Christian faith.

Mussolini and Hitler's Appeal to the Jihadists

For more than sixteen years since Mussolini's regime came to power in 1922, anti-Semitism was rejected by Fascist Italy. Like Kaiser Wilhelm however, Mussolini felt that considerations of power politics ultimately required favoring Muslim sensitivities to keep them as allies or acquire new ones rather than the potential benefits that Italy might derive from favoring the Jews. The Fascist movement in Italy was not favorably disposed towards the Catholic Church and resented the opposition the Vatican had demonstrated to Italian unification. Until the Lateran Treaty (1929) that recognized the sovereignty of the Vatican City State, relations between the Catholic Church and Mussolini's Fascist regime were cold and relations with Nazi Germany reached a low point in 1934 that brought Mussolini into direct confrontation with Hitler over the question of Austria's independence. (See Chapter 12.)

It was however, Mussolini's quest for a new and grand version of ancient Rome with colonial possessions in North Africa, naval supremacy in the Mediterranean ("Our Sea" – "Mare Nostrum"), the Italian desire for revenge against Abyssinia for the disastrous defeat suffered at Ethiopian hands at Adowa in 1896 that resulted in a total change of his position on a possible alliance with Zionism. In his view Italy had sacrificed much in World War I only to be denied the fruits of victory with an expanded colonial role in the Middle East and Africa. This led him to pursue an aggressive campaign that ultimately brought him into an alliance with Nazi Germany and Hitler whose ideology he had previously ridiculed.

In March 1937, Benito Mussolini opportunistically proclaimed himself as "Protector of Islam" following a state visit to the Italian colony of Libya where he opened a new military highway. The occasion was to mark the brutal suppression of resistance to Italian occupation that ended with the execution of a Senussi rebel leader, Omar al-Mukhtar. Italy simultaneously began a propaganda campaign designed to pacify Muslim sentiment around the Mediterranean and deflect anti-colonialist sentiment against the British and French presence in North Africa and the Middle East.

This policy included secret Italian support of the most extreme anti-Zionist of the Palestinian Muslim political figures, Haj Amin al-Husseini who had been installed in office by the British in 1931 even though he finished fourth in an election of Palestine's chief religious leader (mufti) by Muslim notables. The British tried to impress the Arab population that even though they were widely blamed for the Balfour Declaration and the Mandate for Palestine as a "Jewish National Home," they respected Muslim concerns and rights. Ironically, Italian support was provided for the same reason – exploitation of the mufti's appeal to the most radical fundamentalist Muslim religious sentiment in the expectation that they could "outbid" the British for Arab sympathy.

Mussolini, in a typically extravagant and bizarre dramatization of his manly image, and newly established title of Protector of Islam, arranged for a ceremonial girding the "Sword of Islam" in Libya in 1937. At the ceremony in Tripoli, he declared "Italy will always be the friend and protector of Islam throughout the world." Italian Foreign minister Ciano noted that Islam was totally compatible with the Fascist outlook and added that *"The Islamic world, in accordance with its traditions, loves in the Duce, the wisdom of the statesman united to the action of the warrior."*

In the Italian campaign of aggression against Abyssinia, the Catholic Church was exploited by Mussolini to lend its approval to a war it characterized as one on "behalf of Western civilization against African barbarism." Nevertheless, a large proportion of the Italian forces were Muslim recruits from Libya, Eritrea, Somaliland and the Muslim dominated Galla region who were jihad-inspired volunteers, cynically exploited by the Italians to fight against the "infidel" Christian Ethiopians.

Hitler and Germany's Endorsement of Jihad against the Jews

In a telegram to Haj Amin al-Husseini, on November 2, 1943, Heinrich Himmler wrote;

"The National Socialist Movement of greater Germany has since its inception, inscribed upon its flag, the fight against world Jewry. It has therefore followed with particular sympathy the struggle of freedom-loving Arabs, especially in Palestine against Jewish interlopers. In the recognition of this enemy and of the common fight against it lies the firm foundation of the natural alliance that exists between the National Socialist greater Germany and the freedom loving Muslims of the whole world."

To all Muslims aware of the telegram, this meant Germany endorsed the mufti's call to jihad.

When the British quelled an Arab revolt in Palestine in 1938-39, the mufti fled to Iraq where he helped orchestrate a pro-Axis coup and vicious pogrom against the Jews of Baghdad. Thanks to the counteroffensive of the Red Army in front of Moscow in 1941/1942, at Stalingrad in 1942/1943, and the defeat of the German Africa Corps at El Alamein, the Germans never managed to actively intervene militarily in the Middle East. Many Bosnian Muslims were nevertheless recruited by the Mufti and served in a special SS division. For this, he was sentenced to death in absentia after the war by a court in Yugoslavia under Marshall Tito.

The USSR Turns a Blind Eye to Jihad

In spite of Jihad's appeal to the forces of the Far Right regimes of the Kaiser of Imperial Germany, Hitler and Mussolini, the USSR turned a blind eye to the potential threat it posed. The unrest and anti-Western sentiment of Muslim peoples seeking to throw off the yoke of European colonial domination in the Near East, North and East Africa, India and Indonesia all offered the foreign policy of the USSR a fertile field for propaganda and economic and diplomatic initiatives. The USSR imposed its brand of Communism on the subject peoples of central Asia in the Muslim majority republics for seventy years and Islam was strictly regulated and restrained. On the foreign policy front however the USSR could appear as a force opposing Western colonialism and by default, a friend of Islam. Soviet and Czech diplomatic and even military support for the partition of Palestine and aid to the Jewish forces following the invasion of Palestine by regular Arab armies were quickly forgotten as a temporary aberration.

From 1949 until its involvement in Afghanistan and imminent collapse in the late 1980s, the USSR could effectively portray itself as a friend of the Muslims including the extremist Islamist fringe by virtue of its diplomatic, economic and military aid to many Arab regimes, endorsement of extremely critical U.N. resolutions of Israeli policy and the restriction of Jewish emigration to Israel. It is striking however that at no point were Soviet relations with Muslim nations contingent on it adopting a passive or favorable attitude towards the religious concepts and political ramifications of jihad and vice-versa. This was of little matter. Whatever the implications of Marxism and the theories of dialectical materialism, the ruling elites and corrupt dictators in Muslim majority nations who had even schemed with the Nazis to rid themselves of colonial rule, saw mutual benefits to a close relationship with the USSR.

Soviet doctrine and practice offered Colonel Gamal Abdul Nasser more than the traditional means of reliance on the army and authoritarian rule. His was the first Arab regime to institute a model of secret police, concentration camps, predetermined sentences, and show trials. Major arms deals with the Kremlin and its satellite states brought about a closer Russian-Arab relationship than at any time in the past. In spite of initially utilizing the Communists (and the Muslim Brotherhood) to overthrow the regime of King Farouk, Nasser moved against them in January, 1954 when he felt his rule was secure. Both the Communists and the Muslim Brothers (The Far Left and the Far Right of the Egyptian political spectrum) were outlawed and went underground.

As a result the Great Soviet Encyclopedia described Nasser and his colleagues as *"a reactionary officers' group linked to the U.S.A., and a force severely oppressing the workers."* To combat this criticism and widen appeal, Nasser embarked on an ambitious program of land expropriation and seizure of factories from industrialists, but the mechanism to administer and distribute the seized assets was wholly in the hands of a corrupt bureaucracy subservient to Nasser.

The threat of Soviet intervention to halt the Suez campaign in 1956 (supported by the U.S.) won considerable prestige for Nasser and greatly improved Soviet-Egyptian relations, including the provision of educational grants for Egyptian students to study in the USSR and intensive lip service to left-wing ideals of equality. Between 1954 and 1970, Egypt, Syria and Iraq received more than half of the global Soviet military assistance.[2] Ironically, due to the instability of the entire region and the corruption of Arab regimes, much of this Soviet aid was wasted. Muslim opinion in the region continues to look with deep suspicion on the Russians as a Christian nation with devious aims. To counteract this, the Soviet leadership has continued to downplay the threats of jihad and militant Islam even though the new Russian regime has been the target of terrorism in Chechniya and elsewhere.

What is truly amazing today is that much of the political Left in the United States (Michael Moore, Keith Olbermann, et.al.) under obeisance to multiculturalism and what they perceive to be the "underdog" (Muslim immigrants), even reject the existence of a real threat.

The Call for Jihad Against the Jews in Palestine and Israel

The unrest in Palestine during the British Mandate is most frequently presented as a unilateral struggle between rival nationalisms (Arab vs. Jewish). The impulse towards jihad on the part of the Muslim extremists dominating the Arab nationalist cause is downplayed or purposely ignored by Leftwing opinion. In spite of repeated propaganda campaigns by anti-Zionists that the Muslims of Palestine bore no ill will against ultra-orthodox religious (and non-Zionist) Jews, the violent pogrom of 1929 in Hebron was motivated by traditional calls of jihad against the veteran Jewish community in the town resulting in dozens of aged Orthodox men, women and children killed.

Even the official Palestine Royal Commission Report of 1938 gave evidence of the religious fanaticism animating the Palestinian Arab national movement, reporting in detail how the Arab Higher Commit-

---

2 Glassman, Jon D. *Arms for the Arabs*, Johns Hopkins University Press. 1975.

tee under the leadership of the Grand Mufti had employed violence and intimidation against scores of village chieftains and Bedouin as well as moderate Muslim Arab personalities culminating in the murder of Nasr el Din Nasr, the Mayor of Hebron and attempts on the life of Hasan Shukri, the Mayor of Haifa. Christian Arabs were hardly exempt from gross intimidation by the Mufti's leadership to express support for the Palestinian cause. Here too, jihadist calls were frequent to pressure Christian Arabs to give up the *tarboosh* (fez) in favor of the *keffiyah*, for Christian women to wear the veil just as their Muslim counterparts and for Christian shopkeepers to close on the Muslim Sabbath of Friday instead of Sunday.

On May 15, 1948, Abdul Rahman Azzam Pasha, General-Secretary of the Arab League, generally recognized as a "moderate spokesman" for Arab nationalism proclaimed that the conflict with the Jews was unavoidable and promised publicly in classical jihadi religious terms that the Arab invasion of Palestine to crush the Jews *"will be a war of extermination and a momentous massacre which will be spoken of like the Mongolian massacres and the Crusades."* Azzam was an Egyptian who, on many occasions, assured Zionist leaders that he did not wish to see a confrontation but that it would be inevitable and contrary to his moderate position, he would be forced by "Arab public opinion" (the Arab street) to couch his rhetoric in the most extreme position to capitalize on Muslim religious as well as nationalist emotion.[3]

"Islamism" and Jihad vs. The World

In the 1960s, it could be said that the political leadership of every Muslim state had set a course on imitating the Western concept of the nation state and paid lip service only to the idea that all Muslims constituted a world-wide community. These views were shaken by a renewed extremist Islamist campaign in Egypt led by the Muslim Brothers found-

---

3 For an accurate analysis of the role of the Arab League's attempt to aid the Palestinians and crush the new Jewish state see Kurzman, Dan *Genesis 1948; The First Arab-Israeli War* Signet Books, New American Library, 1970. Whatever the real faults and mistakes of the Zionist movement and whatever the extent of compromises proposed, it is clear from the evidence that the Jews were faced with a war of extermination and religious incitement.

ed and inspired by the Islamist theorists Hassan al-Banna (1906-1949) and Sayyad Qutb (hanged by the Egyptian government in 1966), in Pakistan under the influence of the continuing conflict with India and the views of cleric Mawlana Mawdudi (1903-1979), and most dramatically by the triumph of the revolution led by the Grand Ayatollah Khomeini (1902-1989) that overthrew the Shah in Iran.

The credo of the Muslim Brothers (or Brotherhood) for which there is no possibility of misinterpreting states that *"Allah is our goal, the Koran is our constitution, the Prophet is our leader, struggle is our way and death in the path of Allah is our highest aspiration."*

This is the ideology that still animates the "Brothers" who immediately saw their renewed chance during the demonstrations in Tahrir Square in Cairo in February, 2011 urging the resignation of Hosni Mubarak. Almost immediately signs appeared with Mubarak labeled a Jew and the Star of David imprinted on his forehead. He and President Sadat had recovered every inch of Egyptian territory in negotiations with Israel and steered a course that has kept peace in the region for almost 38 years. Like Sadat, Mubarak was marked for assassination, for the Brothers care not a whit for Egypt's progress as a modern nation state or its historical pre-Islamic past.

Mawdudi, who founded the Islamist Jamaat-e-Islami (Muslim Bloc) in Pakistan in1942, argued that the ultimate goal of the jihadi movement is to destroy all those regimes that are opposed to the precepts of Islam and replace them with a world wide government based on Islamic principles.

The emergence of militant Islamism among both Sunnis and Shi'ites and the call for all legislation to be based on the Koran as well as world-wide jihad became as much a threat to the "moderate" rulers in these three states as against the Dar al- Harb. The assassination of Egyptian President Anwar Sadat (by the Muslim Brothers) was a harbinger of the growing jihadi threat and the desire to implement an Islamist solution wiping away the vestiges of Western and secular institutions everywhere in Muslim and Arab countries. Attempts to placate the Islamists in Egypt, Jordan, Algeria, Malaysia, Lebanon and elsewhere have only led to their increased strength.

Hamas is the Palestinian branch of the Muslim Brotherhood and Hizbollah is an Iranian puppet committed to a Shi'ite variety of the same world-wide jihadist call. Western politicians and so-called Leftwing or "progressive" political forces urging or pressuring Israel to "negotiate" with these two Jihadist terror organizations display a willful ignorance and simply refuse to acknowledge the reality of their violent heritage, fascist character and long term goals to destroy the West.

If we are to learn anything at all from history, it is that the Islamist concept of jihad was unequivocally understood as "violent holy war" against the infidels and not subject to interpretation. It remains a political weapon that has been used quite similarly by the last Ottoman Caliph, the Taliban, the Iranian mullahs, Al-Qaeda and rival extremist Sunni and Shi'ite clerics in Iraq today. It is still attractive to much extremist opinion in large parts of the Arab world, Chechniya, the Sudan, Pakistan and even in Indonesia. Its attraction throughout the 20th century for those autocratic and dictatorial European leaders who sought to become "Protectors of Islam" and borrow it, was to exploit its violent and evil appeal for their own purposes.

Our media and government and even more incredibly the forces on the political Left in much of the world have essentially promoted an ignorance of what motivates Muslims to undertake violent acts preferring to focus on their individual problems of being marginalized in Western societies and subject to discrimination and estrangement due to their inability to integrate or be successful.

The look of benign puzzlement on the face of Attorney General Holder when asked about the common factor of "Radical Islam" in the behavior and attempted acts of terrorism by those individuals apprehended and questioned over the past two years of the Obama administration reveals a profound avoidance of following the dictum if it looks like a duck and walks like a duck and quacks like a duck, it must be a duck. No, for Obama and Holder, for *The New York Times* and for a large majority of those who pretend to be journalists not only in the United States, but in practically all Western societies including paradoxically, those like Spain and the U.K. that have already suffered atrocious acts of wanton terrorism, the guilty are "certain people who act from a variety of motives."

On August 5, 2010 even Holder was obliged to use the impermissible T-word (i.e. TERRORISM) in his boasting of the indictments of 14 Americans of Somali origin who had created a *"a deadly pipeline* that has routed funding and fighters to al-Shabab from cities across the United States," Holder said. "*We are seeing an increasing number of individuals -- including U.S. citizens -- who have become captivated by extremist ideology and have taken steps to carry out terrorist objectives, either at home or abroad.*"

A leader such as Saddam Hussein came to power through the Ba'ath political movement in Iraq devoted to "secular" Arab nationalism but when unable to fully mobilize public support for his failed policies, resorted to reforming his regime to make it appear more in line with traditional Islam, imprinting the first principle of Islam (There is no God but Allah and Muhammad is his Prophet) on the country's flag and putting his portrait on the currency in the image of Saladin. In the letter he left to be read after his execution, he wrote:

> Dear faithful people, I say goodbye to you, but I will be with the merciful God who helps those who take refuge in him and who will never disappoint any faithful, honest believer ... God is Great ... God is great ... Long live our nation ... Long live our great struggling people ... Long live Iraq, long live Iraq ... Long live Palestine ... Long live jihad and the mujahedeen."

Jihad, this Sixth Pillar of Islam is not a "marginal" or "perverted interpretation" practiced by a tiny minority. It may lay dormant for generations but has the power overnight to transform tens of millions of Muslims around the globe into a mob craving blood, and "revenge" for what they perceive to be an affront to their dignity and sacred beliefs. The extremist Muslim Brotherhood and its many affiliates operating under a variety of names are either the largest political grouping or a powerful force threatening to impose its program on behalf of Sharia law and jihad in many of the 56 nations that comprise the Organization of the Islamic Conference (OIC).

The Strange Silence, Apathy and Sympathy of the Left for a Resurgent Islam and Failure to Deal with the Threat of Jihad

The massive world-wide demonstrations against American intervention to topple Saddam Hussein and end the Taliban regime in Afghanistan, blind 'sympathy' for the Palestinians and the coordinated and consistent attempts to delegitimize Israel in the United Nations and other international forums, special obsessive pleading for privileges (disguised as 'rights') for Muslims in the United States and Europe as a religious minority to be accorded special treatment and the passivity and the lack of initiative in confronting fifth column terrorist activities and plots are all shared by diverse and so called 'moderate' Leftwing political groups. It is largely a matter of those groups committed to an agenda that takes its starting point from the alleged sins and shortcomings of American society and Western civilization in general. Major Nidal Malik Hasan, the assassin of twelve soldiers, one civilian and the wounding of more than forty others at Ft. Hood, Texas on Nov. 6, 2009 was not joking. Newspapers all over the United States carried headlines on the order of "Army authorities searching for a motive in the massacre", and "Obama finds the crime Incomprehensible." Both the Army and the U.S. President bear complicity for the deaths of these soldiers, killed at the safest location imaginable, yet many observers referred to the crime as "incomprehensible," although Malik had been cited numerous times for extremist Islamist statements, sympathy with Al-Qaeda and his own personal calling card as a "soldier of Allah."

For Faisal Shahzad, the attempted Pakistani (and American citizen) Times Square bomber, sentenced to life imprisonment without parole, and the countless others, it is a wholly vain endeavor to search for some "factor" that somehow "radicalized" them apart from Islam. Just as the many millions of Muslims who participated in the anti-Danish demonstrations, there is only one factor they all hold in common – the trigger pushing them "over the line" is the ever-present allegiance to Islam which means the blind obedience to those in power able to manipulate them by resorting to the appeal of jihad.

Since District Attorney Holder's responses about "certain people" the Department of Justice, apparently stung by criticism over such a nonchalant euphemistic rationalization has carried out more than one hundred indictments – all of them against Muslims residing in the United States.[4]

---

4 For a brief overview of illegal Islamist activity in the United States and the support provided by Leftwing opinion and Arab, especially Saudi funding, see David Horowitz *The Unholy*

The Question Never Asked

Nobody among our leading journalists, politicians, television commentators and pundits and certainly not the President or the Attorney General or the many congressmen and others who had enquired about our policies vis a vis the "Muslim World" have dared ask or tried to answer the following question about their view that Islam is a noble religion and only a tiny minority can be classified as "radical Islamists." Question: Can you name ANY widely regarded, internationally respected, prominent Muslim cleric or the religious authorities in any Muslim religious institution enjoying government support in a Muslim majority state ANYWHERE who has unconditionally condemned either the numerous murderous attacks carried out in the name of jihad against innocent non-Muslim civilians; or the wholly reprehensible malicious attacks against Denmark; or the death threats (Salman Rushdie) as well as actual assassination attempts (against the Danish cartoonist Kurt Westergaard by an axe-wielding Somali now under arrest in Denmark); and murders carried out against writers, intellectuals, film producers and politicians (Pym Fortuyn and Theo Van Gogh in the Netherlands)?

Those few brave and lonely individuals who are indeed moderates hoping to reform Islam such as Irshad Manji and M. Zuhdi Jasser of the American Islamic Forum for Democracy and former Muslims like Ibn Warraq[5] and Walid Shoebat, and women in exile such as Nonie Darwish,[6] Ayaan Hirsi Ali, Wafa Sultan, and Taslima Nasrin are all straws in the wind with no support for help or outreach of any kind from the U.S. government. These individuals are few in number.

The editorial in the April 15th, 2007 issue of the London based *Al-Sharq Al-Awsat*, the leading Arabic International Daily Newspaper, repeated essentially the same message and had this to say:

Alliance, Islam and the American Left Regnery books, 2006. P. David Gaubatz and Paul Sperry, *Muslim Mafia, Inside the Secret Underworld Conspiring to Islamize America* WND Books, New York. 2009. See slso *Allah is Dead* by Rebecca Bynum (New English Review Press 2011) for an in depth analysis of how western misunderstanding of Islam as simply a religion masks the true nature of an aggressive, expansionist belief system.

5 Ibn Warraq, *Why I am Not a Muslim*, Prometheus Books, Amherst, N.Y., 2003.

6 Nonie Darwish, *Cruel and Usual Punishment, The Terrifying Global Implications of Islamic Law* Thomas Nelson, Nashville, 2008..

"To make the picture clearer... This religious war has nothing to do even with the major issues, slogans related to which are raised in the terrorists' literature itself, like Palestine, Iraq, the U.S., etc. These are people who want martyrdom, that is, they want to fight war, anywhere in the world, and for any cause that has a religious angle.

"They are not fighting for money, public reform, or for... the environment, and they are not nationalists, pan-Arabists, or communists... They are not jokers, hippies, or opposition-ists. They are seekers of martyrdom, meaning that they are in a hurry to go to Paradise. They are not interested in the life of this world, and they want to take with them to the grave the greatest number of people possible.

"I know that this is an issue that is difficult for the Western-er to understand. It is also difficult for many of the Muslims themselves to accept this, and they always try to justify it with issues that they consider legitimate and comprehensible. But the truth is that these terrorists want death for the sake of Al-lah... That is, even if the Americans left Iraq tonight, and the Jews fled Palestine, and extremist religious governments were established in Morocco, Algeria, and Egypt - this would not satisfy them... They want Paradise, and for this they will travel to the ends of the earth, to the North Pole and the South Pole, 'to fight the infidels.'"

It is incumbent on all of us to make certain that no connection whatsoever exists between this view of Islam and any request to estab-lish a mosque anywhere. Yet, we have a so called "Director of National Intelligence" (soon to be renamed Director of National Ignorance), James Clapper speaking before Congress (February 10, 2011), who could say *"The Muslim Brotherhood is an umbrella term for a variety of movements. In the case of Egypt, a very heterogeneous group, largely secular, which has eschewed violence and has decried al-Qaeda as a perversion of Islam."* This idiotic remark, typical of the Obama administration, had to immediately be qualified and explained by the office of public affairs for the Director of National Intelligence who said in a statement to ABC News: *"To clarify Director Clapper's point - in Egypt the Muslim Brotherhood makes efforts to work through a political system that has been, under Mubarak's rule, one that is largely secular in its orientation – he is well aware that the Muslim Brotherhood is not a secular organization."*

Attempts to placate radical Islamist militancy in Egypt, Jordan, Algeria, Malaysia, Lebanon and elsewhere have only led to their increased strength. At least, the political leadership in these nations is aware of the threat and knows how to combat it. The same cannot be said of our blind leaders and media. They cannot see the jihadi writing on the wall. It comes straight from Mohammad, the Koran, the Sunna and the Sira, from all four schools of Orthodox Sunni Islam and the Shi'ite thugs in power in Iran.

The Appeal of Jihad and the Cartoon Affair

To understand the latent but decisive appeal of jihad on Muslims who for all intents and purposes are lawful, peace-abiding and "moderate" but who are clay to be molded in the hands of the jihadist masters who dominate political Islam, one only has to look at the Danish cartoon affair throughout 2006.

If anyone doubts the potential for mass violent behavior at the drop of a hat and the instantaneous appeal of jihad, let them carefully study the anti-Danish riots in February 2006 and how quickly the behavior of a violent mob can be turned from focusing on the INFIDEL, if not the Israeli, then the Jew, if not the Jew, than the foreign Christians, if not the foreign Christians, any Christian at hand including Arab Christians.

The anti-Danish demonstrations across the Arab and Islamic world in the wake of the cartoon depiction of the Prophet Muhammad quickly turned violent. In Beirut, anti-Danish demonstrations on Sunday, February 6 unleashed an anti-Christian sectarian riot. Thousands of demonstrators set fire to the Danish embassy in Ashrafieh and then went on to rampage and loot this largely Christian neighborhood, smashing car windows and shop fronts. Hundreds of Lebanese troops and riot police quickly converged on the area, and fired warning shots. A fire truck that had tried to use a hose to disperse the rioters was seized and its crew attacked. Rioters stoned the St. Maroun Church and ripped a metal cross from the entrance to the home of the Greek Orthodox Bishop of Beirut.

The empty ruins of the Danish embassy were still smoking and piles of glass littered the street. The air reeked of smoke. Fortunately, the embassy staff had vacated the week before in anticipation of protests. The Danish government called on all its citizens to leave Lebanon and Syria. Syrian demonstrators had set fire to the Danish and Norwegian embassies in Damascus the day before. Thousands of Sunni Muslims from northern Lebanon converged on Beirut during the morning on their way to the demonstrations, driving along the coastal highway in convoys decked with green and black Islamic flags inscribed with "There is no God but Allah." Among those Sunni political and religious groups participating in the demonstration was Al-Ahbash, an Islamist organization that has close ties to Syria. It has been linked to the assassination of former Lebanese Prime Minister Rafik Hariri.

Denmark has given its Muslim population the same safeguards and protection as all its citizens. It supports their institutions and schools and instituted costly programs designed to ease their integration into Danish society by making allowances for their customs such as dietary restrictions. A Muslim immigrant of Palestinian origin, Naser Khader, was elected to the Folketing (Danish Parliament) from the moderate-centrist "Det Radikale Venstre" Party that has supported Danish policies in Iraq yet, literally, at the drop of a hat, at the call of extremists, Muslims all over the world in their millions were mobilized to demonstrate, threaten, riot, and commit mayhem and violence against the citizens and the flag of a country they knew nothing about.

Khader, like other Danes, was shocked and outraged by the provocation of several Muslim religious leaders in Denmark (imams who had control of the state supported Islamic religious Council) who purposely defamed the country and spread incendiary false stories about the cartoons.

What was entirely missing from the coverage in much of Europe and the United States by the media was the decided split among Danish Muslims. Several hundred contacted Khader to express their support of his brave stand and his new organization of "Democratic

Muslims" the imams misused their power and that ordinary Muslims must support the democratic values of the host society in which they live. Also lacking in international coverage was the growing resistance of Danes who are not racist but have been stirred as in the heroic days of 1943 to stand up and defend their country.

As a result, Danes cancelled more than 100,000 vacation trips to Egypt and Turkey (where violent demonstrations and flag burning rioting in front of the Danish embassies occurred). This is clearly the case even though the ever ready Danish willingness to compromise was present and both former Prime Minister Fogh and the editors of Jyllands-Posten apologized for any unintended offence. This, of course, was insufficient. The call to jihad, no matter from where, launched by the most extremist elements within political Islam always trumps the moderates. The message of Islam is clear – to strike anywhere anytime. It reads *"Yesterday Israel, Today Denmark (or Britain, or Switzerland or Spain again), Tomorrow the World!"*

From the address delivered by Libyan Leader Mu'ammar Al-Qadhafi, which aired on Al-Jazeera TV on February 25, 2010, Benghazi, Libya.

Anyone who doubts what this more than one thousand year old history of jihad and its implications for the West must go on line and witness thousands of ecstatic Libyans dancing in abandon to the words of their leader Mu'ammar Al-Qadhafi:

> "We will not give up Jihad, because it is a religious duty. Jihad constitutes a religious duty and self-defense. It is the defense of the religion, fighting for the sake of Allah, defense of the Prophet Muhammad, of the Koran, of the mosques, defense of the Al-Aqsa Mosque, and of our independence....Whoever destroys the mosques of Allah before the eyes of the Muslims is worthy of having Jihad launched against him. If Switzerland were situated on our border, we would fight it, for destroying the mosques of Allah. Jihad against those who destroy the mosques of Allah and their minarets is [true] Jihad, and not

terrorism....What is the meaning of "wage Jihad with your property and your souls"? It means Jihad.

"Any Muslim who buys Swiss products is an infidel. Let Muslims all over the world know this. There are people here from all over the Islamic world. Any Muslim anywhere in the world who deals with Switzerland is an infidel against Islam, Muhammad, Allah, and the Koran. Switzerland is an infidel and sinful country which destroys mosques. Jihad, with all possible means, should be declared against it. Boycott Switzerland, its products, its planes, its ships, and its embassies. Boycott this sinful infidel community, which attacks the mosques of Allah. They portrayed the Prophet Muhammad in their newspapers in the most abominable way. Yet the Islamic world watches from the sidelines. You think that you are still Muslims? No, you're not. Your Islam is in doubt. You need to reexamine your Islam, your faith. If you continue to have dealings with Switzerland, and the people who portrayed the Prophet Muhammad in the most abominable way in their newspapers... If you continue to have dealings with them, to buy their products, to support them, to accept their tourists, to accept their planes, to accept their ships, and to host their embassies – you are not Muslims. Any Muslim must boycott them. The Muslim masses must head towards all the airports in the Islamic world, and prevent any Swiss plane from landing. They should head to the ports, and prevent any Swiss ship from coming in. They should comb the shops and markets and remove the Swiss products."

At the 35th G8 summit in L'Aquila, Abruzzo, Italy in July, 2009, Libya's leader called for the dissolution of Switzerland, its territory to be divided among France, Italy and Germany.[7] In August 2009, Gaddafi' son, Hannibal stated that if he had nuclear weapons, he would "wipe Switzerland off the map." ISRAEL IS NOT ALONE. Gaddafi, in reference to the Swiss ban on minarets, described Switzerland as an "infidel harlot" and "apostate." All of Gaddafi's invective against Swit-

---

7 *TIME* magazine, Sept. 25, 2009. "Gaddafi's Oddest Idea: Abolish Switzerland"

zerland did not persuade him however to withdraw the huge fortune he has accumulated and is on deposit with Swiss banks.

These are the many dots that connect jihad throughout the last century and the appeal that it continues to exercise for all those who oppose and are terrified by modernity, enlightenment, tolerance, equality and equal rights for women and non-Muslims.

For the reader interested in a brief run-down of the appeal of violent jihad and its consequences, here is a summary of events (including intra-Muslim conflicts) since 1948:

1. The eight-year-long war between Iraq and Iran resulting in almost a million killed.

2. The First Gulf War; Invasion of Kuwait (Aug. 1990-Feb.1991), Operation Desert Storm, the Second Gulf War, and Operation Iraqi Freedom.

3. Massive violence between Muslims and Hindus in India on an unprecedented scale following partition (at Muslim insistence) in 1947 and three India-Pakistan wars, terrorism in Kashmir and India resulting in several million killed and at least fifteen million people displaced.

4. Pakistan-Bangladesh conflict, 1971 (following civil war and secession). This war saw the highest number of casualties in any of the India-Pakistan conflicts. It is believed that from one to three million Bangladeshis were killed as a result of this war. Very little media coverage.

5. Ongoing Yemeni and Somali Civil Wars. Thousands killed. No media coverage.

6. Inter-sectarian Muslim violence between Shias and Sunnis in Syria, Lebanon and Iraq; thousands killed.

7. Border disputes between Syria and Jordan, Syria and Lebanon, Iraq and Kuwait, Bahrain and Iran, Algeria and Morocco, Libya and Chad.

8. Jordan's crackdown on "Black September," 1970. PLO crushed by

Jordanian Legion under command of King Hussein (at least 25,000 killed).

9. Syria's suppression of the Muslim Brothers and opponents of the Assad regime; destruction of the city of Hama (at least 25,000 killed) to wipe out Muslim Brotherhood. Media barred from entering the city. Uprising in Hama by Muslim Brotherhood crushed by Assad regime in Syria Feb. 1982.

10. Al-Qaeda and Taliban violence in Pakistan and Afghanistan (Muslims both perpetrators and largely victims for such crimes as sending girls to school, wearing make-up and listening to Western music).

11. Inter-Palestinian factionalism in Gaza; hundreds killed (Hamas activists threw at least 170 members of Fatah off roofs from high buildings).

12. Decade-long mass violence between Muslim religious extremists (Salafist movement) and Algerian government beginning in 1991 estimated to have cost between 150,000 and 200,000 lives.

13. Sixteen-year-long civil war in Lebanon. The war lasted from 1975 to 1990 and resulted in an estimated 130,000 to 250,000 civilian fatalities. Another one million people (one-third of the population) were wounded, half of whom were left with lifetime disabilities; Christians reduced to a minority.

14. Iraqi, Iranian, and Turkish suppression of Kurdish autonomy; approximately 180,000 Kurds killed, mostly civilians in Iraq, by Saddam Hussein's forces via poison gas attacks.

15. Muslim terror against civilians in Chechnya, and additional hundreds killed in Moscow and other Russian cities including children at primary school. Russia's two biggest terrorist attacks both came from Muslim groups. The Chechnyan separatist "Special Purpose Islamic Regiment" took an estimated 850 people hostage in Moscow in October 2002 at a theater. At least 129 hostages died during the rescue, all

but one killed by the chemicals used to subdue the attackers.

In the September 2004, 1,200 schoolchildren and adults were taken hostage at a secondary school in Beslan, North Ossetia-Alania, which was overrun by an Islamic terror group. About 500 people, including 186 children, died in the attempt to free the hostages. According to the only surviving attacker, Nur-Pashi Kulayev, the choice of a school and the targeting of mothers and young children by the attackers was carried out in order to generate the maximum outrage possible and ignite a wider war in the Caucasus with the ultimate goal of establishing an Islamic Emirate across the whole of the North Caucasus.

16. Muslim secessionist activity and terrorism in the Philippines (with almost monthly reports by American media that do not mention the words "Muslim" or "jihad").

17. Southern Sudan and Darfur; genocidal attacks against mostly non-Muslim Black Sudanese. On July 13, 2008, the prosecutor of the International Criminal Court filed ten charges of war crimes against Sudan's President Omar al-Bashir, charges that included three counts of genocide, five crimes against humanity, and two of murder. Between one and two million civilians killed. The ICC's prosecutors have claimed that al-Bashir "masterminded and implemented a plan to destroy in substantial part" three tribal groups in Darfur because of their ethnicity. Finally, the Southern Sudan seceded from the Muslim dominated north creating a new state in February, 2011 followng a plebiscite approved by 99.6% of the population.

18. Muslim grievances and violence in Thailand; dozens killed.

19. Terrorist activity against the Han Chinese in Western China. Several hundred fatalities.

20. Division of Cyprus to satisfy Turkish Muslim minority.

21. Muslim unrest and violence against Christians in Nigeria and Ghana; several thousand killed. No media interest.

22. Muslim terrorist attacks on 9/11 against the U.S. in New York and Washington. Almost 3,000 civilians killed.

23. Terrorist attacks throughout Europe -- London Underground, Atocha Train Station in Madrid; in Africa at American embassy in Kenya; in Bali nightclub where most victims were Australian tourists; foiled attempts in the U.S. and elsewhere; close to a thousand killed, all civilians.

24. Jihadi-inspired sniper and terror attacks by deranged lone Muslims in the United States against military bases (Ft. Hood), synagogues, and airports, and at Times Square.

25. Continued terrorist attacks against the State of Israel and Jews throughout the world since 1948; several thousand killed.

26. Widespread piracy on a scale not seen for 150 years along the Somali coast of East Africa preying upon international shipping. All the pirates are Muslims and continue to justify their acts because their victims are kafirs (non-Muslims).

27. Indonesian Muslim suppression of East Timor population's (98%) desire for independence. Tens of thousands of civilians killed or died from malnutrition, imprisonment (1974-1998).

28. Continued civil war in West Sahara between the Polisario Movement and Moroccan authorities, low-level guerrilla attacks and hundreds of thousands of displaced refuges.

29. Terrorism against civilian airline passengers committed by operatives of different Palestinian Arab terror organizations.

30., 1992 and 1994 murderous terrorist bombings against civilians in Buenos Aires Argentina at the Israeli Embassy and Jewish Community Center building planned and carried out by Iranian operatives; 117 innocent people at work and passers-by were killed and many hundreds more wounded.

31. The Luxor Massacre took place at an archaeological site located across the Nile from the famous Luxor tourist attraction on November 17, 1997. Six assailants, members of an extreme Islamist organization, *Jihad Talaath-al-Fatah* ("Holy War of the Vanguard of the Conquest") massacred 62 people at the attraction. They descended on the Temple of Hatshepsut at around 08:45 where the tourists were trapped inside and systematically went on a killing spree for 45 minutes. Many of the bodies, especially of women, were mutilated with machetes. A note praising Islam was found inside one disemboweled body. The dead included a five-year-old British child and four Japanese couples on their honeymoons. None of those killed were the often proclaimed enemies of Islam or Arab Nationalism, i.e. Israelis, Americans or Jews. Four Egyptians were killed, three of the police officers and one tour guide. A total of 58 foreign tourists were killed: 36 Swiss, ten Japanese, six Britons, four Germans, and two Colombians. The six assailants were armed with automatic firearms and knives, and had been disguised as members of the security forces. The terrorists fled into the hills where their bodies were found in a cave, after having committed suicide together.

The massacre was so horrible that it provoked spontaneous demonstrations in Luxor by those demanding action by the government and forced Egyptian leader Hosni Mubarak to visit the region a few days later. The day after the attack, Islamic Group leader Rifai Taha claimed the attackers intended only to take the tourists hostage, despite the evidence of the immediate, systematic nature of the slaughter. Others denied Islamist involvement completely. Sheikh Omar Abdel-Rahman blamed Israelis for the killings, and Ayman Zawahiri maintained the attack was the work of the Egyptian police.

32. At the end of May, 2010 one of the most inhuman incidents involving the slaughter of innocent civilians took place in Lahore and several kilometers away in Garhi Shahu, Pakistan. There was essentially no media interest, such as on-the-spot coverage or interviews with survivors. The victims were all Ahmadis, a "deviant" sect within Islam. Ahmadis comprise the sect that is distinguished as being the most tranquil; they have always lived in peace with their neighbors, both Muslim and non-

Muslim. The Ahmadis were attacked by those "mainstream" Muslims who are sympathizers of the Taliban and al-Qaeda in Pakistan. These Muslims attacked the two Ahmadi mosques packed with hundreds of worshipers. At least ninety people were killed. The assaults in Lahore were carried out by at least seven men, including three suicide bombers. Some of the attackers acted as snipers from an adjacent mosque to kill their fellow Muslims.

Ahmadis are reviled as heretics by mainstream Muslims for their belief that their sect's founder was a savior foretold by the Quran, Islam's holy book. The group has experienced years of state-sanctioned discrimination and occasional attacks in Pakistan, but never before in such a large and coordinated fashion.

Not one reputable, representative, acknowledged Muslim religious leader anywhere has seen fit so far to issue a condemnation of the attack. Not one media commentary anywhere (except in Israel) saw fit to mention that the only place within the Middle East where Ahmadis live in peace and harmony with their neighbors and enjoy full civil and religious rights is Israel. The Kababir neighborhood in Haifa was established in 1928. The neighborhood's first mosque on Mount Carmel was built in 1931, and a larger grand mosque was built in the 1970s. The grand mosque has two white minarets standing one hundred feet tall. They dominate the low-rise skyline of the residential neighborhoods on the ridges nearby. The mosque is subsidized entirely by the members of the local Ahmadiyya Muslim Community.

Jihad is directed not "just" against the unbelievers (the kaffirs, i.e., non-Muslims), but all those who have "deviated" -- the Shi'ites, the Alawites, the Ahmadis, the Druze, Bahais, Yazidis, etc. It is holy war by armed resistance to all those who do not accept Muhammad's message as interpreted by the sacred traditions hallowed by all the schools of Sunni jurisprudence across fourteen hundred years of history.

33. Dozens of attacks against Christians at prayer in their churches resulting in hundreds of fatalities in Iraq, Egypt, Pakistan, the Philippines and elsewhere. The most heinous of these and wholly ignored by most

Western media was the attack on the Our Lady of Salvation Chaldean Catholic Cathedral in Baghdad. It occurred during Sunday evening Mass on October 31, 2010 and left at least 58 people dead. "Credit" was taken by the al-Qaeda-linked Sunni insurgent group the Islamic State of Iraq. More than half the Christian population has left Iraq since the fall of Saddam Hussein and the ten million strong Coptic community of Egypt now lives in fear for their continued existence.

No doubt, the list will be very much out of date by the time this book is published.

23

The LEFT and the National Question:
Marx, Stalin and Opportunism

The Marxist explanation of the plight of oppressed peoples without a national homeland was part of what they considered to be based on "firm theoretical foundations" as well as a natural sympathy for the poor and dispossessed. In order to "facilitate" the "construction of socialism" as well as offer aid to help liberate those peoples under foreign rule, Marx and then Stalin developed a theory of a "territorial solution" that led to the support of what might be termed "pseudo-Zion" states. Before the eventual "withering away" of the state, proletarian consciousness would eventually come to be accepted by the workers who would realize the priority of common class interests over and above the divisive and "non-essential" issues of race, nationality, territory and language.

Stalin's Contribution to the National Question

How did Marxism begin to shape a policy of "liberation" with regard to peoples devoid of a national homeland? In 1913, Stalin wrote what has been termed his most important contribution to Marxist theory entitled "The National Question and Social Democracy" This essay won Lenin's approval and made Stalin known internationally. Stalin attacked Socialist leader Otto Bauer who had proposed a model of "cultural autonomy" on the "personal principle" for individuals wherever they lived to choose and maintain their own sense of national identity. Although nationalism like religion was often termed a deviation from the true "class interests of the workers," Stalin asserted that:

"A nation has the right freely to determine its own destiny. It has the right to arrange its life as it sees fit, without, of course, trampling on the rights of other nations. That is beyond dispute."

He immediately qualified this assertion of the nation as a social reality by asking:

"But how exactly should it arrange its own life, what forms should its future constitution take, if the interests of the majority of the nation and, above all, of the proletariat are to be borne in mind? A nation has the right to arrange its life on autonomous lines. It even has the right to secede. But this does not mean that it should do so under all circumstances, or that autonomy, or separation, will everywhere and always be advantageous for a nation."

Stalin rejected the Social-Democratic solution of "cultural autonomy" based on individual rights and insisted that:

"The only correct solution is regional autonomy, autonomy for such crystallized units as Poland, Lithuania, the Ukraine, etc. The advantage of regional autonomy consists, first of all, in the fact that it does not deal with a fiction bereft of territory, but with a definite population inhabiting a definite territory."[1]

This was the format of territorial-ethnic division instituted in the USSR. The so called Marxist principle in the Soviet Union of "*National in form, Socialist in content*" meant however nothing more than a superficial tolerance of folk festivals featuring colorful costumes and songs and dances but not the cultivation of any serious literature or emotional identification with the cherished past of any of the 15 constituent Soviet Republics. These "backward" or "quaint" peoples of re-

---

1 All three of the above quotes are from an English translation of Stalin's 1913 paper, "The National Question and Social Democracy" It was based on research he carried out in Vienna in January-February 1913 (his longest stay outside Russia) It appeared in brochures of the Russian Bolshevik Party and was described by Lenin in an article to Kamenov as "very good" and its author as a "wonderful Georgian." Cited in *Hitler and Staln: Parallel Lives* by Alan Bullock (Harper Colins, 1991) pp. 44-45.

mote provinces would, according to Marxism, soon be brought into closer economic relationships with their national capitals in the states where they lived and through their participation in the national economy they would adopt the national standards of speech, dress, literacy and realize their common interests as workers.

The Postwar Plebiscites According to Stalin's Theory

In several plebiscites held immediately after World War I. The parties defining themselves as Socialist or Communist and adhering to Marxism urged those with identifiable Hungarian and Danish ethnic loyalties to nevertheless vote on the basis of their class interests to become part of Austria and Germany rather than Hungary and Denmark!

Ethnic Danes in the area of South Schleswig (ceded to Germany by Denmark in 1864 after a disastrous defeat) were, like idealistic East European Jews, high up on the "sucker" list. They were loyal to their ideological beliefs and would come to pay a heavy price for their theoretical support of Marxism. In the plebiscite of 1920 they voted for what they believed was a better choice to advance their interests as part of the working class, i.e. inclusion in a German democratic republic with a strong industrial base rather than a "return" to the pre-1864 boundary within the Danish monarchy.

The net result of their foolish vote was to be forced for the second time within a generation to fight and die for a foreign cause including aggression against Denmark. Across the border in North Schleswig, Denmark, the working class voters who chose to return to their ancestral homeland in the 1920 plebiscite progressed much more rapidly in every measure of economic and social progress without regimentation and militarism.

Likewise, in the border area of Burgenland, the Marxist Social Democratic Party urged its members to vote for inclusion in the new Austrian Republic because of the workers' more favorable connections with Vienna in terms of jobs and commuting distance. They also argued that the worker's literacy in German, a language of the "international proletariat and solidarity," rather than the isolated Hungarian tongue would place them in a much better organization framework to advance their interests. Many Burgenlanders of Hungarian and Croatian ethnic origin who were socialists and bilingual in German listened to the very same Otto Bauer (Stalin's opponent in the 1913 debate on what constitutes a nation) instruct them to vote for incorporation into Austria and reject any "narrow" nationalist sentiment that constituted a "backward step" in the class struggle.

Reality versus Theory

The intensified violent conflicts over territory and the demands to impose strict immigration quotas as well as sporadic campaigns in dozens of countries for regional autonomy or special language rights read like a list of defeats for class solidarity. The expected solidarity of the working class across national and linguistic boundaries was a mirage. The calls of the socialist international to prevent the First World War went unheeded except for a tiny minority (most of whom were organized in the "International Workers of the World").

"Authentic internationalism" was not achieved within the international workers' movements or within the multinational states such as the USSR and the so called "People's Democracies." The Marxist dictum that "each kilometer of railroad track and advance in technology would serve as a nail in the coffin of national differences" and eventually eliminate all ethnic distinctiveness in order to forge an authentic working class solidarity was utterly wrong. A rebirth of intense ethnicity and territorial loyalty has occurred among all those groups that even in Marx's time were considered to be on the road to assimilation in larger nationwide frameworks. The Armenians, Basques, Slovaks, Croats, Slovenians, Irish, Scots, Welsh, Catalans, Galicians, Maltese, Moldavians, Ukrainians, Finns, Lithuanians, Latvians, Estonians Georgians, French speaking Quebecois and the Jews who served as a model for Marx's theory on assimilation were all supposed to lose their identity.

The Armenian Homeland and Soviet "Zion-states" for The

Finns and the Jews "Building Socialism"

The Soviets, for their own purposes, seized on the idea of fostering territorial concentration through the creation of two new "Zion states" to build socialism among Jews and Finnish emigres "throughout the world." These projects had their origin in part from Stalin's theory of national identity and the simple fact that Armenians in a far flung Diaspora all over the world including those even unsympathetic to communism looked upon the Soviet Armenian Republic with fond hopes. After all, even under the Czarist regime, Armenian émigrés fleeing persecution at the hands of the Ottoman Turks had struggled to reach Russian territory in 1896 and 1917-1920.

Nevertheless, the need to win the loyalty of the masses often meant that the Communist Parties had to outdo the old prejudices and chauvinism of conservative nationalists. The structure of the Soviet Union with its 15 (later 16, then 15 again after the abolition by decree of the Karelo-Finnish S.S.R.) Soviet Socialist Republics and the support the Communist Parties gave to "national liberation struggles" were intended to win the Party the support of "oppressed nationalities," yet the Soviet Union under Stalin soon attacked the Jews whose assimilation was according to Marxist theory guaranteed, since they lacked the two basic requirements for nationhood -- a common language and territory.

Instead of the class struggle taking precedence over the national question as prescribed in the writings of Marx, Lenin and Stalin, Moscow at times found it expedient to even advocate its own remedy of territorial concentration for Jews and Finns in their own "Zion-states" of Karelia and Birobidjan because those communists choosing this path, were "building socialism" in a territorial homeland.

The Jews were at times labeled as "rootless cosmopolitans" for their tendency to want to assimilate. Stalin even reversed the initial favorable attitude of Lenin towards Esperanto, the international language because its inventor, Dr. L. L. Zamenhof, had at one time been a Zionist, and believed that his devised international language should be cultivated to increase world-wide harmony and unity among the classes as well as the nations.

The Soviet regime promoted Armenian culture and education.

It invited artists and intellectuals from abroad to return to Armenia, and succeeded in creating an environment of greater security than they had known in the aftermath of World War I and the great tribulations of massacres and forced exile they had suffered in Ottoman Turkey and the Middle East. For several decades, it could be said that of all the Soviet republics outside the Slavic core, Armenia probably was the most content.

Marxist theory's doctrines of class warfare and aid to "oppressed nationalities" in the Czarist Empire initially gave what appeared to be an adequate, even "convincing" explanation for the strong support the Communist Party of the U.S.A. received among two immigrant ethnic groups - the Finns and the Jews. It also basked in the sympathy of Armenian emigrants and exiles all over the world who looked upon even the limited framework of the Soviet Armenian Republic as a basis to further develop their national identity and culture and as the only part of their ancestral homeland not under foreign rule.[2]

North American Finnish "Reds"

Throughout the 1920s and well into the mid 1930s, the Finnish language section, representing recent immigrants, in the Great Lakes and adjacent Canadian Prairie Provinces, with a strong proletarian identity and limited knowledge of English, represented the largest group of recruited North American Communist Party members and supporters organized into a specific ethnic organization. The prospects of only limited autonomy and the hope for greater economic opportunity in North America had led to a wave of emigration to the United States and Canada which grew as Russian rule became entrenched. By 1912, the Russian language was granted full official status and more and more Russians had begun to settle in the Duchy, posing a threat that many Finns felt could only be avoided by achieving independence. From the mid 1880s until 1914, more than 200,000 Finns emigrated to the United States and Canada settling in the Great Lakes area and Prai-

---

2 *Karelian Exodus: Finnish Communities in North America and Soviet Karelia During the Depression Era* edited by Ronald Harpelle, Varpu Lindstrom, and Alex Pogorelskin. Special issue of the *Journal of Finnish Studies*. Arpasia Books, Inc. Beavorton, Ontario, Canada, 2004.

rie Provinces. They continued to retain a strong sense of both Finnish and working class identity and followed both the international socialist movement and the nationalist struggle for independence in Finland. (See Chapter 17.)

"Red Finns" with a strong working class consciousness believed that the region of Karelia could be developed with the help of like-minded overseas Finns in America and pose a constant political alternative for the working class in Finland under "White" capitalist control and exploitation. Communist Party leader Edvard Gylling, who had fled from Finland to Soviet Karelia, after the Finnish Civil War (1918-19), imagined the possibility of elevating the autonomous region to a full standing equal Soviet Republic similar in its administrative authority to the other 15 Soviet Republics.

The Depression and Lure of the "Zion-states"

The impact of the Depression had already begun to be felt and thousands of Finnish-Americans who had grown up espousing Left-wing causes and had felt betrayed by the White Victory in the Civil War seriously considered emigration to the Soviet controlled region of Karelia. Much of the enthusiasm was generated by sheer idealism rather than desperation. The movement was aided by the election of President Roosevelt and the establishment of full diplomatic relations between the United States and the Soviet Union.

Hundreds of families in the U.S. and Canada were motivated by "Karelian fever"[3]to migrate and bring with them such luxuries and essential goods as cars, typewriters, industrial machinery and vital materials necessary in the construction of several factories. The new migrants were also given special privileges that included being allowed to buy "luxury" goods with the American dollars they brought with them. Approximately 6,000 American and Canadian migrants reached Karelia, a quarter of whom returned almost immediately.

---

3 Harpelle, Ronald et. Al. (eds.) *Karelian Exodus, Finnish Communities in North America and Soviet Karelia during the Depression Era* from the *Journal of Finnish Studies* Arpasia Books, Inc. 2004.

Karelia and Birobidjan

By 1930, plans were declared to establish a Jewish Autonomous Region in Birobidjan along the Amur River on the Soviet-Chinese border in Manchuria. Birobidjan thus offered a competitive alternative to Zionism and Palestine in an area with absolutely no connection to any Jewish religious or historical memory. Similarly, in the summer of 1930, Gylling was given permission by Soviet authorities to encourage the settlement of American and Canadian-Finns by the 16th Party Congress Resolution calling upon the Karelian Autonomous Region *"to expand the practice of drawing workers and specialists from abroad and inviting foreign engineers, masters and qualified workers to the U.S.S.R."* Priority was given to fishermen, loggers and construction workers.

An Immigration Department was opened in Petrozavodsk - the largest town in the region and a Society to aid the scheme was established in New York on May Day 1931 as well as another branch in Toronto. Approval of the scheme was given by the Finnish language Communist newspaper in Superior Wisconsin, *TuUmies* (Working Man). Somewhere between 10,000 and 15,000 disgruntled Finnish citizens who could not reconcile themselves to life in the Finnish Republic also crossed the border to the new Finnish 'Proletarian Zion' in Karelia.

The inevitable result was immediate resentment and astonishment by the local population who were flabbergasted by the arrival of well to do Americans who had come voluntarily out of idealism to share in the already abysmal life of a depressed backward, marginal region of the Soviet Union. The Birobidjan experiment of the Jewish Autonomous Region was basically similar but perhaps more pathetic and comical for the migrant Jews coming from the United States, Argentina and Western Europe as well as the European parts of the Soviet Union had absolutely nothing in common with the local Mongol population. The selection of this territory without any historic Jewish connection in a remote corner of the USSR in the Far East bordering China and Mongolia was due to Soviet hopes that settlement there might serve their security needs against Japanese expansionism.

Until 1935, migrants to Karelia or Birobidjan wishing to return to Canada and the United States encountered no obstacle as the Soviets had no wish to antagonize the Americans and Canadian governments.

Those who had opted for Soviet citizenship were doomed to remain. After the assassination of Sergei Kirov, the Leningrad Party boss in December 1934, Stalinist paranoia took over and thousands perished in the purges of the late 1930s.

The 1939-40 Winter War of naked Soviet aggression against Finland (see Chapter 17) strained the remaining sentiments of the hardest Communist loyalists. The ethnic Finnish population of Karelia was thrown a bone following the Soviet victory in March 1940 in the form of the creation of the 16th Soviet Socialist Republic -- the Karelian S.S.R. with its own flag (both Republic and flag abolished by decree in 1956 without a whimper) but the change in official status offered little in the way of additional benefits. Soviet territorial gains on the Karelian isthmus including the city of Vipurii were added to the new Soviet Republic, scant reward for those communist idealists who had given up life in the United States, Canada and Finland for their own "Soviet Zion."

Origin of the Jewish Autonomous Region

In 1934, the "Jewish Autonomous Region of Birobidjan" was declared in a region of mostly swamp and forest on the Manchurian frontier in what appeared to be an about-face of original Marxist theory about the "rootless cosmopolitan Jews." Tens of thousands of Jews from the Ukraine and Belarus were "persuaded" to move there and start a new "productive life" as farmers. Appeals were sent via the Communist Parties abroad to attract Jewish sympathizers that the Soviet Union was not only opposed to antisemitism but had actually proposed to establish a Jewish territorial region on socialist principles and Yiddish culture as a counterweight to the "illusion" of Zionism with its roots in religion and the "artificial" recreation of the Hebrew language, supported by what was described as "British imperialism in the Middle East."[4] President Kalinin even promised the eventual establishment of a Jewish Soviet Socialist Republic should the region manage to attract a

---

4 Berdichevsky, Norman "Parallel Zionisms, Chinese, Greek, Armenian and Hungarian Parallels of Nationhood, Diaspora, Genocide, Exile, Partition and Aliya" in *World Affairs*, Winter 2007, vol. 169. No. 3 pp.119-124.

dense Jewish farming and proletarian population of 100,000.

Approximately one thousand foreign Jews, many of them active Communists from the U.S.A, Canada, Argentina and Europe followed their dream of a "Soviet Zion." The Jewish population rose to 45,000 at its peak about 1941 comprising 28% of the total population (the figure today is around 5%). Unwilling to let Jewish refugees from Poland and other areas of Nazi conquered Eastern Europe who found refuge in the USSR reach and settle Birobidjan, the region languished and was thrown into confusion by two developments in 1948-49.

First: The brief Soviet foreign policy initiative supporting the partition of Palestine and active military aid allowing the new Jewish state of Israel enabling it to survive. It thus raised hopes that the Soviet leaders had finally acknowledged the existence of a Jewish nationality. (See Chapter 21.)

Second: A suppression of all Jewish cultural expression including the murder of leading Yiddish writers in the USSR. This was followed by the infamous "Doctors Plot" trials in 1952-53, in which a clear antisemitic trend was evident.

Double About-Face on Zionism and Palestine

The "achievements" of the Jewish Autonomous Region were meager by any measure and ignored by Soviet foreign policy considerations. The classic Stalinist explanation of Marxist theory regarding the Jews was that they had lost the national characteristics of a people speaking their own language and residing in their own territory. Birobidjan had been created as a counterweight to the appeal of Zionism and the hope that Jewish national aspirations within the Soviet Union could find a safety valve for those Jews who were either unsuccessful in their attempts to assimilate or were spurned by the other nationalities within the USSR who regarded them as "foreign" and too influential.

Jewish Marxist theoreticians including several high ranking Party activists, all dedicated anti-religious and anti-Zionist communists, had followed the Party Line and even praised a vicious pogrom by a Muslim mob carried out against ultra-Orthodox Jews in the town of Hebron in Palestine in 1929. The Party Line then was that the Arab masses were demonstrating their anti-imperialist sentiment against British rule and its sponsorship of Zionism. A few years later, they had to feign enthusiasm first for Birobidjan and then perform an even greater hypocritical about-face following Soviet recognition and aid to Israel in 1948-49. Both the *Daily Worker* and the Yiddish language communist daily in the U.S. *Freiheit* (Freedom) outdid one another to explain the new party line that.... *"Palestine had become an important settlement of 600,000 souls, having developed a common national economy, a growing national culture and the first elements of Palestinian Jewish statehood and self-government."*[5]

As early as 1938, just prior to the Hitler-Stalin Non-Aggression Pact, Jewish communists throughout the world were instructed to play on Jewish anger at Nazi Germany to win increased support for the Soviet Union and the Communist Parties. Moissaye Olgin, the veteran editor of *Freiheit*, went to such lengths to follow the new line from Moscow in 1948 that one could imagine him as repenting at Yom Kippur services for all his past animosity to the cause of Jewish self-determination in Palestine (which had been denounced as reactionary Zionism by the *Freiheit* over the previous twenty-five years):

> "We managed to alienate the Jewish masses. More than that we managed to convey an idea that the Communists are hostile to Jewish national aspirations. We fought Zionism which was correct, but in fighting Zionism we forgot that many progressive elements of the Jewish People were Zionistically inclined. We forgot also that the craving, the desire for nationhood is not in itself reactionary, although Zionism is reactionary."

He ended his confession-diatribe with the appeal that the Jewish Communists repudiate "national nihilism" yet, nevertheless, must learn not to scoff at religion and be the "inheritors of the best in Jewish culture"

A 1947 CP-USA resolution entitled "Work Among the Jewish Masses" proclaimed that "Jewish Marxists have not always displayed

---

5 Alexander Bittelman in "Program for Survival; The Communist Position on the Jewish Question" *New Century* 1947. pp. 16, 52-53; cited in Nathan Glazer. *The Social Basis of American Communism.*

a positive attitude to the rights and interests of the Jewish People, to the special needs and problems of our own American Jewish national group and to the interests and rights of the Jewish Community in Palestine."

Stalin's essay on the National Question from 1913 was even dug up again to explain that even though Jewish immigration to Palestine had been fostered by "romantics" or "religious circles" or "bourgeois nationalists," all under the reactionary banner of Zionism, the new reality that had been created in Palestine was a "Hebrew nation" that deserved the right to self-determination. Curiously, the Soviet propaganda machine even praised the far-right underground groups of the Irgun and "Stern Gang" for their campaign of violence against the British authorities.

In what might be termed "poetic justice," the Winter War of 1940 caused a dramatic loss of support for the Communist Party among ethnic Finns in the United States and Canada (see chapter 17). On the other hand, Soviet support for the partition of Palestine and the military aid (through the agency of the Communist Czech government) rendered to the beleaguered Israeli state fighting for its life in 1948-49 helped in furthering a pro-Soviet position among many American Jews who gave considerable support to the far-left candidate, former Vice President Henry Wallace of the Progressive Party in the 1948 election.

The abrupt end of the Soviet honeymoon with Israel in 1950 did not signal any renewed support for Birobidjan. On the contrary, new purges decimated the veteran Jewish population especially among educators, writers, and even authentic "proletarians." Much of the leadership was purged and a new campaign against "rootless cosmopolitans" began. In 1958, Khruschev admitted failure of the region and blamed it on "Jewish individualism." Today, the region has begun to recover and has even attracted some former residents who had migrated to Israel but couldn't find satisfactory jobs and make the transition to Hebrew and a totally different climate.

Opportunism as the Guiding Light

Whenever the supposed international ideology of Marxism collided with the power interests of the USSR, in Palestine, or aid to the Spanish Republicans manipulated by the Spanish Communist Party to exclude and even combat the Trotskyite and anarchist parties, the infamous Hitler-Stalin Pact of 1939, the Soviet invasion of Poland two weeks after the initial German assault unleashing World War II, the Soviet attack on Finland in December 1939, the imposition of brutal dictatorships across Eastern Europe following the end of the war in 1945, Marxist ideology was used as a screen to further the great power interests of the Soviet state. This meant utilizing Great-Russian chauvinism as an important motive to further the standing of the Communist Party at home.

With regard to the "National Question," no real consistent line was followed. It was always subject to the geopolitical and military needs of the Soviet state. Insistence on a territorial definition of nationhood, led to brief support for Black separatism in America, and a temporary "pseudo" or "neo-Zionist solution" to the problems of the world-wide Diaspora of Armenians, Finns, and even Jews "building socialism."

The Palestinian Arab Claim to "Self-Determination"

Current Russian, and much of the world-wide support for the Palestinians in another "homeland," whose claim to a distinct nationhood (NO renowned historical figures, distinctive history, or flag, language, religion, sense of past nationhood, or common historical memory before the Balfour declaration), is suspect at best. It is likely to be as doomed as the Soviet line on the need for a distinct territory for Afro-Americans, Yiddish speaking Jews in Manchuria and the red Puppet State of the Karelian SSR.

It likewise clashes with the excellent relations between the Hashemite Kingdom of Jordan (where Palestinians represent two-thirds of the population) and the Russian Federation and their close cooperation on many international issues including Jordanian condemnation of Islamic extremism and separatism in Chechnya. It is obvious that the Russians resent the loss of what had been strong support of the Communist Party among disaffected Arabs in Israel and in the very sympathetic pro-Russian policies of the PLO. Popular opinion in Gaza and parts of the "West Bank" has now swing toward ultra-Islamist fundamentalist views. Mahmoud Abbas, a long time admirer of the Soviet system who gained a BA in law from Damascus University and a Ph.D. from the Oriental College in Moscow in History, has been a long-time associate of Israeli leftists. He is now threatened by Hamas and is regarded as a collaborator and traitor by many Hamas and Hizbollah activists.

In reality, the class interests of the "oppressed peoples" has repeatedly played second fiddle to the principle of self-determination in nationalist movements everywhere. The only authentic "Zion state" besides Israel is still Armenia, the homeland of a people who are among the most ancient with their distinctive language, alphabet, religious center, and historic memories. The failed pseudo-Zion states didn't succeed because there was no immense and long lasting reservoir of love and devotion to develop and cultivate a historic homeland under the oppressive regimes that failed to offer liberty as well as ethnic pride.

24

Case Closed: The Balance Sheet of Marxism-Leninism

Gerald Posner's brilliant and definitive analysis of the Kennedy assassination, *Case Closed* (Doubleday, 1993), traces the abysmal and pathetic life of the lone assassin Lee Harvey Oswald, a name that will live in infamy. The story is one of repeated failures and a search for martyrdom to find meaning through death for a life completely unfulfilled.

Oswald's search for a just and well functioning Marxist state and society served to assuage his feelings of always being a misfit and outsider longing for fame, recognition or notoriety at any price. Posner's conclusions could very well serve as an analogy for the three generations of doctrinaire Leftwing "activists" who continued to hope against hope that somewhere, sometime, somehow an undefiled Marxist society world arise that would not repeat the errors and catastrophes of the Soviet Union (Stalinism, the purges and forced labor camps of the Gulag), China (The "Great Leap Forward"), or Cuba (a million and a half exiles and an even greater concentration on the production of sugar and tobacco than before the Revolution) or even more absurd candidates such as Romania, Albania, Vietnam and East Germany.

The Unquenchable Thirst for Conspiracy and the Real Socialist Society

In Posner's final pages (469-470), he concludes..."*The search for a darker truth than the lone assassin seems unquenchable. The desire to find a conspiracy in the Kennedy assassination will continue to be answered for years by more "confessions," witnesses who change their testimony to recall disturbing events, the appearance of papers of dubious authenticity, and by writers and researchers who present cases of guilt by association support-ed by rumor and innuendo. But for those seeking the truth, the facts are in-controvertible. They can be tested against credible testimony, documents and the latest scientific advances. Chasing shadows on the grassy knoll will never substitute for real history. Lee Harvey Oswald, driven by his own twisted and impenetrable furies was the only assassin at Dealey Plaza on Novem-ber 22, 1963. To say otherwise in the light of the overwhelming evidence, is to absolve a man with blood on his hands and to mock the President he killed."*

The same can be essentially said for the many critics of capital-ism and American institutions who are driven by the same unquench-able thirst to apply Marxist-Leninist theory to the world's ills. Their insistence that the theory is correct but has somehow always been per-verted is nothing less than the search for new evidence of the conspira-cy that killed JFK which has been hidden by the "establishment." They continue to chase the shadows of an imaginary immaculate socialist or communist society they are convinced should solve all the shortcom-ings of capitalism including war, poverty, crime and prejudice. The in-controvertible evidence of the countless crimes against humanity and the millions of lives snuffed out in the 20th century by those who clung to the Red Flag and hammer and sickle emblems have always been ex-cused, blamed on others, forgotten or denied.

As with Oswald, these critics are incapable of seeing that the Conspiracy Theory Emperor is naked and that the many failures of the past were a direct outcome of that same theory they held so dear in their youth. They acknowledge that the tree can easily be recognized from the fruit it bears but bitter fruit is the inevitable consequence of a diseased tree, or one that has been neglected, or improperly cultivated, no matter how well meaning the gardener was.

The Garbage Can of History

The collapse of the Soviet Union and its satellite regimes in Eastern Europe is a fact of history. The "garbage can of history" to which numerous communist leaders such as Lenin, Stalin, Khruschev, Mao Tse-Tung and Castro assigned capitalism is now full to the brim with the collected works of Marx and Lenin in dozens of languages; their portraits emblazoned on life size statues, red flags, hammer and sickle emblems, medallions and the millions of tons of Soviet and East Bloc military equipment are rusting and rotting on forgotten battle-fields in the Middle East, Africa and Southeast Asia. No economist however skilled has ever really made a full account of this useless waste of capital and human lives and what its potential investment benefit in peaceful resources would have meant for the entire world.

To Have and Have Not

What "solutions" did Marx and Lenin offer to the oppressed workers and nationalities of the world in their time and how relevant, if at all, are these solutions today? Are the problems of unemployment and national identity analyzed by Marx and Lenin in the last century obsolete or solvable by Capitalism and the present world order?

In this partnership, Leninism meant the Soviet way to realize "socialism" by temporarily seizing power and enforcing the Dictator-ship of the Proletariat to carry out the ownership and regulation of the means of production and distribution until such time as the state would wither away. The result was an absolutist state that rivaled the Pharaohs of Egypt. Marxism remains a tool of political and social analysis of the dominant role of economic affairs in human history based on the rec-ognition of a diversity of interests between classes. While there is no dispute that Marx made many wrong predictions such as that the work-ers would seize power first in the most advanced industrial states, there are still many historians, economists and sociologists who argue that Marx's analysis of the struggle between the haves and the have-nots retains its validity.

For Marx, "to have and have not" meant capital and land that put immense power at the disposal of those who owned them whereas the workers possessed only their labor that had to be offered to the highest bidder. The great irony of our time is that this third factor – work is now the critical one. There is not enough "work" (i.e. salaried employment) to satisfy the valuable supply of labor – at least this is a serious political problem in a majority of developed industrial countries in Europe. Jobs, not land or capital are in critically short supply.. A job now is the major criterion by which to divide the haves from the have-nots.

Unemployment benefits exist in all developed countries and provide an economic safety net far beyond the dreams of nineteenth century industrial workers, yet in spite of the progress made in the amount and quality of goods, and a dramatic rise in the standard of living and security from the threat of illness since Marx's time, unemployment remains a grave problem aggravating all others. In this sense, many traditionalists and religious people would agree with Marxists that idleness is the root of all evil.

Work is, was and will always be more than just "the means of production." It is a good in scarce supply, one that allows the individual to attain self-expression, creativity and social development, rather than merely satisfying essential physical needs, food, shelter and clothing. A growing segment of society combining the under 30 year olds who have never been gainfully employed and over 40 year olds who have despaired of finding new jobs after being laid off, threaten the social fabric in all industrial societies. Even the most successful economic powerhouses with low unemployment such as Japan, Taiwan, and Korea fear the social and political consequences of the slightest rise in the jobless rate.

The nineteenth century problems of alcoholism and petty crime that were so prevalent among the unemployed pale in comparison with the drug addiction, violent crime, divorce, and psychological disorders that are widespread today. There is no evidence, however, that these problems were substantially ameliorated or better treated in the USSR and the East European communist states. The reverse was more likely the case. Under the rubric of "psychological care," political opponents of the regime were sent to languish in mental hospitals or forced labor camps.

Direct control of production by the producers themselves has existed briefly within small "island communities" on a limited scale such as the Israeli kibbutzim and the Amish and Mennonite settlements in the United States and Canada. Nevertheless their production was tied to the demand of market forces among consumers. In spite of ideological commitments, these communities have been forced to produce for the highest bidders and not according to need. Moreover, many of them have had to employ labor from outside.

The Mill Town Company Store Analogy

The state's role in guaranteeing employment in the USSR was a mirage. The same can be achieved anywhere by forcing labor to be engaged in prestige projects of no utility to society as a whole. This was what the Pharaohs did in building the pyramids. They too solved the problem of unemployment. On a practical scale, state monopolies of all sources of employment became a weapon in the hands of a bureaucratic and despotic regime that created a new class and made the state more powerful than any old American mill town company store. The immensity of hidden unemployment in the Eastern bloc only became apparent after the collapse of communism and the dismemberment of the state apparatus controlling production and distribution.

Return of the Class Struggle? The Wisconsin State Senate and the Cheeseheads Who Turned the United States into a Banana Republic.

The severe economic downturn that has caused markets and house prices to plummet has resulted in the highest unemployment since the Great Depression in most Western countries. This has provided ample opportunity for those who preach class warfare to trot out the old slogans and insist that once again capitalism has failed and that the "workers" must stand united against their class enemies. This wholly false appeal has not been able to stop the real "revolt of the masses" in the United States – the appearance of an authentic mass movement, namely The Tea Party. The Party's members are a true cross section of the American middle class and are predominantly wage earners or retirees on fixed incomes. Their motives and socio-economic standing as well as their cultural values demonstrate they have joined in a mighty leaderless movement to rise up and give the Democrats under Obama's leadership the "shellacking" he so well deserved and drive him from office.

Those members of labor unions in the public sector who see their favored position and guaranteed security in the most unstable situation for the past seventy years continue to fight tooth and nail under the banner of workers' solidarity that is a myth and a slap in the face of all salaried employees in the private sector and the unemployed. Their interests are diametrically opposed to those teachers, nurses, firemen and other state employees in vital services who occupied the Wisconsin State Capitol Building in Madison in February-March 2011.

The old union songs of "solidarity forever" simply don't apply no matter how the faithful are in good voice as they are dragged off from lying on the floors and barricading the doors of the Senate Building. The unemployed and the less fortunate in the private sector don't understand the solidarity of many of the public sector workers in more than a dozen states over the past few years who have refused compromises resulting in savings that would have allowed state budgets to avoid cuts and firing employees. Governor Walker in Wisconsin has staked a lot on making good a promise to significantly increase employment by not incurring massive deficits or resorting to ever higher taxes that impinge on all others including the unemployed. Workers chained to the class warfare idea of the 1920s and 30s refuse to see the benefits that accrue from creating a more business friendly environment and the willingness to risk new capital ventures that will create private sector jobs.

The "Reverend" Jesse Jackson told Fox News (March 10, 2011), *"You will either have collective bargaining through a vehicle called collective bargaining or you're going to have it through the streets."* Death threats and calls for the use of violence as the "legitimate tool" of the working class have been issued for the first time in a half century in a labor dispute. The most militant of the Wisconsin "Cheeseheads" have brought us to the brink of The Banana Republic in which the rule of law has been superseded by threats and intimidations or the outright destruction of representational government by renegade State Senators who violated their oath of office by flight and subterfuge. The elected Democrat legislators of the Senate who fled to Illinois to prevent the necessary quorum of the Wisconsin Senate defied and ridiculed Wisconsin Constitution Article IV that states the oath of office they swore to uphold.

SECTION 28. Members of the legislature, and all officers, executive and judicial, …. shall before they enter upon the duties of their respective offices, take and subscribe an oath or affirmation to support the constitution of the United States and the constitution of the state of Wisconsin, and faithfully to discharge the duties of their respective offices to the best of their ability.

Unresolved Nationalist Conflicts

The many nationalist conflicts of the twentieth century were not solvable by any Marxist formula of "class solidarity." The expected solidarity of the working class across national and linguistic boundaries was a mirage. The intensified conflicts over territory and the demands to impose strict immigration quotas as well as sporadic campaigns in dozens of countries for regional autonomy, minority, or special language rights read like a list of defeats for class solidarity.

On the other hand, the European Community promises to do away with the old national barriers on the movement of people, goods and capital. Just compare for the sake of argument the burial of the old Franco-German hatred with the savage tribalism unleashed in Yugoslavia and the USSR after decades of preaching international solidarity. The greatest success story in ameliorating old ethnic hatreds and forging a new sense of nationhood without a basis in "blood" is the United States. Its success, based on an open society of liberal capitalism and tolerance contrasts with the inherited blood feuds that are now growing almost everywhere.

The growth of nativist populist and anti-foreign movements such as La Pen in France, other Far Right European political parties, neo-Nazism in Germany, the English "skinheads," the candidacy for Senator in the Republican open primary in 1990 of KKK "Grand Wizard" David Duke in Louisiana (where he actually won close to 60% of the white vote) all drew their strength from the broad segment of the working population that was the targeted core of Marxist parties in the past.

Whatever the international appeal of pop music, the rock sub-culture and football, it has not made the young more tolerant. Internationalism today does not mean anything more than the participation of more than one nation in an organization or event. It does not convey the sense of solidarity across ethnic racial, sexual and linguistic barriers. The International approach envisioned by Marx embodied in the communist anthem, the Internationale, with its call to build a world based one new foundations, had only a brief appeal prior to the First World War. The universal appeal of this internationalism was extinguished in the patriotic fervor unleashed in 1914.

The Balance Sheet - A Huge Minus

While Marxism retains some validity as an analytical tool to examine and explain past economic development, it offers no guiding light to the future. Leninism as the way to seize power and create a classless society has been a failure on all fronts. There are undeniably many serious problems within the advanced capitalist societies yet the progress made by the working class there has far exceeded the dreams of those who only two and three generations ago believed that it was a doomed system. Marxism-Leninism, like the conspiracy theory to explain the Kennedy assassination, could only rely on myths, propaganda and the cultivation of mass appeal of envy towards those who are richer, more talented or more fortunate in life. In the end, it was the ideology that has ended up on the garbage can of history.

Three European Women of Courage and the Moral Defeat of the Left Today

Many individuals have had to confront a torrent of abuse heaped upon them after having proven by word and deed their personal courage and integrity in opposing the forces of evil on the Right but then dared to reveal and openly criticize the equivalent oppression of the politically correct LEFT. Arthur Koestler, George Orwell, Ignazio Silone, Whittaker Chambers, Richard Wright, Andre Gide, Ralph Glasser, Andre Malraux, Milovan Djilas, Albert Camus, Louis Fischer, Stephen Spender, R. H. S. Crossman, Ronald Radosh and David Horowitz immediately come to mind as men drawn to the Party and its front organizations largely through the cynical manipulation of their idealism and the mistaken straw-man image of The Right led them to their choice of Communism only to experience the ultimate disillusionment and sense of betrayal.

Three European women must be mentioned in higher regard as never having been seduced and betrayed by the political extremes. Their integrity and deep commitment to noble ideals exposed them to dangers and risks to their lives, families and careers from the Right and then from the Left. They were even more savagely attacked because they stood up in defense of the historic and human rights of Jews not just as individuals but also for Zionism and the State of Israel or revealed the grotesque misogyny of Muslim culture and thereby exposed themselves to the slander and abuse of colleagues who could not forgive them for such a deviation from the grotesque idolatry of the Left with its frequent cults of personality worshipping Stalin, Mao, Castro, Ceaucescu, Pol Pot, Kim Jung-Il, Yasser Arafat and Ahmadinejad.

Their stories deserve to be told and retold today when many on the Left in Europe and America have defended what amounts to Islamo-Fascism as the solution of convenience by burying their heads in the sand. One was a devout Catholic in an overwhelmingly Protestant country and the other two agnostics or atheists in devoutly Catholic countries, but all three had the immense spiritual power of their convictions and conscience that could not be assuaged by what was politically correct and the conventional wisdom of the moment.

Sigrid Undset

Sigrid Undset (1882-1949) is today largely unknown outside of Norway. Few women made more noble sacrifices in the cause of freedom and women's liberation. Few great writers have had a more difficult struggle in devoting themselves to their art while earning a living and supporting their children. She was born on 20 May 1882, in Kalundborg, Denmark, the eldest of three daughters. When Sigrid was only two, the family moved to Norway and she grew up in Kristiania (Oslo). Her father, Martin, was a respected archaeologist who died at the age of 40 after a prolonged illness when Sigrid was 11. His scholarly involvement with Norse folklore and the sagas greatly stimulated Sigrid's fascination with literature but her widowed mother, with very little means, had to cope with raising three young daughters.

This family tragedy left its mark on Sigrid Undset's childhood and adolescence and all hope of a university education had to be abandoned. After graduating from middle school, she took a one year secretarial training course and got a job with a large German owned engineering company in Oslo where she worked full time for the next ten years to help support her mother and sisters although she hated the work, believing that she was wasting her time and her youth.

Every free moment she had outside of work and family obligations was devoted to reading and writing, and at barely age 16 she made her first attempt at a novel set in the Nordic Middle Ages. Late at night, and during weekends and holidays, she stole the time to write. She read the great classics of Shakespeare, Chaucer, contemporary British authors such as Jane Austen and the Bronte sisters as well as the great Scandinavian writers, Ibsen, Strindberg, and George Brandes, acquiring the university level education that had been denied to her. She published her first work at age 22 and twenty-two years later was awarded the Nobel Prize for Literature!

At age 25 she made a real literary debut with her book *Fru Marta Oulie* with a realistic description of a woman with a lower middle class background in contemporary Kristiania. The opening sentence was a real shocker that scandalized readers: "*I have been unfaithful to my husband,*" the words of the book's main character. The book was rejected at first but eventually accepted on the recommendation of several well known writers. This short realistic novel on adultery created a sensation and she found herself ranked as a promising young author in Norway. Sigrid was one of the first writers to use the technique known as "stream of consciousness" which is why she is still regarded as a "modern" writer. Her best-known work is *Kristin Lavransdatter,* a trilogy about life in Scandinavia during the Middle Ages that portrays a humble woman from birth until death.

In Rome, she met Anders Castrus Svarstad, a Norwegian painter. She was then 30, nine years younger than him and, most likely, he was her first love. When they met, Svarstad was married, and had three children in Norway. This shocked her public for a while but contributed eventually to her reputation as a free spirit and non-conventional feminist. Their meeting must have been a case of love at first sight. It took three years before Svarstad got his divorce and the couple was married in 1912 and had three children together. They went to live in London. Sigrid's second child was a girl who was mentally handicapped as was one of his sons.

Eventually they separated in 1919, and she settled on a farm in Lillehammer, Norway with her daughter and two sons. Anders and stepchildren were frequent visitors to the farm, called Bjerkebæk. Before 1919, she had published a number of novels set in contemporary Kristiania based on her experiences as a lonely secretary working in an impersonal office, the result of her familiarity with the lives of ordinary people who strove to find some happiness in life. Sigrid Unset won respect as an author who could observe people accurately and see through them.

Both her parents had been intellectuals and atheists who were nominal members of the State Lutheran Church. Sigrid's early adult years were spent under the influence of the general agnosticism that prevailed in much of Europe even before World War I but a growing crisis of faith and her deep uneasiness about the ethical decline of the age led her to convert to Catholicism, an unheard of move for anyone already known and respected in Norwegian public life. She was received into the Roman Catholic Church in November 1924, after thorough instruction when she was 42 years old and became a lay Dominican. Her writing more and more developed a deep regard for the mystery of life and all that cannot be explained by reason and human intelligence.

She gave her Nobel Prize money away, 156,000 kroner, part of it going to a foundation established to help families with mentally disabled children. Later in 1940 she also sold her Nobel medal, giving the money to the relief effort for Finnish children after the outbreak of the Winter War between Finland and the Soviet Union. Her books had long been banned in Germany for her outspoken criticism of Nazism and defense of the Jews. During the German invasion of Norway, her elder son Anders, a second lieutenant in the Norwegian Army was killed in the fighting. She joined the Resistance movement but was strongly advised by Norwegian authorities to flee the country. After her departure, the Germans occupied her home in Bjerkebæk and chopped up her writing desk.

In 1940, Sigrid and her younger son left neutral Sweden where they had sought refuge and sailed for the United States. There, she worked to plead her occupied country's cause and that of Europe's Jews, in writings, speeches and interviews. She lived in Brooklyn Heights where she was active in St. Ansgar's Scandinavian Catholic League.

At the end of the war, Undset returned to Norway, where she was awarded the Grand Cross of the Order of St. Olav in 1947, for her "distinguished literary work and for her service to her country." She died in Lillehammer, on June 10, 1949.

The Left both home and abroad that once regarded her work as an expression of a great artist who championed feminism and rose to international recognition from a humble background, turned its back on her in spite of her heroic stand against Nazism. Her deep spirituality, rejection of crass materialism and her "incorrect" emphasis as a feminist on biological destiny with motherhood as the highest duty a woman can aspire to, are all out of fashion now. Tim Page, author of *The*

Unknown Sigrid Undset[1] commented: "She is, one might say, rather like Norway itself, its soul - half Viking, half Christian - torn between bold adventure and stark self-denial."

Orianna Fallaci

Orianna Fallaci (1930-2006) shares many of the same traits of independence and integrity although coming from a very different cultural and social background. Like Sigrid Undset, Orianna took part in the Resistance and was awarded a certificate of valor from the Italian army. She was an atheist but with a deep understanding and appreciation of Italy's Catholic heritage. Her father Edoardo Fallaci, a cabinet maker in Florence, was a political activist struggling to end the Italian fascist regime.

Hers was one of the most passionate voices of the 20th century and refused to compromise her convictions for the sake of some immediate gain in her career as a journalist. In a 1976 collection of her works, she commented that:

> "Whether it comes from a despotic sovereign or an elected president, from a murderous general or a beloved leader, I see power as an inhuman and hateful phenomenon...I have always looked on disobedience toward the oppressive as the only way to use the miracle of having been born."

She absorbed this outlook and integrated it into her journalistic career and never allowed herself to be cowed into submission in order to curry favor with the powerful and acquired the title of the "greatest political interviewer of modern times."

In her powerful bestseller *The Rage and the Pride,* Orianna explains the magnificent courage of her mother that set an example she followed to her dying day. She began her career as a journalist while

---

1 Page, Tim (Author and editor), Undset, Sigrid (author), and Nunnally Tina (translator) *The Unknown Sigrid Undset, Jenny and Other Works.* Steerforth Press. 2001

still in her teens writing a crime column for an Italian daily but was soon promoted to carry out assignments interviewing prominent personalities in the areas of politics and culture. In what was her most famous interview with Secretary of State, Dr. Henry Kissinger she adroitly managed to get him to admit a penchant for seeing himself as *"a cowboy astride his horse in the Wild West,"* an image he transferred to the scene of international relations. He later would reveal that this Fallaci interview was *"the most disastrous conversation I ever had with any member of the press."*

During her lifetime, Fallaci viewed with trepidation the growing strength of the Muslim community in Italy, aided by the unthinking support of Left wing political parties. Like Sigrid, Orianna came to develop an admiration for the Jewish people and their struggle for survival against terrible odds. This alone would have made her an outcast among many in influential Leftwing circles but it was her devastating attacks on many so called iconic "celebrities" (she threatened to kick Jane Fonda in the ass and spit in her face for lying about her coverage of the Vietnam war and betraying the confidence of American POWs) and the ignorance of a large part of the younger generation that resulted in vicious attacks against her. She was made to pay the price of ostracism by much of the Left who trumped up accusations of anti-Arab "racism" to demean her record, her pro-American sympathies, and concern for the survival of European civilization as well as her fervent support of Israel.

Shortly before her death she described how since 9/11 the whole of Europe has become a "Niagara Falls of McCarthyism" – with the new Grand Inquisitors of the Left persecuting and victimizing all others while Europe's own Judeo-Christian civilization is regarded by many of its so called intellectuals as *"a spark of a cigarette – gone."*

Pilar Rahola

One shining light in the gloom of contemporary Spain is Pilar Rahola, a feminist, author, parliamentarian and good friend of Israel who first represented the Catalan Liberal-Republican party (ERC) and then a Catalan Independence Party in the Spanish Cortes (parliament), and who has been compared to Oriana Fallaci and even Dolores Ibarruri, the fiery communist Basque deputy in the Cortes during the 1930s.

Rahola comes from a distinguished family of Catalan nationalists that includes Pere Rahola, the Minister of the Navy during the Spanish Republic, Frederic Rahola, the first public defender in the regionalist government (*Generalitat de Catalunya*); and Carlos Rahola, a writer executed by the Franco regime. She studied Spanish and Catalan Philology at the University of Barcelona and has published several books. She was a member of the Cortes for the leftwing nationalist and republican party *Esquerra Republicana de Catalunya* (ERC: The Republican Left of Catalonia) and is currently a columnist for *La Vanguardia* in Spain; *La Nación* in Argentina; and *Diario de América* in the United States (Miami). She is married and has three children, two of them adopted.

From 1987 to 1990, she directed *Portic*, the Catalan publishing house and covered wars in Africa, the Balkans, the Middle East and the fall of the Berlin Wall. She also served as Vice-Mayor of Barcelona and participated in several committees of investigation. In 1996, Rahola left the ERC to help establish a new political group, *Partit per la Independencia*, but after failing reelection, she concentrated on journalism and writing. Her main areas of interest include women's rights, international human rights, and animal rights and in recent years has spoken out about the galling hypocrisy of left wing politicians with regards to Israel and Zionism.

She has explained the abject failure of the political Left in her country to educate the public and combat antisemitism and the country's surrender in foreign policy to a pro-Arab, anti-Israel, and anti-American stance. Rahola is now a "Prophet without honor in her own country." The Catalan and Barcelona government authorities cancelled "Holocaust Remembrance Day" on January 27th because in their view it would not be proper while the *"Israelis were carrying out a holocaust against the people of Gaza."* The grotesque analogy drawn is a symptom of the absurd time we live in. The most widely read newspaper, the leftwing *El País*, is consistently the most extreme in its constant criticism and often demonization of Israel and Zionism. Jose Maria Bastenier, its international affairs editor, frequently publishes invectives against the

Jewish state, and portrays the Israelis as planning the *"final solution of the Palestinian question."*

The language used in the mass media duplicates the language used by the Far Right propaganda before and during the Spanish Civil War holding "Jews" (or disguised as the "Neocons" today) responsible for the world financial crisis. At the same time, those political forces and media on the Left often seek to excuse blatant examples of Muslim rejection of Western social, moral and political values.

Both Rahola and Fallaci, as women, were more alert to the utter disregard for women's and children's rights in Muslim societies than their male counterparts. Pilar Rahola is disgusted by how her erstwhile allies on the political Left in Spain have violated their principles and continually ignore the brutal viciousness of the worst antisemitism and yet cheer and applaud the use of Palestinian refugees, women and children as cannon fodder by Hamas and Hizbollah.

The previous centrist-right government of Jose Maria Aznar had taken a risk in supporting the American intervention in Iraq thereby "provoking" Islamic extremists. It has however, been established that the plans to make a spectacular terrorist attack had been planned well in advance of the 2004 election and even before the Aznar government sent a token military force to Iraq. The Spanish press, mindful of the long tradition of anti-Americanism evident since the Spanish-American War (1898), strongly supported the criticism of the post-Gonzalez Socialist Party's two favorite targets – Israel and America.[2]

In a reversal of the situation in 1986, when the forces of modernism, democracy and turning away from Spain's old prejudices made the Socialist Party under Felipe Gonzalez welcome relations with Israel, the political Left has since totally embraced the worst prejudices of the past. Spain's Prime Minister since 2004, Jose Luis Rodriguez Zapatero has confirmed the dire and accurate warning made by one of the founding fathers of the Socialist movement in Europe – August Bebel, the head of the SAPD (*Sozialistische Arbeiterpartei Deutschlands,* "Socialist Workers' Party"), renamed the SPD in 1890 – the ancestor of today's major socialist party in Germany. Bebel criticized the tendency of populist political parties to use the Jews as their scapegoat and accu-

---

2 See Berdichevsky, Norman *Spanish Vignettes: An Offbeat Look into Spain's Culture, Society and History* (Santana Books, 2004).

rately proclaimed that "Antisemitism is the Socialism of Fools."

Most Spaniards refuse to accept the reality that the extremist anti-Israel forces among the most radical Palestinian Arabs and the Muslim perpetrators of atrocious attacks on innocent Spaniards are one and the same in their ultimate motives; the desire to "regain" Andalucía, restore the Caliphate, destroy the Jewish state and weaken Western civilization in the process. This policy of appeasement is regarded by the present socialist government as the best means of ensuring Spain's supply of oil (90% provided by Middle Eastern countries) and pacifying Spain's growing Muslim population of 750,000.

As Pilar wrote in recent website articles, *"The Left has always been anti-Western, and therefore not so far removed from some of the obsessions of current Islamic fundamentalism. In any case, it has been said that in Israel, killings in the name of Islamic nihilism have benefited from increasing impunity, and every Israeli victim that is reviled, ignored or despised by Western intelligentsia, has prepared the way for the killings in Atocha (Madrid train station bombing) and London (terrorist attack on the Underground).....As a non-Jew, journalist and Leftist, I have a triple moral duty with Israel, because if Israel is destroyed, liberty, modernity and culture will be destroyed too."*

The deeds and words of these three women inspired me to write this book. They should inspire us all.

Bibliography

Bar-Zohar, Michael *Beyond Hitler's Grasp; The Heroic Rescue of Bulgaria's Jews.* Holbrook, Mass: Adams Media Corporation, 1998.

Beevor, Antony *The Spanish Civil War.* London: Cassell, 1999.

Berdichevsky, Norman *Spanish Vignettes, An Offbeat Look Into Spain's Culture, Society and History.* Fuengirola-Malaga, Spain: Santana Books, 2004.

Billinsley, Kenneth Lloyd "Hollywood's Missing Movies" in reasononline; free minds and free markets. Print edition June 2008, Internet 1/23/2008.

Bosworth, R. J. B. *Mussolini's Italy; Life Under the Fascist Dictatorship, 1915-1945.* New York: Penguin, 2006.

Branner Hans "Den 9. April 1940 – et politisk lærestykke?" Copenhagen: Dansk Udenrigspolitisk Institut, 1987.

Brinkley, Alan *The End of Reform. New Deal Liberalism in Recession and War* New York: Vintage, 1996.

Bruce, Tammy *The Death of Right and Wrong; Exposing the Left's Assault on our Culture and Values. New York:* Three Rivers Press, 2004.

Bynum, Rebecca *Allah is Dead; Why Islam is Not a Religion.* Nashville: New English Review Press, 2011.

Charen, Mona *Useful Idiots; How Liberals Got it Wrong in the Cold War and Still Blame America First.* Washington D.C.: Regnery Publishing Inc., 2003.

Cibotti, Ema *Queridos Enemigos; De Beresford a Maradona – La Verdadera Historia de Las Relaciones Entre Ingleses y Argentinos*. Buenos Aires: Aguilar, 2006.

Clogg, Richard *A Short History of Modern Greece*. London: Cambridge University Press, 1979.

Coulter, Ann *Treason; Liberal Treachery from the Cold War to the War on Terrorism*. New York: Three Rivers Press, 2003.

Crassweller, Robert *Perón y los enigmas de la Argentina*. Buenos Aires: Emecé Editores, 1988.

Darwish, Nonie *Cruel and Usual Punishment*. Nashville: Thomas Nelson, 2008.

De Andrés, Jesus and Cuéllar, Jesus *Atlas Ilustrado de la Guerra Civil Española*. Madrid: Susaeta Ediciones, 2008.

Diggins, John Patrick *Mussolini and Fascism; The View From America*. Princeton: Princeton University Press, 1972.

Evans, F. Stanton *Blacklisted by History; The Untold Story of Senator Joe McCarthy*. New York: Crown Forum, 2007.

Fallaci, Oriana *The Rage and the Pride*. New York: Rizzoli, 2002.

Fray, Michael *Copenhagen* (Methuen Drama Series) London: Random House, 1998.

Goldberg, Jonah *Liberal Fascism; The Secret History of the American Left from Mussolini to the Politics of Meaning*. New York: Doubleday, 2007.

Grover, Warrren *Nazis in Newark*. New Brunswick, N.J.: Transaction Publishers, 2007.

Hammerich, Paul *Skindet pa næsen, 1945-48*; volume one of *En Danmarks Kronike 1945-72*. Denmark: Gyldendals, 1976.

Helmer Pedersen, Erik *Drømmen om Amerika* Politikens Danmarks Historie. Copenhagen, Denmark: Politikens Forlag, 1985.

Horowitz, David *Radical Son*. New York: The Free Press, 1997.

Harpelle, Ronald et. Al. (eds.) "Karelian Exodus; Finnish Communities in North America and Soviet Karelia during the Depression Era" *Journal of Finnish Studies*. Vol. 8, No. 1 August, 2004.

Huntington, Samuel *Who Are We? The Challenges to America's National Identity*. New York: Simon & Schuster Paperbacks, 2003.

Jerasimof Vatikiotis, Panayiotis "Metaxas Becomes Prime Minister". *Popular Autocracy in Greece, 1936–41: a Political Biography of General Ioannis Metaxas* Routledge (1998).

Keen Benjamin and Haynes, Keith *A History of Latin America* Seventh edition. Boston and New York: Haughton Mifflin Co., 2004.

Kravchenko, Victor *I Chose Freedom: The Personal and Political Life of a Soviet Official* New York: Charles Scribners Sons, 1946.

Karsh, Efraim *Palestine Betrayed*. New Haven and London: Yale University Press, 2010.

Kousoudlas, D. George *Modern Greece; Profile of a Nation*. New York: Scribners. 1974.

Lappin, Daniel Rabbi *America's Real War*. Sisters, OR: Multnomah Publishers, Inc., 1999.

Lawlor, Sheila *Churchill and the Politics of War, 1940–1941*. Cambridge University Press. 1993.

Leuchtenburg, William E. *The FDR Years: On Roosevelt and His Legacy*. New York: Columbia University Press, 1995.

Lewis, Sinclair *It Can't Happen Here*. New American Library, 2005 (many previous editions), 1936.

Lichtman, Allam J. *White Protestant Nation; The Rise of the American Conservative Movement*. New York: Atlantic Monthly Press, 2008.

Lindberg, Lars "Arvefjenden; Dansk-svenske kampe på slågsmarker og foldboldbaner fra sagntid til nutid" *Forlaget* Danmark.

Lisboa, José Antonio *España-Israel: Historia de Unas Relaciones Secretas* 2nd ed. Madrid: Temas de hoy, 2002.

Mahin, Dean *One War at a Time; The International Dimension of the American Civil War*. Washington, D.C.: Brassey's, 1999.

Marwick, Arthur *The Sixties, Cultural Revolution in Britain, France. Italy and the United States, 1958-1974*. Oxford: Oxford University Press, 1998.

Mead, Walter Russell, Walter "The New Israel and the Old: Why Gentile Americans Back the Jewish State" *Foreign Affairs*, July/August 2008 .

Merkley, Paul C. *The Politics of Christian Zionism, 1891-1948*. London: Frank Cass, 1998.

Oren, Michael B. *Power, Faith and Fantasy; America in the Middle East 1776 to the Present*. New York: W. W. Norton & Company, 2007.

Payne, Stanley *Falange, A History of Spanish Fascism*. Stanford, California: Stanford University Press, 1961.

Radosh, Ronald *Commies: A Journey Through the Old Left, the New Left, and the Leftover Left*. San Francisco: Encounter Books, 2001.

Bibliography

Read, Anthony and Fisher, David *The Deadly Embrace; Hitler, Stalin and the Nazi-Soviet Pact 1939-1941.* New York: W. W. Norton 7 Company, 1988.

Roussell, Aage *The Museum of the Danish Resistance Movement 1940-1945: A Short Guide.* The National Museum, Copenhagen 1964.

Sebreli Juan José *Comediantes y Mártires; Ensayo Contra Los Mitos (Gardel, Evita, Che and Maradona)* Buenos Aires. Argentina: Debate, 2008.

Shavit, Yaakov *Jabotinsky and the Revisionist Movement, 1925-1948.* London: Frank Cass, 1988.

Steyn, Mark *America Alone: The End of the World as We Know It.* Washington, DC.: Regnery Publishing, 2006.

Trotter, William R. *Frozen Hell, The Russo-Finnish War of 1939-40.* Chapel Hill: Algonquin Books, 2000.

Vidal, César *España Frente al Islam; De Mahoma a Ben Laden* Madrid: la esfera de los libros, 2004.

Warraq, Ibn *Why I Am Not A Muslim.* Amherst, New York: Prometheus Books, 2004.

West, Diana *The Death of the Grown-Up.* New York: St. Martin's Griffin, 2007.

Woolf, S. J. (ed.) *Fascism in Europe.* London and New York: Methuen, 1981.